Scots in New England
1623–1873

Scots

in

New England

1623–1873

David Dobson

Introduction

Scottish emigration to New England was rather a small scale intermittent phenomenon compared to the movement from Scotland to the Carolinas or to Canada. The reason for this may lie in the fact that by the time large scale emigration occurred, opportunities for settlement were greater elsewhere in colonial America than in New England. Nevertheless, from virtually the earliest period in the history of New England there have been Scots, albeit small in number, settled there. Probably the only time that significant numbers of Scots settled in New England was in 1650-1651 when Oliver Cromwell despatched hundreds of Scots prisoners of war, captured after the battles of Dunbar and Worcester, into exile, or in the period immediately before the outbreak of the American Revolution when the Scots American Company of Farmers established a settlement in Vermont. Thoughout the nineteenth century, however, there was a steady stream of skilled industrial workers and granite tradesmen from Scotland to New England attracted by social and economic opportunities there.

This book has been compiled from primary and secondary sources on both sides of the Atlantic over several years. Possibly the most significant sources used were the records of the Scots Charitable Society of Boston. This society had been founded in 1657 and was open to Scots or the sons of Scots, and is possibly the oldest continuous organization of its type in America.

David Dobson,
St Andrews, Scotland

v

References

ARCHIVES

ABA =   Aberdeen Burgh Archives
          APB =   Aberdeen Proprinquity Book

EUL =   Edinburgh University Library

NAS =   National Archives of Scotland, Edinburgh
          AC   =   Admiralty Court
          B   =   Burgh Records
          CC   =   Commissary Court
          CS   =   Court of Session
          GD   =   Gifts & Deposits
          JC   =   Justiciary Court
          RD   =   Register of Deeds
          RS   =   Register of Sasines
          SC   =   Sheriff Court
          SH   =   Services of Heirs

NEHGS   New England Historic Genealogical Society, Boston
          SCS =   Scottish Charitable Society Papers,
                    Mss.B/S.36v.6

OA   =   Orkney Archives

PRO =   Public Record Office, London
          AO   =   Audit Office
          CO   =   Colonial Office
          PCC =   Prerogative Court of Canterbury
          T   =   Treasury

USNA =   United States National Archives, Washington DC
          C   =   US Census, 1850
          PAR =   Passenger Arrival Records

UAL =   University of St Andrews Library, Scotland
          HGP =   Hayden Guest Papers
          StABR   St Andrews Burgess Roll

VHS =   Vermont Historical Society, Whitelaw Papers

Publications

AA	=	American Ancestry
AJ	=	Aberdeen Journal, series
AncH.NE	=	Ancestral Heads of New England Families
ANQ	=	Aberdeen Notes and Queries, series
ANY	=	Biographical Register of the St Andrews Society of New York
AO	=	Annandale Observer, series
BFH	=	Bethune Family History [London, 1893]
BLG	=	Burke's Landed Gentry [London, 1939]
BosGaz	=	Boston Gazette, series
BP	=	Boston Pilot, series
CCNE	=	Colonial Clergy of New England
CCMC	=	Colonial Clergy of the Middle Colonies
CEG	=	Catalogue of Graduates of Edinburgh University [Edinburgh, 1858]
CG	=	Clan Gillean [New York, 1893]
CM	=	Caledonian Mercury, series
CMF	=	Clan MacFarlane [PEI, 1899]
CMM	=	Clan MacMillan Magazine, series
Col.Fams	=	Colonial Families of the United States of America
CTB	=	Calendar of Treasury Books, series
DAB	=	Dictionary of American Biography
DCC	=	Dumfries & Galloway Courier, series
DGH	=	Dumfries & Galloway Herald, series
DJ	=	Dunfermline Journal, series
DNCB	=	Dictionary of North Carolina Biography
DP	=	Dunfermline Press, series
DPCA	=	Dundee, Perth & Cupar Advertiser, series
EAF	=	Founders of Early American Families, 1607/57 [Cleveland, 1975]
EAR	=	Edinburgh Apprentice Records
EC	=	Edinburgh Courant, series
EEC	=	Edinburgh Evening Courant, series
EFR	=	East Fife Record, series
EMA	=	List of Emigrant Ministers to America, G. Fothergill [London, 1904]
F	=	Fastii Ecclesiae Scoticanae, J. Scott [Edinburgh, 1915]

FA	=	Fife Advertiser, series
FFP	=	Fife Free Press, series
FH	=	Fife Herald, series
FPA	=	Fulham Papers in Lambeth Palace Library, WW Manross [Oxford, 1965]
GBR	=	Glasgow Burgess Register
HAR	=	History of Ayrshire and its Families [Ayr, 1847]
HMC	=	Historical Manuscript Commission, series
HNV	=	History of Barnet, Vermont [Burlington, 1923]
HSPC	=	History of the Somonoak Presbyterian Church
ImmNE	=	Immigrants to New England [Salem, 1931]
KCA	=	Officers and Graduates of King's College, P J Anderson [Aberdeen,1893]
LAP	=	List of Alien Passengers .....1847-1851, J.B. Munroe [Baltimore, 1971]
LJM	=	Letters of James Murray, Loyalist [Boston, 1901]
MB	=	The Macleans of Boreray, H. H. Mackenzie [Inverness, 1946]
MNS	=	McNaughton Saga, V V McNitt [Palmer, 1951]
MAGU	=	Matriculation Rolls of the University of Glasgow
NENS	=	'New Englanders in Nova Scotia', F E Crowell [Boston, 1979]
NER	=	New England Register, series
NHM	=	Newport Historical Magazine, series
NNQ	=	Northern Notes and Queries, series
NSHistRev	=	Nova Scotia Historical Review, series
NWI	=	New World Immigrants, M. Tepper [Baltimore, 1980]
NYGaz	=	New York Gazette, series
NYM	=	New York Mercury, series
PaChron	=	Pennsylvania Chronicle, series
PAB	=	Port Arrivals and Immigrants to the City of Boston, W. H. Whitmore [Baltimore, 1973]
PJ	=	People's Journal, series
PTA	=	Passengers to America, M. Tepper [Baltimore,1980]
RAF	=	Robertson's Ayrshire Families [Kilmarnock, 1908]
RPCS	=	Register of the Privy Council of Scotland, series
S	=	Scotsman, series
SA	=	Scottish Americanus, W. Brock [Edinburgh,1982]
SCHR	=	Scottish Church History Records, series
SG	=	Scottish Guardian, series
SGen	=	Scottish Genealogist, series

SI	=	St Clair of the Isles, R W St Clair [NZ, 1898]
SM	=	Scots Magazine, series
SN	=	The Scottish Nation [Edinburgh, 1869]
SPC	=	Calendar of State Papers, Colonial, series
TCF	=	The Calderwood Families [London, 1964]
TSA	=	The Scots in America,
TML	=	The MacLeods [London, 1959]
UJA	=	Ulster Journal of Archaeology, series
VSP	=	Virginia State Papers, series
W	=	Witness, series
WA	=	Who Was Who in America, 1607-1896
1812	=	British Aliens in the United States of America, 1812 [K. Scott, Baltimore, 1979]

Abbreviations

Cnf	=	confirmation of testament
G/s	=	gravestone inscription
OPR	=	Old Parish Register

Scots in New England 1623-1873

ABERCROMBIE, JAMES, admitted as a member of the Scots
    Charitable Society of Boston in 1709. [SCS]

ABERCROMBIE, ROBERT, born in Edinburgh during 1712, a
    minister in Pelham, New England, from 1744 to 1755, died
    there on 3 March 1780. [Imm.NE#1]; Mr Robert Abercromby,
    a minister in New England, son of Andrew Abercromby in
    Kirkcaldy, Fife, 1762. [NAS.B41.7.7/454]

ADAM, PETER, a mason on Fox Island, son of George Adam
    {1808-1881} and Isabella Reid {1810-1880}, died 17
    September 1872, buried in Palmer, Massachusetts.
    [Monymusk g/s, Aberdeenshire]

ADAMS, JAMES, prisoner of war captured after the Battle of
    Dunbar in September 1650, transported on 3 November
    1650 from London to New England on the Unity, employed
    as an indentured servant at the Lynn Ironworks in
    Massachusetts, [NWI]; admitted as a founder member of the
    Scots Charitable Society of Boston on 6 January 1657.
    [SCS]

ADAMS, SAMUEL, of Charlestown, admitted as a member of the
    Scots Charitable Society of Boston in 1742. [SCS]

ADIE, ALEXANDER, admitted as a member of the Scots
    Charitable Society of Boston in 1799. [SCS]

AGNEW, NIVEN, a prisoner of war who was captured after the Battle of Dunbar in September 1650 and transported on 3 November 1650 from London on the Unity to New England, an indentured servant who later settled in Kittery, Berwick, Maine, during 1656, [NWI]; in Kittery, Maine, probate 16 September 1687 Maine Probate Office 1/3. [reference to Peter Grant and his daughter Elizabeth, John Taylor and his daughter Mary]

AIKEN, BETTY, born in 1819, immigrated to Massachusetts aboard the Buena Vista on 15 June 1849. [LAP]

AIKEN, JOHN, from Ayr, member of the Scots Charitable Society of Boston in 1745. [SCS]

AIKEN, WILLIAM, emigrated from Greenock aboard the brigantine Matty, master Thomas Cochrane, on 19 May 1774 bound for New York, arrived there on 22 July 1774, settled Barnet, Vermont. [HBV]

AIKMAN, PATRICK, commander of the Hannibal, admitted as a member of the Scots Charitable Society of Boston in 1715. [SCS]

AIKMAN, WILLIAM, from Glasgow, member of the Scots Charitable Society of Boston 1718. [SCS]

AIKMAN, WILLIAM, admitted as a member of the Scots Charitable Society of Boston in 1731. [SCS]

AINSLIE, THOMAS, possibly from Roxburghshire, emigrated before 1722, Customs Collector in Boston, husband of Elizabeth Martin. [NAS.RD4.275.447/RD4.239.11]

AITCHISON, ANDREW, from Glasgow, then in Boston, admitted as a member of the Scots Charitable Society of Boston in 1800. [SCS][NAS.CS17.1.18/412]

AITCHISON, JOHN, son of John Aitchison of Rosalloch, a merchant in Grenada, died in New London, Connecticut, on 25 August 1770. [SM#32.630]

AITCHISON, JOHN, a merchant in Massachusetts, by 1787. [PRO.AO12.81.36]

AITKEN, HENRY, from Kinghorn, Fife, admitted as a member of the Scots Charitable Society of Boston in 1740. [SCS]

AITKEN, JOHN, admitted as a member of the Scots Charitable Society of Boston in 1732. [SCS]

AITKEN, PETER, born 1852, died in Boston, USA, on 28 June 1887. [Torpichen g/s, West Lothian]

AITON, JOHN, admitted as a member of the Scots Charitable Society of Boston in 1712. [SCS]

AKIN, Mrs MARY, born 1640 in Aberdeen?, widow(?) of David Akin, to Rhode Island before 1675, with sons John born 1663, David born 1664, and James born 1668. [SG.XLIV.2]

ALEXANDER, COSMOS, a painter, son of John Alexander, emigrated to New England before 1772. [NAS.RD4.212.837]

ALEXANDER, GEORGE, son of John Alexander, emigrated to Massachusetts around 1643, in Windsor, Massachusetts, 1644, Northampton, Massachusetts, 1653, a freeman, married Susanna Sage on 18 March 1644, father of John and Ebenezer, died in Northampton, Massachusetts, on 5 May 1703. [EAF][AA.4.208][CAG#1.58]

ALEXANDER, JOHN, born in 1615, emigrated to Massachusetts in 1640, father of George, John and Thomas. [AA#4.208][CAG#1.58]

ALEXANDER, ROBERT, in Boston, Massachusetts, 1684. [Anc.H-NE]; member of the Scots Charitable Society of Boston 1684. [SCS]

ALEXANDER, ROBERT, from Dumfries, admitted as a member of the Scots Charitable Society of Boston in 1758. [SCS]

ALEXANDER, THOMAS, from Edinburgh, admitted as a member of the Scots Charitable Society of Boston in 1772, {possibly} a hosier in Boston, Loyalist, in Nova Scotia 1783. [Loyalists in Nova Scotia, p157][SCS][PRO.AO13.43.69-89]

ALEXANDER, WILLIAM, from Glasgow, admitted as a member of the Scots Charitable Society of Boston in 1758. [SCS]

ALLAN, ALEXANDER, admitted as a member of the Scots Charitable Society of Boston 1685; in Windsor, Connecticut, 1689. [Anc.H.-NE][SCS]

ALLAN, ANDREW, admitted as a member of the Scots Charitable Society of Boston in 1715. [SCS]

ALLEN, DAVID, born in 1739, a farmer from Sandylands, Renfrewshire, and agent for the Scots American Company of Farmers, emigrated from Greenock to America on the brig Matty, master Thomas Cochrane, on 25 March 1773, arrived in Philadelphia on 24 May 1773, settled in Ryegate, Vermont, died in Scotland.[VHS][HGP]

ALLAN, EDWARD, to New England in 1636, settled in Ipswich and in Dedham, Massachusetts, later in Suffield, Connecticut. [Anc.HNE]

ALLAN, GEORGE, from Fife, admitted as a member of the Scots Charitable Society of Boston in 1736. [SCS]

ALLEN, JOHN, admitted as a member of the Scots Charitable Society of Boston in 1712. [SCS]

ALLEN, JOHN, born in Edinburgh on 3 January 1747, emigrated to Nova Scotia in 1749, an army officer, administrator and merchant, settled in Maine during 1784, died on 7 February 1805 at Passamaquoddy Bay. [WA]

ALLEN, THOMAS, from Kirkbean, Galloway, admitted as a member of the Scots Charitable Society of Boston 1819. [SCS]

ALLISTER, CATHERINE, daughter of William Allister in Beveridgewells, Fife, died in Greenville, Connecticut, on 9 September 1870. [DP]

ALLISTER, ISABELLA, born during 1806, relict of Andrew Hoggan, died in Rockville, Connecticut, 30 April 1877. [DJ]

ALLARDYCE, JOHN, admitted as a member of the Scots Charitable Society in Boston on 25 October 1684. [SCS]

ALRON, JOHN, a trader, arrived in Boston on 12 April 1712 on the brigantine Success, master Andrew Gibson, from Glasgow. [PTA#129]

ANDERSON, ALESTER, a prisoner of war transported to New England on the John and Sarah of London, master John Greene, in November 1651.[Suffolk Deeds, 1-56]

ANDERSON, ALEXANDER, settled in Dartmouth, Massachusetts, a Loyalist in 1776. [PRO.AO13.96.53-57]

ANDERSON, DAVID, a prisoner of war transported to New England on the John and Sarah of London, master John Greene, in November 1651. [Suffolk Deeds, 1-56]

ANDERSON, ARCHIBALD, Scots prisoner at Lyn Ironworks, Massachusetts, probate 27 September 1662 Essex County [ref. to Alistair Graeme, John Clark, Allister MacMillan, William Gibson in Boston, Roland McPherson, Malcolm Downing, John Hawthorne, Corporal John Andrews][Essex County Quarterly Court Files, Vol.4.82; Vol.7.37-38]; inventory dated 13 June 1661 at Lyn Ironworks, includes a deposition by Allister Mackmallen aged 30 to prove that Allister Graim was nearest of kin to said Arzbell Anderson deceased, dated 12 December 1661, in Salem Court Records.

ANDERSON, ARCHIBALD, admitted as an honorary member of the Scots Charitable Society of Boston in 1807. [SCS]

ANDERSON, GEORGE, admitted as a member of the Scots Charitable Society of Boston in 1695. [SCS]

ANDERSON, GILBERT, from Crawfordjohn, Lanarkshire, member of the Scots Charitable Society of Boston in 1767. [SCS]

ANDERSON, JAMES, from Greenock, admitted as a member of the Scots Charitable Society of Boston in 1757. [SCS]

ANDERSON, JOHN, a prisoner of war transported to New England on the John and Sarah of London, master John Greene in November 1651. [Suffolk Deeds, 1-56]

ANDERSON, JOHN, admitted as a member of the Scots Charitable Society of Boston 1684. [SCS]

ANDERSON, JOHN, admitted as a member of the Scots Charitable Society of Boston in 1694. [SCS]

ANDERSON, JOHN, admitted as a member of the Scots Charitable Society in 1725. [SCS]

ANDERSON, JOHN, from Dunfermline, Fife, settled in Danbury, Connecticut, probate 6 March 1740 Connecticut

ANDERSON, JOHN, from Glasgow, a member of the Scots Charitable Society of Boston 1759. [SCS]

ANDERSON, JOHN HENDERSON, a draper's assistant in Rhode Island, cnf.1882. [NAS.SC70.1.218]

ANDERSON, NANCY, born in 1799 with Peggy born 1839, immigrated into Massachusetts on board the bark Athol on 2 June 1849. [LAP]

ANDERSON, ROBERT, emigrated from Greenock aboard the brigantine Matty, master Thomas Cochrane, on 19 May 1774 bound for New York, arrived there on 22 July 1774, settled Barnet, Vermont. [HBV]

ANDERSON, TINA, younger daughter of John Anderson, married Ernest T. Holwill from Pittsfield, Massachusetts, in Edinburgh on 5 February 1873.[EC#27563]

ANDERSON, WILLIAM, a prisoner of war transported to New England on the John and Sarah of London, master John Greene, in November 1651. [Suffolk Deeds 1.56]; admitted as a founder member of the Scots Charitable Society of Boston on 6 January 1657. [SCS]

ANDREW, WILLIAM, admitted as a member of the Scots Charitable Society of Boston in 1686. [SCS]

ANDERSON, WILLIAM, from Dunfermline, Fife, settled in Deerfield, Massachusetts, during 1758, married Abigail Hitchcock, died in 1810. [Imm.N.E., 1700-1775, p.3]

ANGUS, WILLIAM, admitted as a member of the Scots Charitable Society of Boston in 1693. [SCS]

ANNAN, DAVID, born in Cupar, Fife, during 1754, son of John Annan, married Mary Smith, settled in Peterborough, New Hampshire, died in Ireland during 1802. [Imm. N.E, 1700-1775, p.5]

ARBUCKLE, ROBERT, admitted as a member of the Scots Charitable Society of Boston in 1687. [SCS]

ARBUCKLE, WILLIAM, admitted as a member of the Scots Charitable Society of Boston in 1684. [SCS]

ARBUTHNOTT, JOHN, admitted as a member of the Scots Charitable Society of Boston in 1712. [SCS]

ARCHER, Reverend JAMES, born in 1801, son of Andrew Archer (1769-1823), died in New Lebanon during 1825. [Tealing g/s, Angus]

ARCHIBALD, FRANCIS, MD, admitted as a member of the Scots Charitable Society of Boston in 1721, [SCS]; a naval surgeon who settled in Boston during 1721. [SA]

ARCHIBALD, JAMES, a printer, arrived in Boston on 22 August 1765 aboard the Jamieson and Peggy, master John Aitken, from Leith. [PAB]

ARCHIBALD, JOHN, a prisoner of war captured after the Battle of Dunbar in September 1650, transported on 3 November 1650 from London to New England on the Unity, an indentured servant at the Lynn Ironworks in Massachusetts. [NWI]

ARKLEY, EVELYN, daughter of Patrick Arkley and his wife Julia, died in Lynn, Massachusetts, in 1869. [Murroes g/s, Angus]

ARMOUR, JOSEPH, admitted as a member of the Scots Charitable Society of Boston in 1819. [SCS]

ARMSTRONG, GREGORY, married Eleanor ....., a widow, in New England during 1638. [NEHGS#II.110]

ARMSTRONG, JOHN, emigrated from Greenock aboard the brigantine Matty, master Thomas Cochrane, on 19 May 1774 bound for New York, arrived there on 22 July 1774, settled Barnet, Vermont. [HBV]

ARMSTRONG, ROBERT, a surveyor in Boston and New Hampshire in 1710, [NAS.NRAS0332.1297/1306]; admitted as a member of the Scots Charitable Society of Boston in 1711. [SCS]

ARNOLD, JOHN, settled in Haddow, Connecticut, before 1855, father of Joseph. [AA#2/4]

ARNOTT, EDWARD, born in Dunfermline, Fife, during 1807, died at Warehouse Point, Connecticut, on 18 August 1870. [FH]

ARNOTT, WILLIAM, a joiner, arrived in Boston on 3 June 1766 aboard the George and James, master Robert Montgomery, from Scotland. [PAB]

ARTHUR, ALEXANDER, a mariner, admitted as a member of the Scots Charitable Society of Boston in 1685. [SCS]

ARTHUR, ROBERT, from Crawforddyke, Renfrewshire, admitted as a member of the Scots Charitable Society of Boston in 1731. [SCS]

ARTHUR, MARY, in Boston, cnf 1887. [NAS.SC70.1.257]

ATKIN, GEORGE, from Kirkcaldy, Fife, admitted as a member of the Scots Charitable Society of Boston in 1730. [SCS]

ATKIN, HENRY, from Kinghorn, Fife, admitted as a member of the Scots Charitable Society of Boston in 1740. [SCS]

AUCHENCLOSS, THOMAS, from Glasgow, a member of the
Scots Charitable Society of Boston in 1769. [SCS]; merchant
in Portsmouth, New Hampshire, Loyalist, settled in Halifax,
Nova Scotia, married Mary Filler, there on 14 May 1777,
died by 1784. [PRO.AO13.96.1-5]

AUCHMUTY, ROBERT, born in Scotland, emigrated to America
around 1720, a lawyer in Boston, later Judge of the
Admiralty Court of Massachusetts 1733-1734, died in Boston
in April 1750. Admitted as a member of the Scots Charitable
Society of Boston in 1717. [SCS][DAB.1.421]
[SM#7.349][NYGB#26.186][WA]

AUCHMUTY, ROBERT NICHOLAS, brother of Major General Sir
S. Auchmuty, died in Rhode Island during 1813. [EA]

BAILEY, ROBERT, a carpenter and farmer who settled in Barnet,
New Hampshire, in 1775. [HGP]

BAILIE, WILLIAM, admitted as a member of the Scots Charitable
Society of Boston in 1698. [SCS]

BAIN, JOHN, a carpet weaver, married Agnes, (baptised on 14
July 1806 in Kilmarnock, Ayrshire), daughter of James
Laughland and his wife Jean Wilson, in Kilmarnock on 14
September 1827, parents of Mary Bain born in
Thomsonville, Connecticut, on 9 August 1830. [Kilmarnock
Old Parish Records]

BAIN, ROBINA, youngest daughter of John Bain in Leslie, Fife,
married George Duncan, a papermaker, in Poquonod,
Hartford, Connecticut, on 21 October 1881. [PJ]

BAIRD, FRANCIS C., Stanford Connecticut, 1876. [NAS.GD2.356]

BAIRD, THOMAS, born 1608, settled in Salem, Massachusetts,
during 1628, died in 1678. [CAG#1.52]

BAKER, ..., a gentleman, and his wife, arrived in Boston on 3
June 1766 aboard the George and James, master Robert
Montgomery, from Scotland. [PAB]

BALEY, JAMES, admitted as a member of the Scots Charitable
Society of Boston in 1734. [SCS]

BALFOUR, ANDREW, baptised on 28 February 1737 in Temple
parish, Midlothian, son of Andrew Balfour of Braidwood and
Margaret Robertson, emigrated with his first wife and
daughter Tibbie from Greenock to Boston in 1772, married
Elizabeth Dayton in Newport, Rhode Island, later settled in
North Carolina, died there on 10 March 1782. [DNCB]

BALFOUR, CHARLES, surgeon, admitted to the Scots Charitable
Society of Boston in 1697. [SCS]

BALFOUR, JANE, daughter of Alexander Balfour in Kirkcaldy, Fife,
married George Elder jr., a merchant from Montreal, in
Boston on 2 August 1845.[W#603]

BALFOUR, JOHN, born on 25 September 1798 in Bowden,
Roxburghshire, son of Reverend William Balfour and Mary
Mein, died in Boston on 15 August 1844. [F.2.172]

BALFOUR, WALTER, born in St Ninians, Stirling, during 1776,
emigrated to America in 1806, a minister, admitted as a
member of the Scots Charitable Society of Boston in 1817,
died in Charlestown, Massachusetts, during 1852.
[SCS][TSA]

BALFOUR, WILLIAM, MD, admitted as a member of the Scots
Charitable Society of Boston in 1715. [SCS]

BALLANTINE, ARCHIBALD, admitted as a member of the Scots
Charitable Society of Boston in 1700. [SCS]

BALLANTINE, JOHN, a merchant from Ayr, in Boston on 25
October 1684; admitted as a member of the Scots
Charitable Society of Boston in 1687. [SCS]

BALLANTYNE, JOHN, a cooper, admitted as a member of the
Scots Charitable Society of Boston in 1684. [SCS]

BALLANTYNE, PATRICK, from Ayr, admitted as a member of the
Scots Charitable Society of Boston in 1717. [SCS]

BALLANTYNE, WILLIAM, born in 1616, emigrated to Boston during 1647, married Hannah Holland, admitted as a founder member of the Scots Charitable Society of Boston on 6 January 1657. [SCS][CAG#1/64]

BALLINGALL, ALEXANDER, arrived in Boston on 22 August 1765 aboard the Jamieson and Peggy, master John Aitken, from Leith. [PAB]

BALLAGH, WILLIAM, from South Carolina, admitted as a member of the Scots Charitable Society of Boston in 1693. [SCS]

BAND, JAMES, admitted as a member of the Scots Charitable Society of Boston in 1686. [SCS]

BANE, ALEXANDER, admitted to the Scots Charitable Society of Boston in 1697. [SCS]

BANK, JOHN, a prisoner of war captured after the Battle of Dunbar in September 1650, transported on 3 November 1650 from London to New England on the Unity, an indentured servant at the Lynn Ironworks in Massachusetts. [NWI]

BARBOUR, PETER, a tailor, admitted as a member of the Scots Charitable Society of Boston 1684, reference to in 1711. [SCS]

BARBER, WILLIAM MCLEOD, born on 31 May 1827 in Fochabers, Morayshire, baptised on 17 June 1827, son of Thomas Barber and Madeline McLeod, emigrated to Newhaven, Connecticut, educated at Yale University, a minister, died during 1889 in Malden, Massachusetts. [TML.2.39]

BARCLAY, ANDREW, born in Cleish parish, Fife, a merchant and bookbinder in Boston, a Loyalist in 1776, with wife Mary Bleigh, via New York to settled in Shelburne, Nova Scotia, 1783. [NSHist.Rev.#3.1.25] [PRO.AO13.24.23]

BARCLAY, GILBERT, a merchant in Boston, 1763. [NAS.CS16.1.115/60]

BARCLAY, JOHN, admitted as a member of the Scots Charitable Society of Boston in 1709. [SCS]

BARCLAY, JOHN, a dyer, arrived in Boston on 16 April 1766 aboard the Stirling Castle, master John Cockburn, from Greenock. [PAB]

BARCLAY, WILLIAM, a clerk, to New England on 30 January 1703. [EMA#12]

BARCLAY, WILLIAM, a smith, arrived in Boston on 27 June 1763 aboard the snow Jenny, master James Orr, from Scotland. [PAB]

BAREY, JAMES, from Glasgow, a member of the Scots Charitable Society of Boston in 1729. [SCS]

BARNETT, ISABELLA, daughter of James Barnett a merchant tailor in Leven, Fife, married Charles B. Owler in Andover, Massachusetts, on 10 April 1846, settled in Charlestown, Boston, during 1862, [FH, 28.4.1896]

BARNETT, JAMES, born during 1820, son of James Barnett a merchant tailor in Leven, Fife, died in Danvers, Massachusetts, on 30 July 1888. [FFP]

BARNETT, THOMAS, born during 1825, youngest son of James Barnett a merchant tailor in Leven, Fife, emigrated to USA in 1845, died in Haverhill, Massachusetts, on 9 December 1884. [FFP]

BARNETT, WILLIAM, born during 1818, a tinplate and sheet metal worker, second son of James Barnett a merchant tailor in Leven, Fife, emigrated to America in 1845, died in Andover, Massachusetts, on 9 December 1884. [FFP]

BARNHILL, JAMES, from Crawforddykes, Renfrewshire, a member of the Scots Charitable Society of Boston in 1759. [SCS]

BARR, JAMES, born in Kilbarchan, Renfrewshire, on 12 December 1752, settled in Ipswich, New Hampshire, during 1773, married Molly Cummings {1764-1845} during 1783, died on 7 March 1829. [Imm.NE#9]

BARRY, JAMES, a prisoner of war captured after the Battle of Dunbar in September 1650, transported on 3 November 1650 from London to New England on the Unity, an indentured servant who settled in Kittery, Berwick, Maine, around 1656. [NWI]

BART, CHARLES, emigrated from Greenock aboard the brigantine Matty, master Thomas Cochrane, on 19 May 1774 bound for New York, arrived there on 22 July 1774, settled Barnet, Vermont. [HBV]

BARTLEY, ROBERT, educated in Edinburgh and in Dublin, MD, emigrated from Greenock aboard the brigantine Matty, master Thomas Cochrane, on 19 May 1774 bound for New York, arrived there on 22 July 1774, settled Barnet, Vermont, later around 1790 in Londonderry, New Hampshire. [HBV][SA#180]

BARTON, WALTER, admitted as a member of the Scots Charitable Society of Boston 1686. [SCS]

BAXTER, FRANCIS, admitted as a member of the Scots Charitable Society of Boston in 1715. [SCS]

BAXTER, GEORGE, admitted as a member of the Scots Charitable Society of Boston in 1713. [SCS]

BAYNE, JOHN, admitted as a member of the Scots Charitable Society of Boston in 1717. [SCS]

BAYNE, WILLIAM, a prisoner of war transported to New England on the John and Sarah of London, master John Greene in November 1651. [Suffolk Deeds, 1-56]

BEAMES, WILLIAM, a prisoner of war transported to New England on the John and Sarah of London, master John Greene in November 1651. [Suffolk Deeds, 1-56]

BEAN, JAMES, admitted as a member of the Scots Charitable Society of Boston in 1800. [SCS]

BEAN, JOHN, emigrated to New Hampshire around 1660, settled in Exeter. [AA#6/53]

BEATON, JOHN, admitted as a member of the Scots Charitable Society of Boston in 1735. [SCS]

BEGG, ADAM, a weaver, arrived in Boston on 28 May 1768 aboard the Glasgow, master John Dunn, from Glasgow. [PAB]

BELL, ALEXANDER, a merchant who arrived in Boston on 31 October 1766 aboard the snow Jenny, master Archibald Orr, from Glasgow. [SG#7.4.15][PAB]

BELL, ISAAC, emigrated to Connecticut in 1640. [CAG#1.577]

BELL, JAMES, from Lanark, admitted as a member of the Scots Charitable Society of Boston 1767. [SCS]

BELL, JOHN, in Charlestown, admitted as a member of the Scots Charitable Society of Boston in 1735. [SCS]

BELL, PATRICK, from Glasgow, admitted as a member of the Scots Charitable Society of Boston in 1718. [SCS]

BELL, ROBERT, from Glasgow, admitted as a member of the Scots Charitable Society of Boston in 1770. [SCS]

BELL, WILLIAM, from Annandale, Dumfriesshire, admitted as a member of the Scots Charitable Society of Boston in 1732. [SCS]

BELL, WILLIAM, born in Paisley, Renfrewshire, settled in New Hampshire before 1780, married Beatrice Barr from Glasgow, died during 1817. [Imm.NE#12]

BENNE, JAMES, a prisoner of war transported to New England on the John and Sarah of London, master John Greene in November 1651. [Suffolk Deeds, 1-56]

BENNE, JOHN, a prisoner of war transported to New England on the John and Sarah of London, master John Greene in November 1651. [Suffolk Deeds, 1-56]

BENNETT, JOHN, admitted as a founder member of the Scots Charitable Society of Boston on 6 January 1657. [SCS]

BENNOCK, JOHN, admitted as a member of the Scots Charitable Society of Boston in 1803. [SCS]

BENSON, DAVID, born in Scotland during 1831, a laborer in Tisbury, Massachusetts, by 1880. [C]

BEREERE, THOMAS, , a prisoner of war transported to New England on the John and Sarah of London, master John Greene in November 1651. [Suffolk Deeds, 1-56]

BERESFORD, ..., son of S.B.Beresford MD, born in Hartford, Connecticut, on 12 March 1837. [S#1788]

BERRY, JAMES, member of the Scots Charitable Society of Boston in 1687. [SCS]

BETHUNE, GEORGE, admitted as a member of the Scots Charitable Society of Boston in 1705. [SCS]

BETHUNE, GEORGE, son of William Bethune of Craigfurdie, emigrated to Boston around 1724, a banker. [BFH]

BETHUNE, JOHN, admitted as a member of the Scots Charitable Society of Boston in 1719. [SCS]

BETHUNE, NATHANIEL, admitted as a member of the Scots Charitable Society of Boston in 1736. [SCS]

BEVERAGE, ..., to New England 1653, settled in Warren, Maine. [Imm.NE.#13]

BEWER, PETER, admitted as a member of the Scots Charitable Society of Boston in 1732. [SCS]

BIGGAR, WILLIAM, from Glasgow, a member of the Scots Charitable Society of Boston in 1748. [SCS]

BINNING, JOHN, admitted as a member of the Scots Charitable Society of Boston in 1702. [SCS]

BINNING, JOHN, from Edinburgh, admitted as a member of the Scots Charitable Society of Boston in 1762. [SCS]

BIRD, ANDREW, to New England 1653, married ... Hathorne, father of Jane, Agnes and Alexander, settled in Cushing. [ImmNE.13]

BISSET, GEORGE, educated in Aberdeen, a Society for the Propagation of the Gospel schoolmaster at Kay's Grammar School and assistant Anglican minister in Newport, Rhode Island, 21 March 1767, married Penelope Honeyman, Loyalist, died in London on 3 March 1788. [FPA.23/230,1][PRO.AO12.75.123,84/2]

BISSET, JOHN, an Episcopalian clergyman in Newport, Rhode Island, on 20 March 1786. [AJ#2024]

BLACK, DANIEL, a prisoner of war transported to New England on the John and Sarah of London, master John Greene in November 1651. [Suffolk Deeds, 1-56]

BLACK, DAVID, merchant in Boston, New England, and his wife Janet Greenlaw, parents of Margaret born 12 August 1775. [Glasgow OPR]; a Loyalist, [PRO.AO12.10.362]; a merchant in Boston 1783. [NAS.CS17.1.2/23]

BLACK, DOUGLAS, admitted as a member of the Scots Charitable Society of Boston in 1731. [SCS]

BLACKADDER, ADAM, born in Troqueer 16...., son of Reverend John Blackadder {died 1686} and Janet Haining, a merchant in New England. [F.2.302]

BLACKADDER, ARCHIBALD, admitted as a member of the Scots Charitable Society of Boston in 1720. [SCS]

BLACKADDER, CHRISTOPHER, from Cockenzie, East Lothian, admitted as a member of the Scots Charitable Society of Boston in 1739. [SCS]

BLACKADDER, JOHN, from St Kitts, admitted as a member of the Scots Charitable Society of Boston in 1740. [SCS]

BLACKADDER, THOMAS, born during the 1660s, son of Reverend John Blackadder and Janet Haining, a merchant in New England. [F#2.302]

BLACKBURN, HUGH, in Boston, son of Basil Blackburn of Prestonpans, East Lothian, 1807. [NAS.RD3.317.299]

BLACKETER, ARCHIBALD, admitted as a member of the Scots Charitable Society in 1725. [SCS]

BLACKIE, JOHN VITIE, admitted as a member of the Scots Charitable Society of Boston in 1827. [SCS]

BLACKLOCK, JOHN, member of the Scots Charitable Society of Boston 1687 [SCS]

BLACKLOCK, THOMAS, in Vermont, 1 November 1860. [NAS.RS.Annan#11/6]

BLACKSTOCK, JAMES, admitted as a member of the Scots Charitable Society of Boston in 1715. [SCS]

BLAIKIE, JAMES, from Eccles, Berwickshire, admitted as a member of the Scots Charitable Society of Boston in 1775. [SCS]

BLAIR, DAVID, emigrated to Massachusetts before 1720, father of Robert (1720-1801). [AA#4/42]; admitted as a member of the Scots Charitable Society in 1724. [SCS]

BLAIR, JAMES, admitted as a member of the Scots Charitable Society in 1724. [SCS]

BLAIR, JOHN, a baker in Boston, a Loyalist who settled in Shelbourne, Nova Scotia, in 1783. [PRO.AO13.25.47]

BLAIR, PATRICK, a doctor in Boston, 1750. [NAS.RD3.210.373]

BLAIR, PETER, from Cockburnspath, East Lothian, settled in Salem, Massachusetts, by 1752. [ImmNE#220]

BLAIR, ROBERT, from Kilbarchan, Renfrewshire, a member of the Scots Charitable Society of Boston in 1766. [SCS]

BLAIR, SARAH, daughter of David Blair of Adamton, wife of … Watkinson, emigrated to America in 17.., mother of David Watkinson a merchant in Hertford, Connecticut. [RAF]

BLAIR, WILLIAM, a merchant, arrived in Boston on 22 August 1765 aboard the Jamieson and Peggy, master John Aitken, from Leith. [PAB]

BLAKE, JOSEPH, born 1795, a farmer who emigrated on the brig Missionary, Captain Sears, in 1821, landed in Boston, Charlestown District. [USNA/par]

BLYTH, MARGARET, or ROLLO, born during 1813, from Newtown, Cupar, Fife, died at the home of her grandson George Rollo in Lumsden, Grenville, Connecticut, on 12 January 1895. [PJ]

BOAG, JOHN, baptised on 13 March 1690 in St Magnus, Kirkwall, Orkney, son of Thomas Boag and Marion Linkletter, emigrated to New England, married Elizabeth Preston on 24 December 1724, settled in Portsmouth, New Hampshire. [Imm.NE.17]

BODMAN, THOMAS, a physician who emigrated to Rhode Island in 1750. [SA#184]

BOGLE, ALEXANDER, admitted as a founder member of the Scots Charitable Society of Boston on 6 January 1657. [SCS]

BOGLE, THOMAS, of Sudbury, admitted as a member of the Scots Charitable Society of Boston in 1719. [SCS]

BOGLE, THOMAS, from Glasgow, admitted as a member of the Scots Charitable Society of Boston in 1747. [SCS]

BOGLE, WILLIAM, admitted as a member of the Scots Charitable Society of Boston in 1685. [SCS]

BOGUE, JOHN, emigrated from Glasgow to East Haddam, Connecticut, during 1680, father of Ebenezer Bogue (1716-1764). [AA#4/202][CAG#1/479]

BOHANNON, ANDREW, born 1709, emigrated to New England before 1734, married Tabitha Fletcher {1709-1810}, father of Sarah, Andrew, John, Jacob, and Annaniah, died ca.1803. [Imm.NE#19]

BOOTH, JAMES, tailor, admitted as a member of the Scots Charitable Society of Boston in 1685. [SCS]

BORLAND, FRANCIS, born 1666, son of John Borland in East Kilbride, Lanarkshire, a minister educated at Glasgow University, member of the Scots Charitable Society of Boston 1684, later in Surinam, Barbados and Darien, died in Lesmahagow, Lanarkshire, in 1722. [F.7.662][HMC.Laing#1.331]

BORLAND, FRANCIS, admitted as a member of the Scots Charitable Society of Boston in 1713. [SCS]

BORLAND, FRANCIS, a merchant in New England, 1743. [NAS.CS16.1.72]

BORLAND, JOHN, merchant, admitted as a member of the Scots Charitable Society of Boston in 1684; a merchant in Boston, New England, presently in London 1699. [NAS.RS42.Lanark.xi67/xii411]

BORTHWICK, WILLIAM, admitted as a member of the Scots Charitable Society of Boston in 1717. [SCS]

BOUCHER, JAMES, from Greenock, admitted as a member of the Scots Charitable Society of Boston in 1735. [SCS]

BOUDEN, JAMES, from Edinburgh, admitted as a member of the Scots Charitable Society of Boston in 1697. [SCS]

BOWMAN, ARCHIBALD, arrived in Boston on 28 May 1768 aboard the Glasgow, master John Dunn, from Glasgow. [PAB]

BOWMAN, JANE MCGRATH, in Lowell, cnf 1895. [NAS.SC70.1.337]

BOWMAN, JOHN, born in 1735, from Glasgow to New England in 1772. [HAR#2.249]

BOWMAN, SAMUEL, from Glasgow, admitted as a member of the Scots Charitable Society of Boston in 1738. [SCS]

BOYD, ALEXANDER, educated at Glasgow University, a minister who emigrated to America in 1743, settled in Georgetown, Maine, from 1748 to 1753, later in Newcastle, Maine, from 1754 to 1758. [CCNE][SA]

BOYD, JAMES, from Kilbride, Ayrshire, admitted as a member of the Scots Charitable Society of Boston in 1741. [SCS]

BOYD, JOHN, from Ayrshire, admitted as a member of the Scots Charitable Society of Boston in 1751. [SCS]

BOYD, JOHN P., admitted as a member of the Scots Charitable Society of Boston in 1829. [SCS]

BOYD, WILLIAM, born in 1874, son of William Boyd and Catherine Graham, died in Norwich, Connecticut, on 18 August 1919, buried in East London. [Bridgend g/s, Dunbarton]

BOYE, JOHN, a prisoner of war transported to New England on the John and Sarah of London, master John Greene in November 1651. [Suffolk Deeds, 1-56]

BOYE, ROBERT, a prisoner of war transported to New England on the John and Sarah of London, master John Greene in November 1651. [Suffolk Deeds, 1-56]

BOYLE, CHARLES, admitted as a member of the Scots Charitable Society of Boston in 1729. [SCS]

BOYLE, DAVID, born in Scotland 1819, a manufacturer, settled in Wolfesboro, Carroll County, New Hampshire, by 1850. [C]

BOYLE, JAMES, admitted as a member of the Scots Charitable Society of Boston in 1701. [SCS]

BOYLE, MARY, born in Scotland 1798, settled in Wolfesboro, Carroll County, New Hampshire, by 1850. [C]

BRABAND, ALEXANDER, a prisoner of war who was captured after the Battle of Dunbar in September 1650, transported on 3 November 1650 from London to New England on the Unity, an indentured servant at the Lynn Ironworks in Massachusetts. [NWI]

BRACE, DAVID, baptised on 28 March 1733 in Sandwick, Orkney, son of Alexander Brass and Marion Button, admitted as a member of the Scots Charitable Society of Boston in 1758, a resident of Boston in 1787. [SCS]

BRACKETT, ANTHONY, emigrated to Portsmouth, New Hampshire, before 1624, father of Thomas (1635-1676), died in 1691. [CAG#1/484]

BRADY, WILLIAM, admitted as a member of the Scots Charitable Society of Boston in 1714. [SCS]

BRAN, ALEXANDER, from Aberdeen, admitted as a member of the Scots Charitable Society of Boston in 1733. [SCS]

BRANDON, JOHN, arrived in Boston aboard the Patience and Judith, from London on 30 June 1716.[BSPL]

BREWER, (?), THOMAS, prisoner of war, captured after the Battle of Worcester in September 1651, transported from Gravesend, Kent, to Boston on the John and Sarah, master John Greene, on 13 May 1652. [NER]

BRICE, NINIAN, from Glasgow, admitted as a member of the Scots Charitable Society of Boston in 1731. [SCS]

BRISLAND, ANDREW, born in 1840, immigrated into Mass. on the New York Packet on 5 July 1849. [LAP]

BRISON, JOHN, emigrated to New England in 1753, settled in Warren, Maine. [Imm.NE#23]

BROCK, ANDREW, from Renfrewshire, settled in Ryegate, New Hampshire, in 1774. [HGP]

BROCK, PETER, admitted as a member of the Scots Charitable Society in 1725. [SCS]

BROCK, THOMAS, in Nantasket, admitted as a member of the Scots Charitable Society of Boston in 1734. [SCS]

BRODY, JOHN, in Kittery, Maine, husband of Sarah ...., probate 6 December 1681, Maine Register of Deeds 5/13

BROUGH, JAMES, admitted as a member of the Scots Charitable Society of Boston in 1711. [SCS]

BROUN, JOHN, a prisoner of war transported to New England on the John and Sarah of London, master John Greene in November 1651. [Suffolk Deeds, 1-56]

BROUNELL, HENRY, a prisoner of war transported to New England on the John and Sarah of London, master John Greene in November 1651. [Suffolk Deeds, 1-56]

BROWN, ADAM, admitted as a member of the Scots Charitable Society of Boston in 1713. [SCS]

BROWN, ADAM, admitted as a member of the Scots Charitable Society of Boston in 1830. [SCS]

BROWN, DAVID, mariner, admitted as a member of the Scots Charitable Society of Boston in 1685. [SCS]

BROWN, DAVID, settled in Boston, Massachusetts, Loyalist, moved to Nova Scotia during 1783. [Loyalists in Nova Scotia.158] [PRO.AO12.10.248]

BROWN, ELIZA, and her three children, had their passages paid to Scotland by the Society in August 1756. [SCS]

BROWN, GEORGE, shipmaster in New England, admitted as a
burgess of St Andrews 18 April 1741. [StABR]; possibly the
George Brown from St Andrews, Fife, who was admitted as
a member of the Scots Charitable Society of Boston in 1744.
[SCS]

BROWN, HENRY, Scots settler in Wells, York County, New
England, ca1675. [York Deeds, Book II folio 167]

BROWN, HUGH, from Glasgow, admitted as a member of the
Scots Charitable Society of Boston in 1746. [SCS]

BROWN, JAMES, son of Nicol Brown in Newmilnes, Ayrshire, a
minister, educated at Glasgow University, admitted as a
member of the Scots Charitable Society of Boston in 1686,
settled in Swansea, Massachusetts.[SCS][F.7.662]

BROWN, JAMES, admitted as a member of the Scots Charitable
Society of Boston in 1706. [SCS]

BROWN, JAMES, of Wenham, Connecticut, admitted as a
member of the Scots Charitable Society of Boston in 1719.
[SCS]

BROWN, JAMES, a shipmaster from Dunbar, East Lothian,
admitted as a member of the Scots Charitable Society of
Boston in 1767. [SCS]

BROWN, JOHN, a Cromwellian prisoner transported to Boston on
the John and Sarah of London, Captain John Greene, in
November 1651, in Cambridge, Massachusetts, in Marlboro,
Massachusetts, 1662, in Falmouth, Maine, 1678, returned to
Watertown, Massachusetts, died after 20 November 1697.
[AncH-NE] [EAF] [Suffolk Deeds, 1/56]

BROWN, JOHN, from Glasgow, admitted as a member of the
Scots Charitable Society of Boston in 1738. [SCS]

BROWN, JOHN, emigrated to New England in 1753, settled in
Warren, Maine, killed by Indians. [Imm.NE#24]

BROWN, JOHN, born in 1782, a weaver from Paisley, Renfrewshire, who emigrated via Liverpool to Maine on the Mexico, master A. P. Patterson, in 1830. [PTA]

BROWN, JOHN, a joiner from Leven, Fife, died in Hartfield, Connecticut, on 15 March 1886. [FFP]

BROWN, JOHN, born 1856, a blacksmith from Leven, Fife, died in Hartfield, Connecticut, on 18 September 1891. [FFP]

BROWN, ROBERT, from Airth, Stirlingshire, admitted as a member of the Scots Charitable Society of Boston in 1729. [SCS]

BROWN, ROBERT, from Wigton, admitted as a member of the Scots Charitable Society of Boston in 1736. [SCS]

BROWN, WILLIAM, merchant from Ayr, admitted as a member of the Scots Charitable Society of Boston in 1684. [SCS]

BROWN, WILLIAM, in Narragansett, admitted as a member of the Scots Charitable Society of Boston in 1713. [SCS]

BROWN, WILLIAM, admitted as a member of the Scots Charitable Society of Boston in 1739. [SCS]

BROWN, WILLIAM, from Glasgow, admitted as a member of the Scots Charitable Society of Boston in 1763. [SCS]

BROWNING, JAMES, born 1672 in Scotland, emigrated via Ireland to New England around 1720, married Elizabeth ..., in Rutland, Maine, during June 1720, father of William, Elizabeth, James, Tristram, Margaret, Joseph, Mary, John, Samuel, and Martha, died on 3 February 1749. [Imm.NE#24/221]

BRUCE, ALEXANDER, from Orkney, admitted as a member of the Scots Charitable Society of Boston in 1761. [SCS]

BRUCE, ARCHIBALD, born in 1777, educated at Edinburgh University around 1799, emigrated to Massachusetts, died during 1818. [SA]

BRUCE, DAVID, born in Edinburgh, a Moravian missionary in Pennsylvania, New York, and New Jersey from 1740 to 1749, died in Sharon, Connecticut on 9 July 1749. [CCMC]

BRUCE, JAMES, from Carsten, Orkney, admitted as a member of the Scots Charitable Society of Boston in 1744. [SCS]

BRUCE, JAMES, shipmaster in Boston, New England, now a mariner in Stepney, London, 1789. [NAS.CS17.1.8/21]

BRUCE, JOHN, admitted as a member of the Scots Charitable Society of Boston in 1729. [SCS]

BRUCE, JOHN, possibly from Edinburgh, settled in Sudbury, Massachusetts, by 1762. [AA#6.36]

BRUCE, ROBERT, born 1740, emigrated via London to New England on the Amherst on 21 March 1774. [NER#63.234]

BRUCE, TIMOTHY, a Scot, married Susanna Joslin 17.., father of Timothy, Thomas, Samuel, and William. [Imm.NE#24]

BRUCE, WILLIAM, admitted as a member of the Scots Charitable Society of Boston in 1734. [SCS]

BRUNTON, GRISEL, born 1750, resident in Perth, emigrated from Greenock to Salem on the Glasgow Packet, master Alexander Porterfield, in April 1775. [PRO.T47/12]

BRUNTON, ELIZA, eldest daughter of John Brunton a shipmaster in Aberdeen, married Ronald C. Macfie from London, Canada West, in Boston, USA, on 3 November 1862. [AJ#5993]

BRYCE, PATRICK, a merchant from Glasgow, admitted as a member of the Scots Charitable Society of Boston on 25 October 1684. [SCS]

BRYDON, JAMES, admitted as a member of the Scots Charitable Society of Boston in 1827. [SCS]

BRYSON, JAMES, emigrated from Greenock aboard the brigantine Matty, master Thomas Cochrane, on 19 May 1774 bound for New York, arrived there on 22 July 1774, settled Barnet, Vermont. [HBV]

BUCHANAN, AGNES, possibly form Glasgow, settled in Chester, Connecticut, during 1755, married William Mitchell. [NNQ#7/89]

BUCHANAN, DAVID, a prisoner of war transported to New England on the John and Sarah of London, master John Greene in November 1651. [Suffolk Deeds, 1-56]

BUCHANAN, DUNCAN, admitted as a member of the Scots Charitable Society of Boston in 1686. [SCS]

BUCHANAN, HENRY, born 1751, a wright from Glasgow, emigrated from Greenock to Salem on the Glasgow Packet, master Alexander Porterfield, in April 1775. [PRO.T47/12]

BUCHANAN, JAMES, from Glasgow, admitted as a member of the Scots Charitable Society of Boston in 1729. [SCS]

BUCHANAN, JEAN, born 1738, a resident of Glasgow, emigrated from Greenock to Salem on the Glasgow Packet, master Alexander
Porterfield, in April 1775. [PRO.T47/12]

BUCHANAN, JOHN, a prisoner of war transported to New England on the John and Sarah of London, master John Greene in November 1651. [Suffolk Deeds, 1-56]

BUCHANAN, JOHN, admitted as a member of the Scots Charitable Society of Boston in 1693. [SCS]

BUCHANAN, JOHN, in Lowell, Massachusetts, died in July 1859, cnf 1878. [NAS.SC70.1.189]

BUCHANAN, WALTER W., M.D., educated at Glasgow University and at Edinburgh University around 1797, emigrated to Massachusetts. [SA]

BUCHANAN, WILLIAM admitted as a member of the Scots
Charitable Society of Boston in 1691. [SCS]

BUCHANAN, WILLIAM, a surgeon, arrived in Boston on 17 August
1767 aboard the snow <u>Jenny</u>, master Hector Orr, from
Glasgow. [PAB]

BUCKLINE, Captain DAVID, in Boston, admitted as a burgess and
guildsbrother of Glasgow on 19 August 1713, [GBR]

BUDGE, WILLIAM, from Caithness, admitted as a member of the
Scots Charitable Society of Boston in 1732. [SCS]

BULL, JONATHAN, admitted as a member of the Scots Charitable
Society of Boston in 1695. [SCS]

BULLMAN, ALEXANDER, admitted as a member of the Scots
Charitable Society of Boston in 1694. [SCS]

BURBEEN, JOHN, a tailor, settled in Woburn, Massachusetts,
before 1660. [Anc.H-NE]

BURCHILL, N. R., born 1800, a farmer who emigrated on the
<u>Cherub</u>, Captain Shepherd, in 1821, landed in Boston,
Charlestown District. [USNA/par]

BURGESS, ALEXANDER, a prisoner of war captured after the
Battle of Dunbar in September 1650, transported to New
England on the <u>Unity</u>, an indentured servant at the Lynn
Ironworks in Massachusetts. [NWI]

BURN, JOHN, Member of the Council of Massachusetts, dead by
1789, Loyalist claim by his widow Ann Burn in Edinburgh,
1789. [PRO.AO13.74.264-265]

BURNETT, DAVID, admitted as a member of the Scots Charitable
Society of Boston in 1745, a resident of Boston in 1787.
[SCS]

BURNETT, JAMES G., of Friendville, Aberdeen, married Mary
Grace Tyrel, youngest daughter of Nathan Tyrel of
Providence, Rhode Island, in New York during 1837.
[AJ#4683]

BURNET, THOMAS, emigrated to Lynn, Massachusetts, before 1640, married Mary Pierson in 1663, father of Daniel. [CAG#1/720]

BURNS, D., born 1793, a clergyman, emigrated on the schooner Victory, Captain Leavet, in 1821, landed in Boston, Charlestown District. [USNA/par]

BURNS, JOHN, born in 1701, son of Thomas Burns and Margaret Leslie, emigrated via Londonderry to New England in 1736, with wife and 3 children. [Imm.NE#26]

BURNTON, WILLIAM, admitted as a member of the Scots Charitable Society of Boston in 1714. [SCS]

BURT, CHARLES, emigrated from Greenock aboard the brigantine Matty, master Thomas Cochrane, on 19 May 1774 bound for New York, arrived there on 22 July 1774, settled Barnet, Vermont. [HBV]

BURTON, WILLIAM, a merchant, arrived in Boston on 15 November 1763 aboard the Diligence, master Charles Robison, from Glasgow. [SG#4.4.14][PAB]

BURTON, WILLIAM, from North Berwick, East Lothian, admitted as a member of the Scots Charitable Society of Boston in 1765, a resident of Boston in 1787. [SCS]

BUTLER, MARY, born in Boston during 1763, daughter of William Butler and Mary Butler, wife of David Laird, died in Strathmartine during 1797. [Strathmartine g/s, Angus]

CADELL, ROBERT, admitted as a member of the Scots Charitable Society of Boston in 1733. [SCS]

CADWELL, EDWARD, emigrated to New England by 1630. [AA#9/66]

CADWELL, MATTHEW, emigrated to New England by 1630. [AA#9/66]

CAHOONE, WILLIAM, probably a prisoner of war banished by
Oliver Cromwell, an indentured servant of Becx and
Company, settled at the Saugus River Iron Works,
Massachusetts, around 1651/1652. [SG#14.2.36]

CAIE, GEORGE, born in 1837, a printer from Aberdeen, died in
Newhaven, Connecticut, on 9 July 1866. [AJ:9.7.1866]

CAIRNS, JOHN, admitted as a member of the Scots Charitable
Society in 1723. [SCS]

CAKLE, ROGER, emigrated to New England in 1773.
[Imm.NE#27]

CALDER, ROBERT, admitted as a member of the Scots
Charitable Society of Boston in 1719. [SCS]

CALDER, WILLIAM, admitted as a member of the Scots
Charitable Society of Boston in 1733. [SCS]

CALDER, WILLIAM, possibly from Aberdeenshire, settled in
Hartfield,
Connecticut, before 1809. [NAS.SH.6.7.1809]

CALDERWOOD, JAMES, and his wife Margaret, emigrated via
Londonderry, Ireland, to America in 1725, settled at English
Range, North Beaver Pond, Londonderry, New Hampshire.
[TCF]

CALDWELL, CHARLES, emigrated from Beith, Ayrshire, to New
England in 1718. [NER#58/36]

CALDWELL, JAMES, husband of Agnes .... in Falkirk,
Stirlingshire, a seaman on HMS Captain, died in Boston,
New England, probate September 1774 PCC

CALDWELL, JOHN, admitted as a member of the Scots Charitable
Society of Boston in 1716. [SCS]

CALDWELL, JOHN, (brother of Charles above), emigrated from
Beith, Ayrshire, to New England in 1718. [NER#58/36]

CALDWELL, JOHN, admitted as a member of the Scots Charitable Society in 1723. [SCS]

CALHOUN, JOHN, in Taunton, Massachusetts, 1845. [NAS.GD1.814.10]

CALLENDAR, ALESTER, a prisoner of war transported to New England on the John and Sarah of London, master John Greene in November 1651. [Suffolk Deeds, 1-56]

CALLENDAR, DAVID, a prisoner of war transported to New England on the John and Sarah of London, master John Greene in November 1651. [Suffolk Deeds, 1-56]

CALLENDAR, JAMES, a prisoner of war transported to New England on the John and Sarah of London, master John Greene in November 1651. [Suffolk Deeds, 1-56]

CALLO, MARGARET, arrived in Boston on 28 October 1763 aboard the Douglas, master James Montgomerie, from Scotland. [PAB]

CAMERON, DONALD, a laborer, arrived in Boston on 26 July 1764 aboard the snow Douglas, master Robert Manderston, from Greenock. [PAB][SG#7.4.14]

CAMERON, FINLAY, arrived in Boston on 1 June 1768 aboard the snow Jenny, master Hector Orr, from Glasgow. [PAB]

CAMERON, JOHN, from Inverness, admitted as a member of the Scots Charitable Society of Boston in 1733. [SCS]

CAMERON, JOHN, a millwright, emigrated from Greenock on the snow Douglas, master Robert Manderston, to Boston, arrived there on 26 July 1764. [SG#7.4.14][PAB]

CAMERON, WILLIAM, from Greenock, admitted as a member of the Scots Charitable Society of Boston in 1731. [SCS]

CAMPBELL, ARCHIBALD, son of Colin Campbell in Rosneath, Dunbartonshire, a marine who died in Boston, Massachusetts, in 1775. Probate 1775 PCC

CAMPBELL, CUTHBERT, baptised on 3 February 1661, son of Alexander and Barbara Campbell in Langa near Campbeltown, emigrated before 1714, a freeman of Rhode Island on 1 May 1718, postmaster there, died there. [SG.40.4.132]; admitted as a member of the Scots Charitable Society of Boston in 1713. [SCS]

CAMPBELL, DANIEL, admitted as a member of the Scots Charitable Society of Boston in 1693. [SCS]

CAMPBELL, DANIEL, admitted as a member of the Scots Charitable Society of Boston in 1694. [SCS]

CAMPBELL, DANIEL, born in 1696, emigrated to New England in 1716, died on 8 March 1744 in Rutland, Maine. [Imm.NE#28/221]

CAMPBELL, DAVID, admitted as a member of the Scots Charitable Society of Boston in 1686; bookseller in Boston, a benefactor of Glasgow University in 1692. [MUG#442][SCS]

CAMPBELL, DAVID, born in 1692, emigrated to New England, father of William, settled in Litchfield, New Hampshire, died 1777. [Imm.NE#28]

CAMPBELL DONALD, son of Malcolm Campbell in Fortingall, Perthshire, servant to ... McDonald, a Jacobite, captured at the Siege of Preston in 1715, transported to the West Indies, settled in New England, died there before 1748, [CM, January 1748]

CAMPBELL, DUNCAN, bookbinder, admitted as a member of the Scots Charitable Society of Boston in 1684. [SCS]

CAMPBELL, DUNCAN, late of Boston, probate 19 May 1704 New York. [Liber 3/4, fo.386]

CAMPBELL, D., admitted as a member of the Scots Charitable Society of Boston in 1826. [SCS]

CAMPBELL, EDWARD, admitted as a member of the Scots Charitable Society of Boston in 1735. [SCS]

CAMPBELL, Mrs ELIZABETH, with her mother and four daughters, emigrated from Glasgow on the snow Amity, master Nathaniel Breed, to Boston, arrived there on 14 May 1716. [SG#7.4.14]

CAMPBELL, GEORGE, admitted as a member of the Scots Charitable Society of Boston in 1721. [SCS]

CAMPBELL, GEORGE, from Burbreck, Argyll, Captain of the Royal Marines, admitted as a member of the Scots Charitable Society of Boston in 1762. [SCS]

CAMPBELL, HUGH, a merchant who settled in Boston, Massachusetts, before 1679. [Insh#191]

CAMPBELL, JAMES, a prisoner of war transported to New England on the John and Sarah of London, master John Greene in November 1651. [Suffolk Deeds, 1-56]

CAMPBELL, JAMES, admitted as a member of the Scots Charitable Society of Boston in 1711. [SCS]

CAMPBELL, JAMES, probably from Newton Stewart, Wigtonshire, settled in Connecticut by 1842. [NAS.SH.29.12.1842]

CAMPBELL, JOHN, a prisoner of war transported to New England on the John and Sarah of London, master John Greene in November 1651. [Suffolk Deeds, 1-56]

CAMPBELL, JOHN, merchant, from Glasgow, admitted as a member of the Scots Charitable Society of Boston on 25 October 1684; boxmaster on 4 February 1695. [SCS]

CAMPBELL, JOHN, born in Scotland 1653, married Mary Clarke, father of Sarah and Elizabeth, settled in New England around 1695, a journalist (published the Boston Newsletter from 1704-1722) and postmaster in Boston from 1702-1718, died on 4 March 1728. [DAB.3.456][WA, p162][NAS.GD152.200]

CAMPBELL, JOHN, from Jamaica, admitted as a member of the Scots Charitable Society of Boston in 1707. [SCS]

CAMPBELL, JOHN, settled in Lancaster, Massachusetts, in 1732. [AA#6/87]

CAMPBELL, JOHN, born around 1690, a minister and physician, settled in Massachusetts, died in 1761. [SA#179]

CAMPBELL, JOHN, a merchant, arrived in Boston on 1 May 1769 from Glasgow on the Nancy, Captain James Moody. [PAB]

CAMPBELL, JOHN GILLIS, emigrated to New England, married Jeanette Baird, in Boston, died in Warren, Maine, during 1809. [Imm.NE#29]

CAMPBELL, JOSEPH, master of the Jenny of Wiscafull, Lincoln County, Massachusetts, in 1793. [NAS.RD2.254.813]

CAMPBELL, LIONEL, arrived in Boston on 28 October 1763 aboard the Douglas, master James Montgomerie, from Scotland. [PAB]

CAMPBELL, MATHEW, admitted as a member of the Scots Charitable Society of Boston in 1690. [SCS]

CAMPBELL, NEIL, a prisoner of war transported to New England on the John and Sarah of London, master John Greene in November 1651. [Suffolk Deeds, 1-56]

CAMPBELL, PETER, a house carpenter, arrived in Boston on 17 August 1767 aboard the snow Jenny, master Hector Orr, from Glasgow. [PAB]

CAMPBELL, ROBERT, commander of the Truth and Daylight, admitted as a member of the Scots Charitable Society of Boston in 1716. [SCS]

CAMPBELL, ROBERT, admitted as a member of the Scots Charitable Society in 1724. [SCS]

CAMPBELL, ROBERT, emigrated to New England before 1760, married Margaret ...{1759-1810}, settled in New Ipswich, died after 1791. [ImmNE#29]

CAMPBELL, SUSANNAH, admitted to the Scots Charitable Society of Boston in 1696. [SCS]

CAMPBELL, THOMAS, admitted as a member of the Scots Charitable Society of Boston in 1717. [SCS]

CAMPBELL, THOMAS BOSTON, admitted as a member of the Scots Charitable Society of Boston in 1802. [SCS]

CAMPBELL, WILLIAM, admitted as a member of the Scots Charitable Society of Boston in 1719. [SCS]

CAMPBELL, WILLIAM, a shipmaster in Rhode Island, son of George Campbell of Carsegownie and his wife Grizel Ogilvy, 1755, 1759. [NAS.CS16.1.95/105; CS16.1.103/202]

CAMPBELL, WILLIAM, born in Cowal, Argyll, during 1741, emigrated to Massachusetts in 1768, a merchant in Worcester, Massachusetts, before the Revolution, a Loyalist who moved to Halifax, Nova Scotia, later settled in St John, New Brunswick, died there during 1823. [PRO.AO.13.24.72/4][The Loyalists of Massachusetts, p.76]

CANNING, CATHERINE, born in 1834, immigrated into Massachusetts on board the Mary Ann on 31 August 1849. [LAP]

CANNING, JOHN, born in 1848, immigrated into Massachusetts on the brig Harmony 7 November 1850. [LAP]

CARGILL, JAMES, elder of the First Church of Christ, Portsmouth, New Hampshire, 1765. [Loyalists of Massachusetts.23]

CARGILL, LOUISA, in Boston, cnf.1893. [NAS.SC70.1.326]

CARLE, ROBERT, admitted to the Scots Charitable Society of Boston in 1697. [SCS]

CARLISLE, ALEXANDER, emigrated to New England in 1743, settled in Boston, Massachusetts; admitted as a member of the Scots Charitable Society of Boston in 1744. [ImmNE#30][SCS]

CARMICHAEL, JOHN, a prisoner of war captured after the Battle of Dunbar in September 1650, transported to New England, an indentured servant, settled in New Hampshire, and later in York, Maine. [NWI]

CARMICHAEL, WILLIAM, a prisoner of war transported to New England on the John and Sarah of London, master John Greene in November 1651. [Suffolk Deeds, 1-56]

CARNEGIE, PATRICK, from Glasgow, admitted as a member of the Scots Charitable Society of Boston in 1750. [SCS]

CARNES, EDWARD, in Boston, admitted as a member of the Scots Charitable Society of Boston in 1765. [SCS]

CARNES, JOHN, admitted to the Scots Charitable Society of Boston in 1696. [SCS]

CARNS, MUNGO, from Ackford, admitted as a member of the Scots Charitable Society of Boston in 1756. [SCS]

CARR, JOHN, admitted as a member of the Scots Charitable Society of Boston in 1732. [SCS]

CARRAN, ELIZABETH, arrived in Boston on 28 October 1763 aboard the Douglas, master James Montgomerie, from Scotland. [PAB]

CARRICK, JAMES, son of James Carrick in Balveard Mill, Abernethy, Fife, a merchant who settled in Boston, Massachusetts, before 1754. [NAS.SH.5.4.1754]; admitted as a member of the Scots Charitable Society of Boston in 1747. [SCS]

CARRUTHERS, JAMES, from Edinburgh, admitted as a member of the Scots Charitable Society of Boston in 1761. [SCS]

CARRUTHERS, Reverend JAMES, born in Ecclefechan, Dumfries-shire, in 1771, died in Portland, Maine, on 28 November 1857. [AO]

CARRUTHERS, WILLIAM, born in 1804, died in Almesbury Village, Boston, on 6 March 1860. [AO]

CARSON, JOHN, born in 1812, with Helen Carson, born in 1812, William Carson born in 1839, Elizabeth Carson born in 1841, John Carson born in 1843, Helen Carson born in 1846, and Janet Carson born in 1849, immigrated into Massachusetts aboard the brig Lydia on 20 May 1850. [LAP]

CARSON, JAMES, son of James Carson a shipmaster and Elspeth Cowan, settled in Boston before 1855. [Dumfries g/s]

CARSON, JOHN, born around 1702, son of John Carson, emigrated to New England by 1756, married Mary Livingstone, settled in New Boston and in Francistown, New Hampshire, died during 1792. [ImmNE#30]

CARSON, WILLIAM, born 1722, son of John Carson, emigrated to New England before 1770, married Isabel Johnson in Lyndborough, settled in Lyndborough and in Francistown, New Hampshire, died in 1818. [Imm.NE#30]

CARSWELL, JOHN, emigrated to New England in 1753, settled in Warren, Maine. [ImmNE#31]

CARTER, NEIL, a prisoner of war transported to New England on the John and Sarah of London, master John Greene in November 1651. [Suffolk Deeds, 1-56]

CARY, SAMUEL, from Glasgow, a merchant and planter in Grenada, settled in Boston during 1791, died in 1800. [Massachusetts Historical Society MS]

CASWELL, MARGARET, born in Glasgow during 1695, married Gowen Fulton, settled in Topsham, Maine, died during 1791. [Imm.NE]

CATHCART, ANDREW admitted as a member of the Scots Charitable Society of Boston in 1691. [SCS]

CATHCART, ANDREW, from Kingston, Jamaica, died in Rhode Island during 1792. [NAS.CS16.1.173/206]

CATHCART, ROBERT, admitted as a member of the Scots Charitable Society of Boston in 1707. [SCS]

CHALMERS, JAMES, from Greenock, admitted as a member of the Scots Charitable Society of Boston in 1757. [SCS]

CHALMERS, JAMES, from Elie, Fife, admitted as a member of the Scots Charitable Society of Boston in 1771. [SCS]

CHARITY, JAMES, a merchant who settled in Boston, Massachusetts, before 1765. [NAS.SC36.63.8.168]; from Glasgow, admitted as a member of the Scots Charitable Society of Boston in 1762. [SCS]

CHARTERS, HARRY, from Dundee, a Captain in General Loudon's Regiment of Foot, admitted as a member of the Scots Charitable Society of Boston in 1757. [SCS]

CHARTERS, WILLIAM, admitted as a member of the Scots Charitable Society of Boston in 1705. [SCS]

CHASE, WILLIAM, in Brookline, Norfolk County, Massachusetts, cnf 1896. [NAS.SC70.1.351]

CHEAP, PATRICK, a trader, from Glasgow to Boston on the brig Success, master Andrew Gibson, on 2 April 1712; admitted as a member of the Scots Charitable Society of Boston in 1712. [SCS][PTA#129]

CHIENE, JAMES M. M., youngest son of Patrick Chiene, Abercromby Place, Edinburgh, died in Boston on 28 September 1857. [EEC#21236]

CHISHOLM, HUGH, in Portland, Maine, 1885, grandson of Colin Chisholm of Fanellan, died 1862, and Isabel McConnell, died in Kerrow 1816. [Clachan Comair, Kerrow, g/s]

CHISHOLM, WILLIAM, born 1843, died in Boston on 26 January 1911. [Creich g/s]

CHRISTIAN, ELIZABETH, arrived in Boston on 28 October 1763 aboard the Douglas, master James Montgomerie, from Scotland. [PAB]

CHRISTIE, BETSY, wife of Henry Christie, third daughter of George Christie at the Mains of Lindores, Fife, died in Chelsea, Massachusetts, on 14 February 1859. [FH]

CHRISTIE, DAVID, from Fraserburgh, Aberdeenshire, admitted as a member of the Scots Charitable Society of Boston in 1743. [SCS]

CHRISTOPHER, JAMES, admitted as a member of the Scots Charitable Society of Boston in 1732. [SCS]

CLERK, JAMES, son of Sir James Clerk of Penicuik, Midlothian, a merchant in Boston, Massachusetts, before 1716. [NAS.GD158]

CLARK, JAMES, settled in Durham, Otter Creek, Charlotte County, Vermont, in 1772, a Loyalist in Montreal 1787 [PRO.AO12.31.13]

CLARK, JAMES, son of John Clark {1820-1902} and Margaret Irving {1809-1851}, died in Boston on 15 January 1890. [Whithorn g/s, Wigtownshire]

CLARK, JOHN, prisoner of war captured after the Battle of Dunbar in September 1650, transported on 3 November 1650 from London to New England on the Unity, an indentured servant at the Lynn Ironworks in Massachusetts, [NWI]; admitted as a founder member of the Scots Charitable Society of Boston on 6 January 1657. [SCS]

CLERK, JOHN, a Covenanter from Argyll, transported from Leith to New England on 9 July 1685. [RPCS.11.94]

CLARK, JOHN, from Greenock, admitted as a member of the Scots Charitable Society of Boston in 1737. [SCS]

CLARK, JOHN, born in 1739, a merchant in Halifax, Nova Scotia, died in Roxburgh, near Boston, New England, on 17 August 1761. [AJ#710]

CLARK, JOHN, administrator of Archibald Anderson's will, 10 October 1661. [Salem Quarterly Court Records, Vol.4, p 82]

CLARK, JOHN, admitted as a member of the Scots Charitable Society of Boston in 1713. [SCS]

CLARK, JOHN, admitted as a member of the Scots Charitable Society of Boston in 1717. [SCS]

CLARK, JOHN, a shoemaker, arrived in Boston on the snow Douglas, master Robert Manderston, on 26 July 1764 from Glasgow. [SG#7/15][PAB]

CLARKE, JOHN, graduated MA from Glasgow University in 1764, a minister in Boston, graduated Doctor of Divinity of Edinburgh University on 12 September 1795. [CEG][MAGU#109]

CLARK, JOHN, born 1749, a farmer in Stirlingshire, emigrated from Greenock to New York on the Matty, master Thomas Cochrane, during May 1774, landed in New York on 22 July 1774, settled in Barnet, New Hampshire. [PRO.T47.12][HGP]

CLARK, JOHN, eldest son of Robert Clark, late of Windmill, Annan, Dumfries-shire, then in Clark's Mill, Oneida County, New York, died in Hartford, Connecticut, on 2 March 1864. [AO]

CLARK, JOSIAS, admitted as a member of the Scots Charitable Society of Boston in 1687. [SCS]

CLARK, ROBERT, a trader, from Glasgow to Boston on the brig Success, master Andrew Gibson, on 2 April 1712, admitted as a member of the Scots Charitable Society of Boston in 1712. [SCS][PTA#129]

CLARK, THOMAS, settled in Ryegate, Vermont, before 1780. [VHS]

CLARK, THOMAS, emigrated from Greenock aboard the brigantine Matty, master Thomas Cochrane, on 19 May 1774 bound for New York, arrived there on 22 July 1774, settled Barnet, Vermont. [HBV]

CLARK, WILLIAM, from Glasgow, admitted as a member of the Scots Charitable Society of Boston in 1753. [SCS]

CLEGHORN, JAMES, a prisoner of war, transported to New England in 1650 or 1651, an indentured servant of Bernard Lambert in Barnstable, later settled at Martha's Vineyard, Massachusetts. [NWI]

CLELAND, JAMES, admitted as a member of the Scots Charitable Society of Boston in 1715. [SCS]

CLELAND, WILLIAM, admitted as a member of the Scots Charitable Society of Boston in 1716. [SCS]

CLEMY, ALEXANDER, admitted as a member of the Scots Charitable Society of Boston in 1688. [SCS]

CLEWSTON, JAMES, baptised on 15 June 1734, son of Henry Clewston and Anna Robertson in Stenness, Orkney, admitted as a member of the Scots Charitable Society of Boston in 1751. [SCS]

CLEWSTON, WILLIAM, a prisoner of war transported to New England on the John and Sarah of London, master John Greene in November 1651. [Suffolk Deeds, 1-56]

CLEWSTON, WILLIAM, from Orkney, admitted as a member of the Scots Charitable Society of Boston in 1756. [SCS]

CLOUSTON, THOMAS, a shipmaster in Newberry, New England, son of Robert Clouston, carpenter and sailor in Stromness, Orkney, 17 June 1776. [NAS.RS.Orkney.133]

CLOUSTON, WILLIAM, admitted as a member of the Scots Charitable Society of Boston in 1800. [SCS]

CLUNIE, MARY, wife of Forbes Dick from Kirkcaldy, died in Torryton, Connecticut, on 9 August 1901. [FFP]

CLYDE, DANIEL, born in Lanarkshire during 1683, a joiner who emigrated via Ireland to New England in 1730, settled in Boston on 9 September 1730, married Esther Rankin, died in June 1753. [Imm.NE#35]

COCHRAN, ALEXANDER, admitted as a member of the Scots Charitable Society of Boston in 1736. [SCS]

COCHRANE, ALEXANDER, in Rhode Island in 1777. [EUL.Laing Writs, Dundonald]

COCHRAN, HUGH, born in Scotland or Ulster, deserted the Newport, Rhode Island Regiment in 1760. [NYM 5 May 1760]

COCHRAN, JOHN, admitted as a member of the Scots Charitable Society of Boston in 1687. [SCS]

COCHRAN, ROWLAND, admitted as a member of the Scots Charitable Society of Boston in 1710. [SCS]

COCHRAN, THOMAS, emigrated from Glasgow to Boston on the Jenny, master Archibald Orr, landed in Boston on 31 October 1766. [SG#7.4.15][PAB]

COCHRAN, WILLIAM, in Charlestown, admitted as a member of the Scots Charitable Society of Boston in 1684. [SCS]

COCHRAN, WILLIAM JOHNSTON, admitted as a member of the Scots Charitable Society of Boston in 1826. [SCS]

COCKBURN, JOHN, mariner, resident in Bristol, Massachusetts, wife Mary Cockburn in London, executors John Borland and John Maxwell merchants in Boston, and William Ralston of Newport, probate 5 January 1702, Bristol County, Massachusetts

COCKBURN, WILLIAM, admitted as a member of the Scots Charitable Society of Boston in 1715. [SCS]

COLE, ALEXANDER, admitted as a member of the Scots Charitable Society of Boston in 1684. [SCS]

COLE, MARY, residing in Augusta, Maine, daughter of Samuel S. Cole of Greenvale, married John Black, ship chandler in Barony parish, Glasgow, 16 June 1850. [Barony OPR]

COLLINGHAM, BARNARD, in Providence, Rhode Island, cnf 1881. [NAS.SC70.1.200]

COLQUHOUN, JAMES, from Glasgow, admitted as a member of the Scots Charitable Society of Boston in 1759. [SCS]

COLQUHOUN, JOHN, a prisoner of war transported to New England on the John and Sarah of London, master John Greene in November 1651. [Suffolk Deeds, 1-56]

COLQUHOUN, JOHN, son of John Colquhoun in Paisley, Renfrewshire, emigrated via Liverpool to America in November 1841, settled in Rhode Island. [NAS.GD1.814.9]

COLSON, DAVID, admitted as a member of the Scots Charitable Society of Boston in 1710. [SCS]

COLVILLE, CHARLES, from Ayrshire, admitted as a member of the Scots Charitable Society of Boston in 1747. [SCS]

COLVILLE, WILLIAM, from Liberton, Edinburgh, admitted as a member of the Scots Charitable Society of Boston in 1774. [SCS]

COLVIN, JAMES KENNEDY, an ironfounder in Providence, Rhode Island, cnf 1896. [NAS.SC70.1.350]

COMEY, DAVID, in Woburn, Massachusetts, 1663, later in Concord, Massachusetts, 1664. [Anc.H-NE]

COMREY, ALEXANDER, emigrated from Greenock aboard the brigantine Matty, master Thomas Cochrane, on 19 May 1774 bound for New York, arrived there on 22 July 1774, settled Barnet, Vermont. [HBV]

CONE, DANIEL, born around 1626, settled in Middlesex County, Connecticut, by 1660, a farmer and landowner, married (1) Mehitable Spencer in 1662, (2) Mrs Rebecca Walkley in 1692, died on 24 October 1706. [AA#9/135][Massachusetts Historical Society, Winthrop MS]

CONKIE, DAVID, from Twynholm, Galloway, admitted as a member of the Scots Charitable Society of Boston in 1767. [SCS]

CONNELL, GEORGE, admitted as a member of the Scots Charitable Society of Boston in 1801. [SCS]

CONNEL, JAMES, a schoolmaster who emigrated from Greenock on the Stirling Castle, master James Cockburn, to Boston, arrived there on 6 April 1766. [SG#7.4.15][PAB]

COOK, ANSEL G., born in Scotland during 1862, in Tisbury, Massachussetts, by 1880. [C]

COOK, Mrs HARRIET A, born in Scotland during 1824, a housekeeper in Tisbury, Massachusetts, by 1880. [C]

COOPER, ALEXANDER, prisoner of war captured after the Battle of Dunbar in September 1650, transported on 3 November 1650 from London to New England on the Unity, an indentured servant who settled in Berwick, Kittery, Maine, died 11 February 1684. probate 28 February 1684, Maine Register of Deeds 5/27. [refs. only son John Cooper, Richard Nason sr., James Warren sr., Peter Grant, John Taylor, George Gray, and Patrick Bryce traveller][NWI]

COPELAND, LAURENCE, born in 1599, settled in Braintree, Massachusetts, by 1651. [Anc.H-NE]

CORBETT, WILLIAM, son of James Corbett a merchant burgess of Glasgow, a merchant who settled in Boston, Massachusetts, died on 4 January 1768 [GA.B10.15.7234/7137]; admitted as a member of the Scots Charitable Society of Boston in 1756. [SCS]

CORCORAN, HUGH, of the Olive of Glasgow, admitted to the Scots Charitable Society of Boston in 1726. [SCS]

CORDINER, JOHN, a merchant, son of John Cordiner in Glasgow, admitted as a member of the Scots Charitable Society of Boston in 1686, a merchant in Boston, father of Christina, died in Boston by 1712. [NAS.SH.17.10.1712][SCS]

CORKAN, CATHERINE, arrived in Boston on 28 October 1763 aboard the Douglas, master James Montgomerie, from Scotland. [PAB]

CORLED, ROBERT, arrived in Boston on 28 October 1763 aboard the Douglas, master James Montgomerie, from Scotland. [PAB]

CORLED, SIMON, arrived in Boston on 28 October 1763 aboard the Douglas, master James Montgomerie, from Scotland. [PAB]

CORMACK, GILBERT, admitted as a member of the Scots Charitable Society of Boston in 1694. [SCS]

CORRIE, JOHN, in Providence, Rhode Island, 1740. [NAS.CS16.1.69]

CORRIE, MARGARET, born in 1821 daughter of Robert Corrie and Jane Haining in Hollows, Torthorwald, Dumfries-shire, emigrated to Rhode Island, died there on 18 December 1898, buried in River Bend Cemetery there. [Torthorwald g/s, Dumfries-shire]

CORRIE, WALTER, in Providence, Rhode Island, 1740. [NAS.CS16.1.69]

CORRIGALL, JOHN, admitted as a member of the Scots Charitable Society of Boston in 1719. [SCS]

CORSAR, JOHN, born in 1678, emigrated to New England by 1716, married Tabitha Kenny in Newbury during 1716, settled in Boscawen, New Hampshire, died in 1776. [ImmNE#39]

COSSAR, HERCULES, admitted as a member of the Scots Charitable Society of Boston in 1659. [SCS]

COSSAR, WILLIAM, admitted as a founder member of the Scots Charitable Society of Boston on 6 January 1657, boxmaster of the Society in April 1661. [SCS]

COULTER, HUGH, from Glasgow, admitted as a member of the Scots Charitable Society of Boston in 1747. [SCS]

COULTER, JAMES, admitted as a member of the Scots Charitable Society of Boston in 1722. [SCS]

COUPLAND, EDWARD, MRCS, died in Boston on 1 May 1877. [EC#29891]

COURTNEY, THOMAS, from Foggo, Berwickshire, admitted as a member of the Scots Charitable Society of Boston in 1770. [SCS]

COWAN, JOHN, emigrated from Scotland to America around 1655, settled in Scituate, Massachusetts, in 1656. [SG#7.3.84]

COWE, ALESTER, a prisoner of war transported to New England on the John and Sarah of London, master John Greene in November 1651. [Suffolk Deeds, 1-56]

CRABB, WILLIAM, born in Leven, Fife, emigrated to USA during 1870, settled in Lowell, Massachusetts, then in Newark, New Jersey, died on 19 May 1890. [FH, 25.6.1890]

CRAIG, GEORGE, a merchant, arrived in Boston on 29 December 1765 aboard the brig Wolf, master Richard Hambleton, from the Orkney Islands. [PAB]

CRAIG, JOHN, a prisoner of war transported to New England on the John and Sarah of London, master John Greene in November 1651. [Suffolk Deeds, 1-56]

CRAIGE, ROBERT, from Irvine, Ayrshire, admitted as a member of the Scots Charitable Society of Boston in 1748. [SCS]

CRAIGE, ROBERT, a sailor at the house of Sarah Smith in Boston 1762. [SCS]

CRAIG, ROBERT, admitted as an honorary member of the Scots Charitable Society of Boston in 1805. [SCS]

CRAIGEN, JOHN, a prisoner of war transported to New England on the <u>John and Sarah of London</u>, master John Greene in November 1651. [Suffolk Deeds, 1-56]

CRAIGIE, GEORGE, from Orkney, later in Portsmouth, New Hampshire, dead by 1836. [NAS.NRAS.0627.5.7]

CRAIGIE, HUGH, admitted as a member of the Scots Charitable Society of Boston in 1715. [SCS]

CRAIGHEAD, ANDREW, admitted as a member of the Scots Charitable Society of Boston in 1716. [SCS]

CRANSTOUN, Dr JAMES, from Scotland to America in 1638, in Portsmouth, Rhode Island, 1644, Governor of Rhode Island, father of William, died in Newport, Rhode Island, 12 March 1680. [EAF][possibly the John, son of William Cranstoun in Newbattle, apprenticed to John Davidson, surgeon in Edinburgh, 8. February 1615 - at Edinburgh University 1617?]

CRAWFORD, ALEXANDER, from Edinburgh, admitted as a member of the Scots Charitable Society of Boston in 1740. [SCS]

CRAWFORD, DAVID, from Greenock, admitted as a member of the Scots Charitable Society of Boston in 1735. [SCS]

CRAWFORD, GIDEON, born in Lanark on 26 December 1651, emigrated to Providence, Rhode Island, in 1670, admitted as a member of the Scots Charitable Society of Boston in 1692, died on 10 October 1707, probate 5 November 1707 Rhode Island. [SCS]

CRAWFORD, HUGH, admitted as a member of the Scots Charitable Society of Boston in 1720. [SCS]

CRAWFORD, JAMES, admitted as a member of the Scots Charitable Society of Boston in 1706. [SCS]

CRAWFORD, JAMES, from Glasgow, admitted as a member of the Scots Charitable Society of Boston in 1733. [SCS]

CRAWFORD, JAMES, from Glasgow, admitted as a member of the Scots Charitable Society of Boston in 1750. [SCS]

CRAWFORD, JAMES, merchant in Boston, a Loyalist who died in 1777, husband of Margaret who settled in Shelburne, Nova Scotia. [PRO.AO.12.10.253]

CRAWFORD, JANET, in Southbridge, Massachusetts, cnf 1886. [NAS.SC70.1.251]

CRAWFORD, JOHN, merchant from Ayr, admitted as a member of the Scots Charitable Society of Boston on 25 October 1684. [SCS]

CRAWFORD, JOHN, son of John Crawford a merchant in Ayr, admitted as a member of the Scots Charitable Society of Boston on 25 October 1684. [SCS]

CRAWFORD, Dr JOHN, died in Boston (?) by 4 May 1762. [SCS]

CRAWFORD, JOHN, born 1717, emigrated to New England in 1753, settled in Stirling, Maine, died in 1809. [ImmNE#42]; possibly from Glasgow, admitted as a member of the Scots Charitable Society of Boston in 1757. [SCS]

CRAWFORD, LAWRENCE, born 1787, a weaver in Paisley, Renfrewshire, emigrated via Liverpool to Maine on the Mexico, master A. P. Paterson, in 1830. [PTA]

CRAWFORD, MATHEW, from Glasgow, admitted as a member of the Scots Charitable Society of Boston in 1700. [SCS]

CRAWFORD, MUNGO, merchant, admitted as a member of the Scots Charitable Society of Boston in 1684. [SCS]

CRAWFORD, ROBERT, from Glasgow, admitted as a member of the Scots Charitable Society of Boston in 1750. [SCS]

CRAWFORD, WILLIAM, a merchant, from Port Glasgow to New England on the Goodhope of Boston in February 1685, admitted as a member of the Scots Charitable Society of Boston 1687. [NAS.E72.19.9][SCS]

CRAWFORD, WILLIAM, of Elizabeth River, Virginia, admitted as a member of the Scots Charitable Society of Boston in 1689. [SCS]

CREER, JOHN, arrived in Boston on 28 October 1763 aboard the Douglas, master James Montgomerie, from Scotland. [PAB]

CREER, WILLIAM, arrived in Boston on 28 October 1763 aboard the Douglas, master James Montgomerie, from Scotland. [PAB]

CREIGHTON, WILLIAM, admitted as a member of the Scots Charitable Society of Boston in 1832. [SCS]

CREIGHTON, WILLIAM CHARTERS, baptised on 19 February 1850 in Buittle, Kirkcudbrightshire, son of Alexander Creighton and Elisa McRobert, died on Clark's Island, Maine, 11 May 1895. [Dalbeattie g/s, Kirkcudbrightshire][Buittle Old Parish Register]

CREKER, ALEXANDER, admitted as a member of the Scots Charitable Society of Boston in 1686. [SCS]

CRIGHTON, JAMES, admitted as a member of the Scots Charitable Society of Boston in 1830. [SCS]

CRIE, JOHN, emigrated to New England in 17..?, settled in Martinicus, Maine, [ImmNE#43]

CROCKFORD, JAMES, a prisoner of war transported to New England on the John and Sarah of London, master John Greene in November 1651. [Suffolk Deeds, 1-56]

CROMARTY, JAMES, possibly baptised 4 February 1728 in Holm & Paplay, Orkney, son of James Cromarty and Christian Spence, admitted as a member of the Scots Charitable Society of Boston in 1750. [SCS]

CROMBIE, WILLIAM, from Morayshire, admitted as a member of the Scots Charitable Society of Boston in 1745, a resident of Boston in 1787 [SCS]; son of William Crombie in Elgin, Morayshire, a saddler who settled in Boston, Massachusetts, before 1764. [NAS.SH.22.2.2.1764]

CROOME, JOHN, a prisoner of war transported to New England on the <u>John and Sarah of London</u>, master John Greene in November 1651. [Suffolk Deeds, 1-56]

CROOM, JOHN, a seaman in Boston, 26 May 1854, [NAS.RS.Edinburgh#65/117]

CROOKSHANKS, JAMES, from Airth, Stirlingshire, settled in Salem, Massachusetts, by 1750. [ImmNE#223]

CROSS, DAVID, admitted as a member of the Scots Charitable Society of Boston in 1695. [SCS]

CROSS, JAMES, admitted as a member of the Scots Charitable Society in 1725. [SCS]

CROSS, JAMES, from Galloway, settled in Barnet, New Hampshire, in 1775. [HGP]

CROSSHONE, PATRICK, a prisoner of war transported to New England on the <u>John and Sarah of London</u>, master John Greene in November 1651. [Suffolk Deeds, 1-56]

CROWGEN, WILLIAM, admitted as a member of the Scots Charitable Society of Boston in 1743. [SCS]

CRUICKSHANK, A. A., born in 1845, late of Boston, USA, died in Inverarity, Angus, on 4 December 1877. [Fern g/s, Angus]

CRUICKSHANK, ANDREW MICHAEL, born on 16 September 1821, parish of Old Machar, son of William Cruickshank and Mary Farquhar, late of Aberdeen, died in Woolcotville, Connecticut, on 14 December 1855. [AJ:16.1.1856]

CRUICKSHANK, ALEXANDER, a goldsmith, arrived in Boston on 29 August 1768 aboard the snow <u>Catherine</u>, master Hugh Morris, from Scotland. [PAB]

CRUICKSHANKS, ALEXANDER, from Banffshire, admitted as a member of the Scots Charitable Society of Boston in 1769. [SCS]

CRUICKSHANK, ANDREW MICHAEL, baptised on 16 September 1821 in Old Machar, Aberdeen, son of William Cruickshank and Mary Farquhar in Aberdeen, died in Wolcottville, Connecticut, 14 December 1855. [AJ#5636][Old Machar OPR, Aberdeen]

CUMMINGS, ALEXANDER, MD, admitted as a member of the Scots Charitable Society in 1724. [SCS]

CUMMING, GEORGE, from Midlothian, admitted as a member of the Scots Charitable Society of Boston in 1769. [SCS]

CUMMING, HELEN, daughter of Sir Alexander Cumming of Culter, Aberdeenshire, married Robert Cumming, settled in Concord, Massachusetts, before 1725. [NAS.GD105.338/48]

CUMMING, JOHN, probate September 1663 Salem, Massachusetts

CUMMING, MATHEW, from Glasgow, admitted as a member of the Scots Charitable Society of Boston in 1719. [SCS]

CUMMING, ROBERT, from Port Glasgow, admitted as a member of the Scots Charitable Society of Boston in 1689. [SCS]

CUMMING, ROBERT, admitted as a member of the Scots Charitable Society of Boston in 1717. [SCS]

CUMMING, ROBERT, a merchant in Boston, New England, father of John baptised in Aberdeen during March 1728. [St Paul's Episcopal Church Register, Aberdeen]

CUMMING, THOMAS, emigrated to New England in 1773, settled in Portland, Maine, [ImmNE#45]

CUNNINGHAM, ANDREW, born in 1654, emigrated to Boston around 1684, married Sarah Gibson in 1685, father of Sarah, Andrew, Elizabeth, William, David, James, Sarah, and John, died in 1735. [AA#5/66][CAG#1/574]

CUNNINGHAM, ANDREW, a glazier, admitted as a member of the

Scots Charitable Society of Boston in 1684; keykeeper of the poor-box on 4 February 1695. [SCS]

CUNNINGHAM, ANDREW, admitted as a member of the Scots Charitable Society of Boston in 1734. [SCS]

CUNNINGHAM, ARCHIBALD, admitted as a member of the Scots Charitable Society of Boston in 1695. [SCS]

CUNNINGHAM, ARCHIBALD, from Haddington, East Lothian, admitted as a member of the Scots Charitable Society of Boston in 1765, [SCS]; a Loyalist merchant in Boston during 1776, moved via New York to settle in Shelburne, Nova Scotia. [NENS#133] [PRO.AO13.24.96]

CUNNINGHAM, JAMES, born in Govan, Glasgow, during 1801, emigrated to America in 1823, a shipowner and mechanical engineer in New York, Boston and San Francisco, died in Irvington on Hudson on 28 April 1870. [ANY]

CUNNINGHAM, JEAN, born 1749, resident of Stirling, emigrated from Greenock to Salem on the Glasgow Packet, master Alexander Porterfield, in April 1775. [PRO.T47/12]

CUNNINGHAM, JOHN, admitted as a member of the Scots Charitable Society in 1724. [SCS]

CUNNINGHAM, JOHN, from Glasgow, admitted as a member of the Scots Charitable Society of Boston in 1734. [SCS]

CUNNINGHAM, JOHN, born in 1752, an architect from Dumfries-shire, died in Chelsea, Massachusetts, on 25 November 1872. [AO]

CUNNINGHAM, JOSEPH, born in 1802, immigrated into Massachusetts on board the Mary Ann on 31 August 1850. [LAP]

CUNNINGHAM, NATHANIEL, admitted as a member of the Scots Charitable Society in 1725. [SCS]

CUNNINGHAM, ROBERT, arrived in Boston on 29 May 1712 aboard the Expedition, master David Preshaw. [PTA#131]

CUNNINGHAM, ROBERT, admitted as a member of the Scots Charitable Society of Boston in 1721. [SCS]

CUNNINGHAM, SUSANNAH, wife of James Dalrymple, daughter of Nathaniel Cunningham in Massachusetts, 1785. [NAS.CS17.1.3/123]

CUNNINGHAM, THOMAS, from Kilmarnock, Ayrshire, admitted as a member of the Scots Charitable Society of Boston in 1732. [SCS]

CUNNINGHAM, WILLIAM, admitted as a member of the Scots Charitable Society of Boston in 1687. [SCS]

CUNNINGHAM, WILLIAM, admitted as a member of the Scots Charitable Society of Boston in 1716. [SCS]

CUNNINGHAM, WILLIAM, from Glasgow, admitted as a member of the Scots Charitable Society of Boston in 1747. [SCS]

CURRIE, JANE, born in 1836, wife of James Piercy of Dover, New Hampshire, died on 8 December 1870. [AO]

CURRIE, ROBERT, possibly from Linlithgow, West Lothian, settled in Providence, Rhode Island, by 1738. [NAS.CS16.1.68]

CURRIE, WALTER, possibly from Linlithgow, West Lothian, settled in Providence, Rhode Island, by 1738. [NAS.GD119.140][NAS.CS16.1.68]

CURRIE, WALTER, from Glasgow, admitted as a member of the Scots Charitable Society of Boston in 1756. [SCS]

CURRY, WILLIAM, admitted as a member of the Scots Charitable Society of Boston in 1695. [SCS]

DAIRSIE, MARGARET, daughter of John Dairsie and Agnes Robertson, wife of William Sturgeon, died on Westerley, Rhode Island, during May 1849. [Anstruther Easter g/s, Fife]

DALGLEISH, ANDREW, a merchant, arrived in Boston on the Douglas, master Robert Manderston, on 26 July 1764 from Greenock. [SG#7/14][PAB]

DALL, WILLIAM, from Forfar, Angus, admitted as a member of the Scots Charitable Society of Boston in 1760, a resident of Boston in 1787. [SCS]

DALRYMPLE, ALEXANDER, from Salem, New England, late of HMS Woolwich, probate February 1747 PCC

DALRYMPLE, JOHN, admitted as a member of the Scots Charitable Society of Boston in 1711. [SCS]

DALRYMPLE, ROBERT, from Burntisland, Fife, admitted as a member of the Scots Charitable Society of Boston in 1739. [SCS]

DALYELL, ANDREW, a merchant, arrived in Boston on the Douglas , master Robert Manderston, on 26 July 1764 from Greenock. [SG#7/14][PAB]

DANE, ROBERT, admitted as a member of the Scots Charitable Society of Boston in 1686. [SCS]

DANFORTH, JEDEDIAH, a laborer who emigrated to New England by 1740. [ImmNE#46]

DANIELSON, JAMES, a prisoner of war captured after the Battle of Dunbar in September 1650, transported on 3 November 1650 from London to New England on the Unity, an indentured servant at Lynn Ironworks in Massachusetts, later settled on Block Island. [NWI]

DARLING, GEORGE, prisoner of war captured after the Battle of Dunbar in September 1650, transported on 3 November 1650 from London to New England on the Unity, an indentured servant at Lynn Ironworks in Massachusetts, [NWI]; see Ingram Moodie's testament 1693 Essex County #7168. [born in Scotland around 1615, married Katherine Gridley in Lynn, Marblehead, Essex County, Massachusetts, on 31 March 1657, father of John, died in 1693]

DARLING, THOMAS, born 29 December 1834, son of John Darling and his wife Elizabeth Bonnar in Dunfermline, died in Rowayton, Connecticut, on 28 January 1909. [Dunfermline Abbey g/s, Fife]

DAVIDSON, ALEXANDER, from Aberdeen, admitted as a member of the Scots Charitable Society of Boston in 1769. [SCS]

DAVIDSON, CHARLES FELIX, in Augusta, Maine, cnf 1887. [NAS.SC70.1.259]

DAVIDSON, DANIEL, prisoner of war transported to New England in 1651, settled in Massachusetts, died after 5 December 1693. [EAF]

DAVIDSON, GEORGE, admitted as a member of the Scots Charitable Society of Boston in 1802. [SCS]

DAVIDSON, HENRY, admitted as a member of the Scots Charitable Society of Boston in 1799. [SCS]

DAVIDSON, or MCLAREN, JANET, possibly from Callendar, Stirlingshire, in Lincoln Center, Maine, 1881. [NAS.SH.1881]

DAVIDSON, WILLIAM, from Peeblesshire, Captain of the 52nd Regiment of Foot, died in Boston, probate 1776 PCC

DAVIDSON, WILLIAM, in Boston 1872, grandson of William Davidson and Agnes Turnbull in Langton. [NAS.SH.1872]

DAVIE, AMBROSE, born in 1813, from Dunfermline, Fife, died in Boston on 13 July 1848. [Dunfermline Abbey g/s, Fife]

DAVIS, ANGIE, born in Scotland during 1852, a housekeeper in Tisbury, Massachusetts, by 1880. [C]

DAVIS, JAMES, born in Scotland during 1855, a laborer in Tisbury, Massachusetts, by 1880. [C]

DAY, Mrs JANET, widow, late of Boston, New England, married David Barclay, merchant in Water Lane, London, in Edinburgh 7 August 1768. [Edinburgh OPR]

DEAN, JOHN, admitted as a member of the Scots Charitable
Society of Boston in 1805. [SCS]

DEAN, THOMAS, admitted as a member of the Scots Charitable
Society of Boston in 1803. [SCS]

DEANE, WILLIAM, admitted as a member of the Scots Charitable
Society of Boston in 1684. [SCS]

DEE, JOHN, admitted as a member of the Scots Charitable
Society of Boston in 1722. [SCS]

DELL, WILLIAM, a prisoner of war transported to New England on
the John and Sarah of London, master John Greene in
November 1651. [Suffolk Deeds, 1-56]

DENNISON, ROBERT SCARTH, baptised 28 September 1841 in
Sandwick, Orkney, son of James Dennison, {1806-1875},
and Margaret Wallace, {1798-1874}, settled in Winsted,
Connecticut. [St Magnus g/s, Kirkwall]
[Lady g/s, Stronsay][Sandwick OPR]

DENNY, JAMES, admitted as a member of the Scots Charitable
Society of Boston in 1736. [SCS]

DENNY, JOHN, admitted as a member of the Scots Charitable
Society of Boston in 1735. [SCS]

DEWAR, ANDREW, from Leith, admitted as a member of the
Scots Charitable Society of Boston in 1761. [SCS]

DEWAR, DAVID, admitted to the Scots Charitable Society of
Boston in 1696. [SCS]

DEWAR, DAVID, in Massachusetts, cnf 1869. [NAS.SC70.1.142]

DEWAR, MARY, born on 20 May 1810, daughter of Dr Henry
Dewar of Lassodie, married Gilman Kimball MD, died in
Lowell, Massachusetts, on 7 July 1869. [Dumfries g/s]

DEWAR, SAMPSON, admitted as a member of the Scots
Charitable Society of Boston in 1692. [SCS]

DEWAR, SAMPSON, admitted as a member of the Scots
Charitable Society of Boston in 1719. [SCS]

DEWAR, THOMAS, admitted as a founder member of the Scots
Charitable Society of Boston on 6 January 1657, boxmaster
of the Society in April 1662. [SCS]

DICK, ROBERT, from Galloway, admitted as a member of the
Scots Charitable Society of Boston in 1737. [SCS]

DICK, WILLIAM, born in 1868 son of William Dick and Christina
Robb, died in Ansonia, Connecticut, 27 October 1889.
[Longforgan g/s, Perthshire]

DICKMAN, JAMES, born in 1749, a farmer in Perthshire,
emigrated from Greenock to Salem on the Glasgow Packet,
master Alexander Porterfield, in April 1775. [PRO.T47/12]

DICKSON, JOHN, admitted as a member of the Scots Charitable
Society of Boston in 1690. [SCS]

DICKY, JOHN, from Ayrshire, admitted as a member of the Scots
Charitable Society of Boston in 1751. [SCS]

DIKE, SAMUEL, born 14 June 1722, emigrated to New England, a
weaver, married Mary Perkins, settled in Hamilton and in
Bridgewater, Massachusetts, died on 22 October 1800.
[ImmNE#49]

DILLON, FRANCIS, born in 1844, with Rosanna Dillon, born in
1846, immigrated into Massachusetts on board the Sesostris
16 August 1850. [LAP]

DINWOODY, LAURENCE, admitted as a member of the Scots
Charitable Society of Boston in 1713. [SCS]

DISTANT, WILLIAM, from Leith, admitted as a member of the
Scots Charitable Society of Boston in 1693. [SCS]

DIXON, WILLIAM, from Haddington, East Lothian, admitted as a
member of the Scots Charitable Society of Boston in 1769.
[SCS]

DOCHERTY, BERNARD, born in 1810, immigrated into Massachusetts aboard the brig Lydia on 20 May 1850. [LAP]

DOCHERTY, DANIEL, a merchant, arrived in Boston aboard the Douglas master Robert Manderston, on 26 July 1764 from Greenock. [SG#7/14][PAB]

DODD, JAMES, master of the Nancy and of the Holbeach of Boston, Massachusetts, died in Boston, son of William and Margaret Dodd in Berwick on Tweed, probate 1774 PCC

DODS, THOMAS, emigrated to New England by 1712, married Elinor Black in Boston on 30 December 1712. [ImmNE#50]

DOLE, ANTHONY, an image maker, arrived in Boston on 16 April 1766 on the Stirling Castle, master James Cockburn, from Greenock. [SG#7/15][PAB]

DONAHAN, ANDREW, arrived in Boston on 11 November 1766 aboard the George and James, master Robert Montgomery, from Glasgow. [PAB]

DONALD, ANDREW, admitted as a member of the Scots Charitable Society of Boston in 1728. [SCS]

DONALD, LAWRENCE, from James Place, Dunfermline, married Edith J. F. Chappell, in Providence, Rhode Island, on 3 July 1888. [DJ]

DONALDSON, JOHN, admitted as a member of the Scots Charitable Society of Boston in 1690. [SCS]

DONALDSON, ROBERT, an engineer, husband of Isabella Hunter, son of Alexander Donaldson a blacksmith in Linktown, Kirkcaldy, died in Waterbury Hospital, Connecticut, on 14 October 1904. [FFP],

DOUGAL, ALEXANDER, a prisoner of war captured after the Battle of Dunbar in September 1650, transported on 3 November 1650 from London to New England on the Unity, an indentured servant at Lynn Ironworks in Massachusetts. [NWI]

DOUGAL, EDWARD, a prisoner of war transported to New England on the <u>John and Sarah of London</u>, master John Greene in November 1651. [Suffolk Deeds, 1-56]

DOUGALL, WILLIAM, a prisoner of war transported to New England on the <u>John and Sarah of London</u>, master John Greene in November 1651. [Suffolk Deeds, 1-56]

DOUGHNY, JOHN, arrived in Boston on 28 October 1763 aboard the <u>Douglas</u>, master James Montgomerie, from Scotland. [PAB]

DOUGLAS, ALEXANDER, admitted as a member of the Scots Charitable Society of Boston in 1717. [SCS]

DOUGLAS, CORNELIUS, from Gifford, Midlothian, admitted as a member of the Scots Charitable Society of Boston in 1753. [SCS]

DOUGLAS, HENRY, admitted as a member of the Scots Charitable Society of Boston in 1709. [SCS]

DOUGLAS, JOHN, born about 1695, emigrated to Boston, New England, around 1707, married Eunice Rattliff, died 12 November 1795. [ImmNE#51]

DOUGLAS, JOHN, admitted as a member of the Scots Charitable Society of Boston in 1754. [SCS]

DOUGLAS, JOHN, born in Scotland around 1799, via 'Island Jamacia' to Boston in 1816, naturalised in Washington, DC, in 1828. [NWI]

DOUGLAS, ROBERT, born around 1639 son of William Douglas and Anne Mottle, emigrated to Boston around 1640, settled in New London, Connecticut, married Mary Hempstead on 28 September 1665, father of William, died on 15 January 1715. [AA#4/67]

DOUGLAS, SAMUEL, born 18 May 1699 son of Samuel Douglas and Hepzibah Farrar, emigrated to New England about 1730, married Hepzibah Richardson in Scotland during

1723, settled in Townsend, Massachusetts, Brookline, New Hampshire, and Littleton, New Hampshire, died in 1793. [ImmNE#51]

DOUGLAS, WILLIAM, born 9 August 1610, son of Robert Douglas, married Ann Mattle around 1636, emigrated to New England in 1640, settled Gloucester, then Boston, then Ipswich, Massachusetts, and in New London, Connecticut, a cooper and town clerk, died in New London 26 July 1682. [Col.Fams#6.87][BLG#2663][AncH-NE]

DOUGLASS, WILLIAM, born around 1691 in Gifford, East Lothian, a physician and author educated in Edinburgh, Leyden, and Paris, settled in Boston during 1718, member of the SCS by 1727, died on 21 October 1752. [WA] [SCS][SA#179]

DOUGLAS, WILLIAM, admitted as a member of the Scots Charitable Society of Boston in 1713. [SCS]

DOUGLAS, WILLIAM, MD, admitted as a member of the Scots Charitable Society of Boston in 1716. [SCS]

DOWALL, JAMES, admitted as a member of the Scots Charitable Society of Boston in 1811. [SCS]

DOWNIE, WALTER, emigrated to New England in 1735, settled in Bridgwater, returned to Scotland. [ImmNE#51]

DOWNING, JAMES, admitted as a member of the Scots Charitable Society of Boston in 1689. [SCS]

DOWNING, MALCOLM, prisoner of war captured after the Battle of Dunbar in September 1650, transported on 3 November 1650 from London to New England on the Unity, an indentured servant at Lynn Ironworks in Massachusetts, [NWI]; reference to in Archibald Anderson's will 25 September 1662. [Essex Court Files, Vol.7, 38]

DOWNS, ALEXANDER, born 1822, died in Canton, Massachusetts, on 18 January 1865. [South Leith g/s, Edinburgh]

DRUMMOND, ANDREW, admitted as a member of the Scots

Charitable Society of Boston in 1767, in Boston 1787. [SCS]

DUDGEON, CATHERINE, born in 1832, immigrated into Massachusetts on 20 May 1850 aboard the brig Lydia. [LAP]

DUDLEY, HUGH, Scots prisoner of war, transported to New England, indentured to William Pyncheon on 9 September 1650, a merchant in Springfield for 4 years, later assigned to Henry Smith in Springfield for 5 years. ["Pyncheon Court Record" in Colonial Justice in Western Massachussetts, 1639-1702, p224, {J H Smith, Cambridge, Mass., 1961}]

DUFF, WILLIAM, from Banffshire, admitted as a member of the Scots Charitable Society of Boston in 1760. [SCS]

DULEN, EDWARD, a prisoner of war transported to New England on the John and Sarah of London, master John Greene in November 1651. [Suffolk Deeds, 1-56]

DUNBAR, GEORGE, of Rhode Island, admitted as a member of the Scots Charitable Society of Boston in 1721. [SCS]

DUNBAR, JAMES, admitted as a member of the Scots Charitable Society of Boston in 1716. [SCS]; settled in Rhode Island before 1717. [NAS.GD298]

DUNBAR, JAMES, admitted as a member of the Scots Charitable Society of Boston in 1718. [SCS]

DUNBAR, JOHN, a merchant, a Jacobite prisoner of war who was transported from Liverpool to Virginia on the Elizabeth and Anne, on 29 June 1716, arrived at Sandy Point on the James River, Virginia, later settled in Newport, Rhode Island, as a merchant skipper. [NAS.GD298] [SPC.1716.310][CTB.31.208][NAS.GD103][VSP.1.185]

DUNBAR, ROBERT, born 1630 son of Ninian Dunbar of Georgehill, settled in Hingham, Massachusetts, during 1650, died there on 19 September 1693. [EAF][AncH-NE]

DUNBAR, SIMON, son of John Dunbar of Burgie, a mariner who settled in Newport, Rhode Island, before 1748. [NAS.GD199.99]

DUNBAR, WILLIAM, born on 13 November 1740, son of Robert Dunbar in Dyke, Forres, Morayshire, admitted as a member of the Scots Charitable Society of Boston in 1766. [SCS]

DUNCAN, ALEXANDER, born on 25 May 1805, settled in Providence, USA, died in Knossington on 14 October 1889. [Craig Inchbrioch g/s]; born on 26 May 1805, son of Alexander Duncan of Parkhill, Arbroath, Angus, emigrated via Liverpool to New York during 1821 on the Amity, educated at Yale and Brown Universities, a lawyer in Canandaigua, New York, and in Rhode Island, settled in England during 1863, died in London on 14 October 1889. [ANY#2.298] ; cnf 1890 [NAS.SC70.1.283]

DUNCAN, ALEXANDER, educated at Edinburgh Academy, emigrated to Providence, Rhode Island, before 1835. [EAR#156]

DUNCAN, ANDREW, a planter in Massachusetts, 1783. [NAS.CS17.1.2/289]

DUNCAN, ANDREW, from Glasgow, a merchant in Worcester, Massachusetts, in 1768, a Loyalist during the American Revolution, died during 1787. [PRO.AO13.24.72][NAS.CS16.1.161]

DUNCAN, DAVID, a baker from Aberdeenshire, admitted as a member of the Scots Charitable Society of Boston in 1767. [SCS]

DUNCAN, JAMES, from Leith, admitted as a member of the Scots Charitable Society of Boston in 1734. [SCS]

DUNCAN, JESSY SCOTT, born during 1831, eldest daughter of Alexander Duncan in Providence, Rhode Island, died in New York on 24 November 1847. [EEC#21596]

DUNCAN, Lieutenant NATHANIEL, sent to Plymouth, New England, in October 1642. [Mass. Colonial Records#II.32]

DUNCAN, PETER, referred to in Henry Muddle's will probate April 1663 Salem, Massachusetts.

DUNCAN, ROBERT, from Glasgow, admitted as a member of the Scots Charitable Society of Boston in 1759. [SCS]

DUNCAN, SAMUEL ALEXANDER, infant son of Alexander Duncan, died in Providence, Rhode Island, on 29 December 1845. [EEC#21300]

DUNCAN, WILLIAM, a merchant in Glasgow then in New England, 1778. [NAS.CS16.1.173/88]

DUNCAN, WILLIAM, son of Henry Duncan (died 1833) and Catherine Bell (died 1842), emigrated to Salem, Massachusetts. [St Andrews g/s, Fife]

DUNCAN, WILLIAM BUTLER, born in Edinburgh on 17 March 1830, son of Alexander Duncan, educated at Edinburgh University and at Brown University, Rhode Island, a banker and entrepreneur, died in New York on 20 June 1912. [ANY.2.274]

DUNCAN, ..., admitted as a member of the Scots Charitable Society of Boston in 1722. [SCS]

DUNCAN, Dr ..., of Barnstable, admitted as a member of the Scots Charitable Society in 1733. [SCS]

DUNCANSON, ALEXANDER, born in 1825 son of Archibald Duncanson, educated at Glasgow University around 1840, a minister in Alloa and Falkirk, emigrated to Boston in 1856. [MUG#14234]

DUNDAS, ALEXANDER, admitted as a member of the Scots Charitable Society in 1724. [SCS]

DUNDAS, ALEXANDER, from Greenock, admitted as a member of the Scots Charitable Society of Boston in 1747. [SCS]

DUNDAS, ELIZABETH, born in 1817, died in Boston on 12 March 1892. [Edzell g/s, Angus]

DUNDAS, JAMES, admitted as a member of the Scots Charitable Society of Boston in 1686. [SCS]

DUNDAS, JAMES, emigrated to New England before 1762, married Elenor Shaddock in Marblehead on 13 November 1762, settled in Salem, Massachusetts. [ImmNE#53]

DUNDAS, JAMES, born 1842, settled in Boston, died in New York 16 January 1890. [Edzell g/s, Angus]

DUNDAS, JOHN, admitted as a member of the Scots Charitable Society of Boston in 1715. [SCS]

DUNDAS, WILLIAM, admitted as a member of the Scots Charitable Society of Boston in 1687. [SCS]

DUNDAS, WILLIAM, born in 1816, died in Boston on 12 March 1892. [Edzell g/s, Angus]

DUNLOP, ALEXANDER, emigrated via Nova Scotia to New England by 1740, settled in Deering, Windham, New Hampshire, [ImmNE#53]

DUNLOP, COLIN, admitted as a member of the Scots Charitable Society of Boston in 1738. [SCS]

DUNLOP, JAMES, from Irvine, Ayrshire, admitted as a member of the Scots Charitable Society of Boston in 1738. [SCS]

DUNLOP, JOHN, a minister from Dolphinton, Lanarkshire, settled in Cambridge [Massachusetts?] before 1774.
[Dolphinton g/s]

DUNLOP, WILLIAM, admitted as a member of the Scots Charitable Society in 1724. [SCS]

DUNLOP, WILLIAM, admitted as a member of the Scots Charitable Society of Boston in 1734. [SCS]

DUNLOP, WILLIAM, from Glasgow, admitted as a member of the Scots Charitable Society of Boston in 1744. [SCS]

DUNLOP, WILLIAM, from Glasgow, admitted as a member of the Scots Charitable Society of Boston in 1751. [SCS]

DUNMORE, JOHN, born in 1763, a resident of Glasgow,
    emigrated from Greenock to Salem on the Glasgow Packet,
    master Alexander Porterfield, in April 1775. [PRO.T47/12]

DUNMORE, MARY, born in 1748, a resident of Glasgow,
    emigrated from Greenock to Salem on the Glasgow Packet,
    master Alexander Porterfield, in April 1775. [PRO.T47/12]

DUNNET, GEORGE, born in 1845, died in Boston on 7 May 1891.
    [Dunnet g/s, Caithness]

DUNSMORE, JAMES, a prisoner of war captured after the Battle
    of Dunbar in September 1650, transported on 3 November
    1650 from London to New England on the Unity, an
    indentured servant at Lynn Ironworks in Massachusetts.
    [NWI]

DYSART, JOHN, admitted as a member of the Scots Charitable
    Society in 1723. [SCS]

EATON, ALEXANDER, a prisoner of war captured after the Battle
    of Dunbar in September 1650, transported on 3 November
    1650 from London to New England on the Unity, an
    indentured servant at Lynn Ironworks in Massachusetts.
    [NWI]

EDGAR, JOHN, from Dumfries, admitted as a member of the
    Scots Charitable Society of Boston in 1694. [SCS]

EDMONSTONE, JOHN, prisoner of war, captured after the Battle
    of Worcester in 1651, transported from Gravesend, Kent, to
    Boston on the John and Sarah, master John Greene, on 13
    May 1652. [NER#I.378]

EDWARDS, BENJAMIN, admitted as a member of the Scots
    Charitable Society of Boston in 1737. [SCS]

ELDER, JOHN, born in Crail, Fife, during 1806, emigrated to
    America in 1840, settled in Patterson, New Jersey, died in
    Hartford City [Connecticut?] during 1898. [EFR. 23.12.1898]

ELLIOT, WALTER, admitted as a member of the Scots Charitable

Society of Boston in 1710. [SCS]

ENGLISH, JAMES, a prisoner of war transported to New England on the John and Sarah of London, master John Greene in November 1651. [Suffolk Deeds, 1-56]

ENGLISH, PATRICK, a prisoner of war transported to New England on the John and Sarah of London, master John Greene in November 1651. [Suffolk Deeds, 1-56]

ERBURY, HARRY, son of John Erbury a merchant in Kirkwall, Orkney, was apprenticed to Captain John Charnock, commander of the Malborrow of Boston, New England, on 25 September 1711. [NAS.GD217.661]

ERSKINE, ARCHIBALD, a merchant, admitted as a member of the Scots Charitable Society of Boston in 1684. [SCS]

ERSKINE, CHRISTOPHER, born in 1701, settled in Bridgewater, Massachusetts, in 1725, married Susannah Robinson (1714-1784), father of John born in 1732, died in 1775. [CAG#1.447/975]

ERSKINE, JOHN, from Edinburgh, admitted as a member of the Scots Charitable Society of Boston in 1740. [SCS]

ERSKINE, PATRICK, admitted as a member of the Scots Charitable Society of Boston in 1717. [SCS]

ERSKINE, ROBERT, Captain of HMS Canterbury, admitted as a member of the Scots Charitable Society of Boston in 1748. [SCS]

ERVING, ANN, born 1741, daughter of Hon. John Erving, late of Boston, New England, widow of Duncan Stewart of Ardshiel, died in Edinburgh on 25 December 1804. [St Cuthbert's g/s, Edinburgh]

ERVING, EDWARD, admitted as a member of the Scots Charitable Society of Boston in 1736. [SCS]

ERVING, GEORGE, graduated MA from Glasgow University in 1762, a Loyalist in Boston who moved to Halifax, Nova

Scotia, and later to London. [MAGU#181]

ERVING, WILLIAM, admitted as a member of the Scots Charitable
Society of Boston in 1788. [SCS]

ESSON, ROBERT, from Greenock, admitted as a member of the
Scots Charitable Society of Boston in 1766. [SCS]

EWAN, PATRICK, admitted as a member of the Scots Charitable
Society of Boston in 1728. [SCS]

EWING, ALEXANDER, admitted as a member of the Scots
Charitable Society of Boston in 1827. [SCS]

EWING, JAMES, from Glasgow, admitted as a member of the
Scots Charitable Society of Boston in 1748. [SCS]

FAED, WILLIAM, admitted as a member of the Scots Charitable
Society of Boston in 1687. [SCS]

FALLAS, WILLIAM, admitted as a member of the Scots Charitable
Society in 1727. [SCS]

FALLS, JAMES, a merchant, arrived in Boston on 29 August 1768
aboard the snow Catherine, master Hugh Morris, from
Scotland. [PAB]

FARQUHAR, JEAN, in Rosendale, Boston, cnf 1893.
[NAS.SC70.1.322]

FARQUHAR, WILLIAM, from Aberdeen, emigrated to
Londonderry, New Hampshire, in 1700, later settled in
Maryland. [CAG#1.102]

FARQUHAR, WILLIAM P., in Storbridge, Worcester,
Massachussetts, cnf 1882. [NAS.SC70.1.215]

FARQUHARSON, JAMES, a prisoner of war transported to New
England on the John and Sarah of London, master John
Greene in November 1651. [Suffolk Deeds, 1-56]

FENNY, THOMAS, born in 1826, immigrated into Massachusetts
on the Lydia, a brig, 31 May 1850. [LAP]

FERGUSON, ADAM, in Newport, Rhode Island, probate February 1802 PCC

FERGUSON, ALEXANDER, a merchant who arrived in Boston aboard the Lovely Betsy, master William Hayman, on 7 August 1766, from Scotland. [SG#7.4.15][PAB]

FERGUSON, ARCHIBALD, merchant in Marblehead, member of the Scots Charitable Society of Boston 1684. [SCS]

FERGUSON, ARCHIBALD, in Marblehead, admitted to the Scots Charitable Society of Boston in 1697. [SCS]

FERGUSON, DANIEL, a prisoner of war captured after the Battle of Dunbar in September 1650, transported from London on 3 November 1650 to New England on the Unity, an indentured servant, settled in Kittery, Maine. [NWI]

FERGUSON, DANIEL, emigrated from Greenock aboard the brigantine Matty, master Thomas Cochrane, on 19 May 1774 bound for New York, arrived on 22 July 1774, settled Barnet, Vermont. [HBV]

FERGUSON, GEORGE, born during 1818 in Ayrshire, settled in Roxburgh, Massachusetts, died in Gold Run, California, on 17 July 1851. [W#1260]

FERGUSON, JAMES, admitted as a member of the Scots Charitable Society of Boston in 1715. [SCS]

FERGUSON, JAMES, emigrated from Greenock aboard the brigantine Matty, master Thomas Cochrane, on 19 May 1774 bound for New York, arrived there on 22 July 1774, settled Barnet, Vermont. [HBV]

FERGUSON, JANET, born 1855, died in Pawtucket, USA, 27 March 1889. [Coupar Angus g/s, Perthshire]

FERGUSON, JOHN, emigrated to New England during 1725, a clothier, married Ann Johnson in Boston 23 September 1729, settled in Pelham, New Hampshire. [ImmNE#59]

FERGUSON, JOHN, born in 1736, emigrated to Rhode Island in 1767, died in 1820. [CAG#1.534]

FERGUSON, JOHN, emigrated from Greenock aboard the brigantine Matty, master Thomas Cochrane, on 19 May 1774 bound for New York, arrived there on 22 July 1774, settled Barnet, Vermont. [HBV]

FERGUSON, PETER, arrived in Boston on 31 October 1766 aboard the snow Jenny, master Archibald Orr, from Scotland. [PAB]

FERGUSON, ROBERT, born in 1719, shipmaster based in Newport, Rhode Island, Loyalist in 1776, settled in Perth, Scotland. [PRO.AO.12.84.2]

FERRY, DAVID, from Renfrewshire, settled in Ryegate, Vermont, on 23 May 1774. [VHS]

FERRY, JOHN, from Irvine, Ayrshire, a member of the Scots Charitable Society of Boston in 1748. [SCS]

FESSENDEN, THOMAS, admitted as an honorary member of the Scots Charitable Society of Boston in 1807. [SCS]

FIDDES, ROBERT, a merchant who arrived in Boston in the Lovely Betsy, master William Hayman, on 7 August 1766. [SG#7.4.15]

FIFE, SAMUEL, admitted as a member of the Scots Charitable Society of Boston in 1717. [SCS]

FINLAY, ALEXANDER, admitted as a member of the Scots Charitable Society of Boston in 1705. [SCS]

FINLAY, JAMES, admitted as a member of the Scots Charitable Society of Boston in 1736. [SCS]

FINDLAY, JOHN, member of the Scots Charitable Society of Boston 1687. [SCS]

FINDLAY, WILLIAM, a gardener in Rhode Island around 1859, son of William Findlay a gardener in Edinburgh. [NAS.SH.1859]

FINLAY, WILLIAM, from Fife, admitted as a member of the Scots Charitable Society of Boston in 1739. [SCS]

FINLAYSON, WALLACE, admitted as a member of the Scots Charitable Society of Boston in 1713. [SCS]

FINNEY, ANDREW, from Greenock, admitted as a member of the Scots Charitable Society of Boston in 1732. [SCS]

FISHER, ARCHIBALD, from Glasgow, admitted as a member of the Scots Charitable Society of Boston in 1758. [SCS]

FISHER, DONALD, settled in Salem before 1750, later moved to Pawlet, Vermont. [MNS]

FISHER, JOHN, admitted as a member of the Scots Charitable Society of Boston in 1800. [SCS]

FISHER, MARGARET, widow of Duncan McNaughton, settled in Pawlet, Vermont, before 1750, mother of Andrew, Malcolm, Finlay, Daniel, Duncan, Jennie, Mary and Margaret. [MNS]

FITCH, JOHN, admitted as a member of the Scots Charitable Society of Boston in 1731. [SCS]

FLEMING, JOHN, a merchant, arrived in Boston on 20 August 1764 aboard the sloop Ann, master Joshua Aitken, from Scotland. [PAB]

FLEMING, JOHN, from Edinburgh, admitted as a member of the Scots Charitable Society of Boston in 1764. [SCS]

FLEMING, JOHN, a printer who arrived in Boston on 31 October 1766 from Glasgow in the Jenny, [SG#7.4.15][PAB]; publisher of the Boston Chronicle, 1767-1770, married Alice Church on 8 August 1770, died in France. [WA#253]; possibly from Newliston, West Lothian, a printer in Boston, 1770. [NAS.CS16.1.141/189][Imm.NE#62]

FLETT, ELIZABETH, daughter of John Flett in Gruthay, Orkney, wife of Alexander Ross, settled in New England before 1772.

[NAS.SH.10.12.1772]

FLETT, JOHN, born during 1737 in Gentha, Orkney, settled in
Portland, Maine, died on 23 March 1760.
[ImmNE#63][Portland, East Cemetery g/s, Maine]
[NAS.GD263.167]

FLORIN, BART, an imagemaker, from Glasgow to Boston on the
Jenny, master Archibald Orr, 31 October 1766. [NWI.1.459]

FLORIN, LUCAS, an image maker, arrived in Boston on 16 April
1766 aboard the Stirling Castle, master John Cockburn, from
Greenock. [PAB]

FORBES, ALEXANDER, admitted as a member of the Scots
Charitable Society of Boston in 1710. [SCS]

FORBES, ALEXANDER, a printer from Edinburgh, and his wife,
arrived in Boston on 22 August 1765 aboard the Jamieson
and Peggy, master John Aitken, from Leith. [PAB]; admitted
as a member of the Scots Charitable Society of Boston in
1767. [SCS]

FORBES, DANIEL, probably a prisoner, to America around 1655,
in Cambridge 1660, died in Concord, Marlborough, 2
October 1687. [EAF]

FORBES, JAMES, a prisoner of war captured after the Battle of
Dunbar in September 1650, transported from London to New
England on the Unity on 3 November 1650, an indentured
servant, settled on Goodwin's farm, Hartford, Connecticut, in
1659, married Katherine .... In Hartford around 1660, father
of John, Mary, Sarah, David, Dorothy and James, died on 27
March 1692.

FORBES, JOHN, son of Reverend John Forbes (1568-1634) and
Christian Barclay, emigrated to America with his wife
Constance Mitchell and her sister on the Little Anne in 1623,
settled in Sudbury, Massachusetts, 1636, and in
Bridgewater, Massachusetts, 1645, father of Edward, died in
1661. [Anc.H-NE][BAF]

FORBES, JOHN, admitted as a member of the Scots Charitable

Society of Boston in 1708. [SCS]

FORBES, JOSEPH, admitted as a member of the Scots Charitable Society of Boston in 1702. [SCS]

FORBES, WILLIAM, born around 1630, prisoner of war captured after Battle of Dunbar 3 September 1650, transported from London to Boston on 11 November 1650 in the Unity, an indentured servant at Kittery Sawmills, married Rebecca ..., died 21 March 1701 in Kittery, Maine. [SG.34.4][NWI]

FORBES, WILLIAM, admitted as a member of the Scots Charitable Society of Boston in 1711. [SCS]

FORD, WILLIAM, a merchant from Glasgow, settled in Boston by 1819. [NAS.CS17.1.38/267]

FORDYCE, Mr ...., born in Scotland during 1670, died in Stratford, Connecticut, in 1772. [Pa.Chron: 30.3.1772]

FORREST, ARTHUR, from Edinburgh, admitted as a member of the Scots Charitable Society of Boston in 1739. [SCS]

FORRESTER, ANDREW, admitted as a member of the Scots Charitable Society of Boston in 1715. [SCS]

FORSYTH, ALEXANDER, admitted as a member of the Scots Charitable Society of Boston in 1716. [SCS]

FORSYTH, MATTHEW, born 1699, via Ireland to New England ca1730, married Esther Graham, settled in Chester, New Hampshire, died 1791. [ImmNE#64]

FFOSSEM(?), MICHAEL, Scots prisoner of war transported from London to Boston on the John and Sarah of London, master John Green, May 1652. [NER#I.378]

FOSTER, EDWARD, Scots indentured servant, indented to William Pyncheon for 9 years, assigned to Elizur Holyoake in Springfield, Massachusetts, tenant of William Pyncheon 1668 to 1703. ["Pyncheon Court Records" in Colonial Justice in Western Massachusetts, 1639-1702 p224, {J H Smith, Cambridge, Massachusetts, 1961}]

FOSTER, WILLIAM, admitted as a member of the Scots Charitable Society in 1727. [SCS]

FOTHERINGHAM, DAVID, admitted as an honorary member of the Scots Charitable Society of Boston in 1822. [SCS]

FOTHERINGHAM, JAMES, in New Hampshire, cnf 1877. [NAS.SC70.1.186]

FOTHERINGHAM, ..., Captain of General Phillips' regiment, admitted as a member of the Scots Charitable Society of Boston in 1746. [SCS]

FOULIS, JAMES, a tailor, admitted as a member of the Scots Charitable Society of Boston in 1684. [SCS]

FOWLER, THOMAS, from Dumfries, admitted as a member of the Scots Charitable Society of Boston in 1734. [SCS]

FOX, JAMES, admitted as a member of the Scots Charitable Society of Boston in 1716. [SCS]

FRASER, ALEXANDER, from Inverness-shire, settled in Guilford, Connecticut, by 1744. [AA#10.141]

FRASER, ALEXANDER, from Edinburgh, admitted as a member of the Scots Charitable Society of Boston in 1746. [SCS]

FRASER, DAVID, from Parbroath, Fife, admitted as a member of the Scots Charitable Society of Boston in 1743. [SCS]

FRAZER, JAMES, admitted to the Scots Charitable Society of Boston in 1726. [SCS]

FRASER, JOHN, of Pitculzean, born 1658, a minister and a Covenanter, banished to the Plantations, transported from Leith to East New Jersey on the Henry and Frances of Newcastle in September 1685, landed in New Jersey, minister of Woodbury, Connecticut, married Jean Moffat in America, returned to Scotland ca.1688, died in Alness on 7 November 1711. [F.7.26/663][RPCS.11.154]

FRASER, JOHN, admitted as a member of the Scots Charitable Society of Boston in 1690. [SCS]

FRASER, JOHN, from Ross-shire, admitted as a member of the Scots Charitable Society of Boston in 1734. [SCS]

FRASER, JOHN, from Inverness, admitted as a member of the Scots Charitable Society of Boston in 1758. [SCS]

FRAZIER, SIMON, a laborer, arrived in Boston on the snow Douglas, master Robert Manderston, on 26 July 1764, from Greenock. [SG#7.4.14][PAB]

FRENCH, PATRICK, a Scotch-Irishman, admitted as a member of the Scots Charitable Society of Boston in 1716. [SCS]

FRENCH, ROBERT, merchant from Kilpatrick in Annandale, admitted as a member of the Scots Charitable Society of Boston in 1685. [SCS]

FRETTER, HUGH, admitted as a member of the Scots Charitable Society of Boston in 1695. [SCS]

FRISSELL, EDWARD, a prisoner of war transported to New England on the John and Sarah of London, master John Greene in November 1651. [Suffolk Deeds, 1-56]

FRIZELL, GEORGE, admitted as a member of the Scots Charitable Society of Boston in 1686. [SCS]

FRIZELL, JOHN, admitted as a member of the Scots Charitable Society of Boston in 1694. [SCS]

FRIZELL, Captain JOHN, in Boston, New England, overseer of the SCS poorbox in 1713, [SCS]; admitted as a burgess and guildsbrother of Glasgow on 11 September 1716. [GBR]

FRIZELL, JOHN, admitted to the Scots Charitable Society of Boston in 1726. [SCS]

FRISSELL, WILLIAM, a prisoner of war transported to New England on the John and Sarah of London, master John

Greene in November 1651. [Suffolk Deeds, 1-56]

FULLARTON, ALEXANDER, admitted as a member of the Scots Charitable Society of Boston in 1699. [SCS]

FULLERTON, ALEXANDER, admitted as a member of the Scots Charitable Society of Boston in 1801. [SCS]

FULLARTON, JAMES, in Manchester, New Hampshire, 1889. [NAS.GD1.19.79]

FULLARTON, JOHN, admitted as a member of the Scots Charitable Society of Boston in 1802. [SCS]

FULLERTON, THOMAS, admitted as a member of the Scots Charitable Society of Boston in 1687. [SCS]

FULTON, ALEXANDER, admitted as a member of the Scots Charitable Society of Boston in 1689. [SCS]

FULTON, ANDREW, possibly from Leith, master of the 70 ton sloop Queen of Newport, Rhode Island, 1720. [NAS.AC9.714]

FULTON, GEORGE, from Coldingham, Berwickshire, admitted as a member of the Scots Charitable Society of Boston in 1762. [SCS]

FULTON, Dr WILLIAM, a merchant possibly from Leith, settled in New Bristol, New England, before 1699, [SPC.1699.501]; there in 1720, father of Andrew Fulton master of the 70 ton sloop Queen of Newport. [NAS.AC9/714]

FULTON, WILLIAM, admitted as a member of the Scots Charitable Society of Boston in 1687. [SCS]

FUSSELL, JOHN, settled in Braintree, Massachusetts, by 1664. [AncH-NE][Dy.Anc.Heads]

FYVIE, WILLIAM, born in Aberdeen 1790, a Congregational minister, settled in Tisbury, Dukes County, Massachusetts, by 1850. [C]

GALBRAITH, ARCHIBALD, from Glasgow, admitted as a member of the Scots Charitable Society of Boston in 1758. [SCS]

GALBRAITH, JOHN, emigrated from Greenock aboard the brigantine Matty, master Thomas Cochrane, on 19 May 1774 bound for New York, arrived there on 22 July 1774, settled Barnet, Vermont. [HBV]

GALBRAITH, JOHN, from East Barns, East Lothian, admitted as a member of the Scots Charitable Society of Boston in 1817. [SCS]

GALL, JOHN, admitted as a member of the Scots Charitable Society of Boston in 1695. [SCS]

GALLOWAY, BARBARA SIMPSON, youngest daughter of Andrew Galloway, Denburn Place, Kirkcaldy, married John Reid, an engineer, in Holyoke, Massachusetts, on 1 September 1899. [FFP]

GALLOWAY, HUGH, a merchant, arrived in Boston on 1 May 1769 from Glasgow on the Nancy, Captain James Moody, [PAB]

GALLOWAY, JESSIE, in Andover, Massachusetts, around 1851, daughter of William Galloway a baker in Brechin, Angus. [NAS.SH.1851]

GALLOWAY, MARGARET, daughter of William Galloway a baker in Brechin, Angus, wife of ... Middleton, settled in Andover, Massachusetts, before 1851. [NAS.SH.1851]

GARDEN, ALEXANDER, a merchant in Boston, 1754. [NAS.AC7.46.101]

GARDNER, ARCHIBALD, from Greenock, admitted as a member of the Scots Charitable Society of Boston in 1743. [SCS]

GARDNER, JOHN, admitted as a member of the Scots Charitable Society of Boston in 1736. [SCS]

GARDINER, JOHN, an MD in Boston, graduated MA from Glasgow University in 1755. [MAGU#211]

GARDNER, ROBERT, from Irvine admitted as a member of the Scots Charitable Society of Boston in 1719. [SCS]

GARDNER, ROBERT, a wigmaker from Glasgow, settled in Boston by 1729. [Imm.NE#67]

GARDNER, ROBERT, admitted as a member of the Scots Charitable Society of Boston in 1732. [SCS]

GARNES, ANDREW, admitted as a member of the Scots Charitable Society of Boston in 1701. [SCS]

GARNOCH, ELIZABETH, indentured in Edinburgh with Andrew Alexander for four years service in East New Jersey on 29 May 1684, emigrated there in November 1684, assigned to Andrew Winton in Fairfield, Connecticut, later settled in Boston. [East Jersey Deeds#D325] [BostonRec.Com.Rep. 9] [Stratford TR2]

GARNOCH, HUGH, admitted as a member of the Scots Charitable Society of Boston in 1691. [SCS]

GARRIOCH, CHARLES, admitted as a member of the Scots Charitable Society of Boston in 1731. [SCS]

GARRIOCH, GEORGE, admitted as a member of the Scots Charitable Society of Boston in 1722. [SCS]

GAULT, SAMUEL, via Londonderry to New England 1721, married Elsie Carlton, died after 29 January 1789. [ImmNE#68]

GAULT, WILLIAM, admitted as a member of the Scots Charitable Society of Boston in 1736. [SCS]

GEAR, JOHN, from Inverness, admitted as a member of the Scots Charitable Society of Boston in 1745. [SCS]

GEDDES, ALEXANDER, admitted as a member of the Scots Charitable Society of Boston in 1803. [SCS]

GEDDES, CHARLES, from Edinburgh, admitted as a member of the Scots Charitable Society of Boston in 1774. [SCS]

GEMMELL, JAMES, admitted as a member of the Scots Charitable Society of Boston in 1695. [SCS]

GENTLEMAN, DAVID, from Montrose, Angus, admitted as a member of the Scots Charitable Society of Boston in 1716. [SCS]

GIBBS, JOHN, admitted as a member of the Scots Charitable Society of Boston in 1695. [SCS]

GIBBS, Dr WILLIAM, admitted as a member of the Scots Charitable Society of Boston in 1693. [SCS]

GIBSON, ANDREW, admitted as a member of the Scots Charitable Society of Boston in 1695. [SCS]

GIBSON, BENJAMIN, admitted as a member of the Scots Charitable Society of Boston in 1705. [SCS]

GIBSON, HUGH, born around 1792, son of Gabriel Gibson a weaver in Irvine, Ayrshire, educated at Glasgow University in 1807, a minister in Biggar, Lanarkshire, settled in Otis, Massachusetts, in 1840 and later Chesterhills, Massachusetts. [MAGU#7276]

GIBSON, JAMES, from Edinburgh, admitted as a member of the Scots Charitable Society of Boston in 1734. [SCS]

GIBSON, WILLIAM, shoemaker, admitted as a founder member of the Scots Charitable Society of Boston on 6 January 1657, boxmaster of the Society in July 1665 and in October 1684. [SCS]

GIBSON, WILLIAM JOHN, graduated MA from Glasgow University in 1888, a teacher at the Boys Latin School in Boston 1889-1890. [MAGU#218]

GIFFORD, JOHN, admitted as a member of the Scots Charitable Society of Boston in 1800. [SCS]

GILBERT, ANDREW, born in 1821, from Edinburgh, died in Chelsea, Massachusetts, on 25 July 1873. [EC#27725]

GILBERT, THOMAS, born during 1610, a minister in England, emigrated to New England in 1661, minister in Topsfield from 1663 to 1671, died in Charlestown on 28 October 1673. [CCNE]

GILCHRIST, JAMES, admitted as a member of the Scots Charitable Society of Boston in 1715. [SCS]

GILCHRIST, JOHN, admitted as a member of the Scots Charitable Society of Boston in 1687. [SCS]

GILCHRIST, PETER, a brewer in Woodbury, Connecticut, 1781. [see John McCallum's will probate 11 April 1781 New York]

GILCHRIST, WILLIAM, in Boston during 1753 en route for Jamaica. [OA.Watt-MS]

GILL, OBADIAH, admitted as a member of the Scots Charitable Society of Boston in 1694. [SCS]

GILLESPIE, ANDREW, from Linlithgow, West Lothian, emigrated via London to New England before 1759, a tobacconist at North End, Boston, admitted to the Scots Charitable Society of Boston in 1761, a resident of Boston in 1787. [SCS][Imm.NE#69]

GILLESPIE, GEORGE, born in Glasgow during 1683, educated at Glasgow University, a Presbyterian minister, emigrated to New England in 1712, ordained as an Anglican clergyman in 1713, a minister in New Jersey and Delaware from 1713 to 1741, died on 2 January 1760. [WA][SA]

GILLESPIE, JAMES, in Boston, cnf 1898. [NAS.SC70.1.23]

GILLESPIE, JOHN, a shipmaster in Boston 1774. [NAS.CS16.1.161]

GILLIES, ROBERT, a merchant, arrived in Boston on 7 August 1766 on the Lovely Betty, master William Hayman, from Scotland. [SG#7.4.15][PAB]

GILLESPIE, WILLIAM, emigrated from Greenock aboard the

brigantine Matty, master Thomas Cochrane, on 19 May 1774 bound for New York, arrived there on 22 July 1774, settled Barnet, Vermont. [HBV]

GILMORE, ANDREW, a Scot, drowned in the wreck of the schooner Nancy at Cape Ann, near Pigeon Hill, Essex County, Massachusetts, 19 October 1752. [HCSI.V.157]

GILMOUR, CHARLES, admitted as a member of the Scots Charitable Society of Boston in 1717. [SCS]

GILMORE, JOHN, born in Paisley, Renfrewshire around 1660, emigrated via Ulster to Massachusetts, in 1700, died in Raynham, Massachusetts. [H]

GILMOUR, JOHN K., only son of Matthew Gilmour in Glasgow, died in Newhaven, Connecticut, on 17 December 1849. [W#XI/1079]

GIMBLE, WILLIAM, of Gammell, admitted as a member of the Scots Charitable Society of Boston in 1734. [SCS]

GIMISON, GEORGE, emigrated to New England by 1718, married Mary Vale in Boston 26 October 1718. [ImmNE.70]

GIVEN, JOHN, distiller, admitted as a member of the Scots Charitable Society of Boston in 1684. [SCS]

GLASS, JAMES, admitted as a member of the Scots Charitable Society of Boston in 1695. [SCS]

GLASSFORD, JAMES, from Glasgow, admitted as a member of the Scots Charitable Society of Boston in 1763. [SCS]

GLEN, GEORGE, settled in Wolfborough, Strafford County, New Hampshire, in 1774, a Loyalist in 1776, returned to Scotland in 1780. [PRO.AO12.100.98]

GLEN, WALTER, a weaver from Paisley, settled in Boston by 1771. [NAS.CS16.1.146/19]

GLEN, WILLIAM, born in 1713, emigrated from Scotland to New England by 1740, a gardener. [Imm.NE#70]

GLEN, WILLIAM, emigrated via Ayr on the Nelly, Captain Breckinridge, to America in November 1766, merchant in Newhaven, Connecticut, a Loyalist who returned to Scotland in 1776.[PRO.AO12.92.5]

GLENCROSS, WILLIAM, admitted as a member of the Scots Charitable Society of Boston in 1701. [SCS]

GLENNIE, PATRICK, born in 1844, from Ballater, Aberdeenshire, died in Thomastown, Connecticut, on 8 April 1873. [AJ:7.5.1873]

GOODWILLIE, DAVID, born on 31 December 1749 son of James Goodwillie and Mary Davidson in Kirkcaldy, Fife, a minister who settled in Barnet, Vermont, around 1789, died on 2 August 1830. [AA#8.10]

GOODWILLIE, Reverend THOMAS, from Barnet, Caledonia County, Vermont, married Alison, youngest daughter of Reverend James Hogg in Kelso, Roxburghshire, in Edinburgh on 11 April 1833. [DPCA, 26.4.1833]

GOODWILLIE, JOSEPH, born in 1751 son of James Goodwillie and Mary Davidson in Kirkcaldy, Fife, settled in Barnet, Vermont, by 1774. [AA#8.10]

GOODWILLIE, WALTER, son of Thomas Goodwillie in Kirkcaldy, Fife, settled in Vermont by 1800. [AA#8.9]

GORDON, ALEXANDER, a prisoner of war captured after the Battle of Worcester in September 1651, transported to New England "in Captain Allen's ship", an indentured servant of Samuel Stratton in Watertown, Massachusetts, 15 October 1652, in Exeter, New Hampshire, 1654. [Anc.H-NE]; wife Mary, daughter of Nicolas Lyson, father of Nicholas and John, died 1697, probate 1698 New Hampshire, vol.3, p.137. [SG.VII.4.27][NWI]

GORDON, ALEXANDER, MD, admitted as a member of the Scots Charitable Society of Boston in 1713. [SCS]

GORDON, ALEXANDER, admitted as a member of the Scots

Charitable Society of Boston in 1721. [SCS]

GORDON, ALEXANDER, a merchant, settled in Boston,
Massachusetts, by 1754.
[NAS.AC7.46/101][NAS.CS16.1.107]

GORDON, Captain ALEXANDER, in Boston, claim by his widow
Jane later in Edinburgh 1784. [PRO.AO12.105.102]

GORDON, Mrs JEAN, relict of Alexander Gordon in Boston, died
at 19 Princes Street, Edinburgh, on 22 June 1789.
[GM#XII.601.212]

GORDON, CHARLES, admitted as a member of the Scots
Charitable Society of Boston in 1736. [SCS]

GORDON, DANIEL, a prisoner of war transported to New England
on the John and Sarah of London, master John Greene in
November 1651. [Suffolk Deeds, 1-56]

GORDON, DANIEL, settled in New Hampshire around 1760.
[AA#4.155]

GORDON, EVA EMILY, daughter of Hugh Gordon, died in
Strathbogie, New England, 27 May 1856. [AJ#5670]

GORDON, GEORGE, admitted as a member of the Scots
Charitable Society of Boston in 1721. [SCS]

GORDON, JAMES, a prisoner of war transported to New England
on the John and Sarah of London, master John Greene in
November 1651. [Suffolk Deeds, 1-56]

GORDON, JAMES, a prisoner of war captured after the Battle of
Dunbar in September 1650, transported to New England on
the Unity, an indentured servant at Lynn Ironworks in
Massachusetts. [NWI]

GORDON, JAMES, admitted as a member of the Scots Charitable
Society of Boston in 1695. [SCS]

GORDON, JAMES, admitted as a member of the Scots Charitable
Society of Boston in 1721. [SCS]

GORDON, JOHN, a prisoner of war transported to New England on the <u>John and Sarah of London</u>, master John Greene in November 1651. [Suffolk Deeds, 1-56]

GORDON, JOHN, admitted as a member of the Scots Charitable Society in 1727. [SCS]

GORDON, JOHN, to New England by 1770, married {1} Mary Boyle, {2} Esther Snow, settled in Antrim, New Hampshire, later in Carmell? [ImmNE#72]

GORDON, JOHN, settled in Antrim, New Hampshire, during 1763, later in Chelsea, Vermont, a tailor and soldier of Fraser's Highlanders, died in 1798. [AA#4.155][Imm.NE#72]

GORDON, LAUGHLAN, a prisoner of war transported to New England on the <u>John and Sarah of London</u>, master John Greene in November 1651. [Suffolk Deeds, 1-56]

GORDON, Reverend PATRICK, son of Alexander Gordon, a weaver burgess of Aberdeen, matriculated at Marischal College, Aberdeen, in 1658, missionary of the S. P. G. in New England in 1702, died on Long Island in July 1703. [ANQ]

GORDON, ROBERT, from Aberdeen, admitted as a member of the Scots Charitable Society of Boston in 1769. [SCS]

GORDON, THOMAS, admitted as a member of the Scots Charitable Society of Boston in 1832. [SCS]

GORDON, WILLIAM, from Aberdeen, admitted as a member of the Scots Charitable Society of Boston in 1733. [SCS]

GORMACK, PATRICK, admitted as a member of the Scots Charitable Society of Boston in 1699. [SCS]

GOULD, JOHN, from Renfrewshire, admitted as a member of the Scots Charitable Society of Boston in 1769. [SCS]

GOURLAY, WILLIAM, from Old Monklands, Lanarkshire, admitted to the Scots Charitable Society of Boston in 1766, [SCS]; a merchant in Boston, 1769. [NAS.CS16.1.134/187]

GOVAN, DONALD, a merchant burgess of Glasgow who had been admitted as a burgess and guildsbrother of Glasgow on 25 September 1673 by right of his father Donald Govan a merchant burgess of Glasgow, [GBR]; admitted as a member of the Scots Charitable Society of Boston on 25 October 1684. [SCS]

GOW, GEORGE, in Johnsonville, New Hampshire, around 1872, possibly from Kirkcaldy, Fife. [NAS.SH.1872]

GOWAN, LEMUEL, admitted as a member of the Scots Charitable Society of Boston in 1716. [SCS]

GOWAN, WILLIAM, a prisoner of war captured after the Battle of Dunbar in September 1650, transported to New England on the Unity, an indentured servant who settled in Kittery, Maine, around 1656. [NWI]

GOWRIE, ALEXANDER, from Orkney, admitted as a member of the Scots Charitable Society of Boston in 1765. [SCS]

GRAHAM, ALEXANDER, prisoner of war captured after the Battle of Dunbar in September 1650, transported to New England on the Unity, an indentured servant at Lynn Ironworks in Massachusetts, [NWI]; possibly the ALLISTER GREIME, a Scot, administrator of the estate of Archibald Anderson, Salem, Massachusetts, November 1662. [Salem Quarterly Court Records, Vol.4, page 82]

GRAHAME, ALEXANDER, from Glasgow, admitted as a member of the Scots Charitable Society of Boston in 1747. [SCS]

GRAHAM, Mrs ELLA, born in Anna, Dumfries-shire, during 1820, wife of Richard Graham, assistant Superintendent of Newport Hospital, died in Newport, Rhode Island, on 14 December 1877. [AO]

GRAHAM, JAMES, admitted as a member of the Scots Charitable Society of Boston in 1689. [SCS]

GRAHAME, JAMES, admitted as a member of the Scots

Charitable Society of Boston in 1713. [SCS]

GRAHAM, JAMES, admitted as a member of the Scots Charitable Society in 1727. [SCS]

GRAHAM, JAMES, admitted as a member of the Scots Charitable Society of Boston in 1729. [SCS]

GRAHAME, JAMES, from Kirkwall, son of Reverend Andrew Grahame {1688-1746} and Christian Flett in Orkney, a houswright in Boston, admitted as a member of the Scots Charitable Society of Boston in 1754. [F.7.236][SCS]

GRAHAM, JAMES, a chairmaker from Rousay, Orkney, admitted as a member of the Scots Charitable Society of Boston in 1767, a resident of Boston in 1787. [SCS]

GRAHAM, JANE, wife of Thomas Morland in Montreal, died in Boston on 13 December 1856. [CM#20987]

GRAHAM, JOHN, admitted as a member of the Scots Charitable Society of Boston in 1686. [SCS]

GRAHAM, JOHN, born in Edinburgh during 1694, educated at Glasgow University in 1714, emigrated to Londonderry, New Hampshire, in 1718, a minister and a physician in Stafford and in Woodbury, Connecticut from 1723 to 1774, died in Southbury, Connecticut, on 11 December 1774. [CCNE][TSA]

GRAHAM, JOHN, emigrated from Greenock aboard the brigantine Matty, master Thomas Cochrane, on 19 May 1774 bound for New York, arrived there on 22 July 1774, settled Barnet, Vermont. [HBV]

GRAHAM, JOHN, a draper in Rhode Island around 1852, possibly from Stirlingshire. [NAS.SH.1852]

GRAHAM, PETER, admitted as a member of the Scots Charitable Society of Boston in 1728. [SCS]

GRANT, ALESTER, a prisoner of war transported to New England on the John and Sarah of London, master John Greene in

November 1651. [Suffolk Deeds, 1-56]

GRANT, ALEXANDER, a prisoner of war transported to New England on the <u>John and Sarah of London</u>, master John Greene in November 1651. [Suffolk Deeds, 1-56]

GRANT, ALEXANDER, admitted as a founder member of the Scots Charitable Society of Boston on 6 January 1657. [SCS]

GRANT, DANIEL, a prisoner of war transported to New England on the <u>John and Sarah of London</u>, master John Greene in November 1651. [Suffolk Deeds, 1-56]

GRANT, DONALD, from Inverness-shire, emigrated to New England during 1760, settled in Newtown, Connecticut. [Imm.NE#74][AA#3.161]

GRANT, DONALD FRASER, in Newport, Rhode Island, cnf 1884. [NAS.SC70.1.231]

GRANT, EBENEZER, settled in Littlefield, Connecticut, by 1756. [AA#7.114]

GRANT, JAMES, a prisoner of war transported to New England on the <u>John and Sarah of London</u>, master John Greene in November 1651. [Suffolk Deeds, 1-56]

GRANT, JAMES, admitted as a founder member of the Scots Charitable Society of Boston on 6 January 1657. [SCS]

GRANT, JAMES, a prisoner of war captured after the Battle of Dunbar in September 1650, transported from London on 3 November 1650 to New England on the <u>Unity</u>, an indentured servant who settled in New Hampshire, later in York, Maine, {RD5.28} probate 11 January 1694 Maine; [NWI]

GRANT, Captain JAMES, a merchant in Boston, admitted as a burgess and guildsbrother of Glasgow 12 October 1703, [GBR]

GRANT, JAMES, a Lieutenant of the 42nd Regiment, settled in Salem, Mass., in 1762, married Mary Hicks. [Imm.NE#74]

GRANT, JOHN, master of the Handmaid arrived in Plymouth, New England, on 29 October 1630 with about 60 passengers; master of the James arrived in Massachusetts Bay in October 1633. [Plymouth Colonial Records#1/20]

GRANT, JOHN, a prisoner of war transported to New England on the John and Sarah of London, master John Greene in November 1651. [Suffolk Deeds, 1-56]

GRANT, JOHN, admitted as a member of the Scots Charitable Society of Boston in 1711. [SCS]

GRANT, JOHN, born in Inverness during 1788, emigrated to America in 1800, settled in Portsmouth, New Hampshire, naturalised there in March 1839. [New Hampshire Court Records]

GRANT, JOSHUA, born in 1750, from Grandholm, Aberdeenshire, settled in Bennington, Vermont, by 1775, died in 1812. [AA#2.47]

GRANT, PATRICK, a prisoner of war transported to New England on the John and Sarah of London, master John Greene in November 1651. [Suffolk Deeds, 1-56]

GRANT, PATRICK, a passenger on the Glasgow Packet, master Alexander Porterfield, bound for Boston, was recruited into the 84th [Royal Highland Emigrant] Regiment on 23 October 1775. [NAS.GD174/2093]

GRANT, PATRICK, born on 25 July 1777, fifth son of John Grant a merchant in Leith, and of Castlehill, Edinburgh, settled in Boston, Massachusetts, as a merchant during 1802, married Anna Powell, drowned in the wreck of the Esther sailing for Baltimore on 20 November 1812. [AJ#3409][BLG#2719]

GRANT, PETER, (possibly the Patrick Graunt a prisoner of war transported from London to New England on the John and Sarah of London, master John Greene, November 1651); a prisoner, in Saugus, Massachusetts, 1654, in Dover 1659, dead by 2 March 1713. [EAF]; founder member of the Scots Charitable Society of Boston in 1657. [SCS]

GRANT, PETER, a prisoner of war captured after the Battle of Dunbar in September 1650, transported from London on 3 November 1650 in the Unity to New England, an indentured servant who settled in Kittery, Maine, around 1656. [NWI]

GRANT, PETER, a prisoner of war captured after the Battle of Dunbar in September 1650, transported from London on 3 November 1650 in the Unity to New England, an indentured servant at the Lynn Ironworks in Massachusetts. [NWI]

GRANT, SWITHIN, admitted to the Scots Charitable Society of Boston in 1726. [SCS]

GRANT, THOMAS, a prisoner of war transported to New England on the John and Sarah of London, master John Greene in November 1651. [Suffolk Deeds, 1-56]

GRANT, WILLIAM, a prisoner of war transported to New England on the John and Sarah of London, master John Greene in November 1651. [Suffolk Deeds, 1-56]

GRAY, ANDREW, from Glasgow, admitted as a member of the Scots Charitable Society of Boston in 1758. [SCS]

GRAY, DAVID, a merchant, arrived in Boston on 1 June 1768 aboard the snow Jenny, master Hector Orr, from Glasgow. [PAB]

GRAY, GEORGE, a prisoner of war captured after the Battle of Dunbar in September 1650, transported from London on 3 November 1650 in the Unity to New England, an indentured servant settled in Kittery, Maine. [NWI]

GRAY, JOHN, admitted as a member of the Scots Charitable Society of Boston in 1687. [SCS]

GRAY, JOHN, admitted as a member of the Scots Charitable Society of Boston in 1690. [SCS]

GRAY, JOHN, a weaver, arrived in Boston on 28 May 1768 aboard the Glasgow, master John Dunn, from Glasgow. [PAB]

GRAY, JOHN, from Renfrewshire, emigrated to America in April 1774, settled in Ryegate, Vermont, before 1780. [VHS]

GRAY, JOHN, born 1783, a gentleman, arrived in Waldboro [Maine?] during 1821 on the Lydia, Captain Adams. [USNA/par]

GRAY, MICHAEL, eldest son of Ebenezer Gray a manufacturer in Grafton, New Hampshire, matriculated at Glasgow University in 1808. [MAGU#234]

GRAY, THOMAS, a merchant in Glasgow, settled in Boston, Massachusetts, before 1766. [NAS.B10.15.7234]

GRAY, WILLIAM, from London admitted as a member of the Scots Charitable Society of Boston in 1691. [SCS]

GRAY, WILLIAM, admitted to the Scots Charitable Society of Boston in 1726. [SCS]

GRAY, WILLIAM, from Glasgow, admitted as a member of the Scots Charitable Society of Boston in 1747. [SCS]

GREEN, GEORGE, born 1835, son of James Green {1813-1900}, a carpenter in Fochabers, Morayshire, and Susan Bremner {1804-1858}, died in Bernardstown, Massachusetts, on 1 July 1860. [Bellie g/s, Morayshire]

GREENLAW, JOHN, from Calder near Glasgow, admitted as a member of the Scots Charitable Society of Boston in 1762. [SCS]

GREENLAW, WILLIAM, emigrated to New England by 1753, settled in Warren, Maine, and on Deer Island, Maine. [ImmNE#77]

GREGG, JAMES, born in Ayrshire during 1690, emigrated via County Antrim to New England in 1718, settled in Londonderry, New Hampshire, married Janet Cargill. [Imm.NE#78]

GREGORY, DAVID, admitted as a member of the Scots Charitable Society of Boston in 1714. [SCS]

GREGORY, JAMES, admitted as a member of the Scots Charitable Society of Boston in 1740. [SCS]

GREIG, ROBERT, born 1806, son of Mrs Greig a midwife in Dunfermline, Fife, died in Danvers, Massachusetts, on 6 December 1871. [DP]

GREIG, ROBERT, born in Dunshalt, Fife, emigrated to America in 1854, died at Wells River, Vermont, on 3 May 1881. [PJ]

GREIG, WILLIAM, from Aberdeen, admitted as a member of the Scots Charitable Society of Boston in 1731. [SCS]

GREIVES, JAMES, admitted as a member of the Scots Charitable Society of Boston in 1731. [SCS]

GUILD, JOHN, born 1612, settled in Dedham, Massachusetts, during 1636, married Elizabeth Crooke in Roxbury during 1645, died on 4 October 1682. [BLG#2723][AA#6.39]

GULLES, JOHN, arrived in Boston on 28 October 1763 aboard the Douglas, master James Montgomerie, from Scotland. [PAB]

GUNN, DANIEL, a prisoner of war transported to New England on the John and Sarah of London, master John Greene in November 1651. [Suffolk Deeds, 1-56]

GUNN, RICHARD, admitted as an honorary member of the Scots Charitable Society of Boston in 1822. [SCS]

GURLEY, WILLIAM, born around 1665, from Inverness, settled in Northampton, Massachusetts, around 1685, died 1700. [CAG#1/573]

GURNER, JAMES, a prisoner of war transported to New England on the John and Sarah of London, master John Greene in November 1651. [Suffolk Deeds, 1-56]

GUTHRIE, JOHN, from Edinburgh, settled in Litchfield County, Connecticut, died in 1730. [DAB#8.62]

GUTHRIE, WILLIAM, a farmer in Ryegate, Vermont, around 1867. [NAS.SH.1867]

HAGOMAN, JOHN, a prisoner of war transported to New England on the John and Sarah of London, master John Greene in November 1651. [Suffolk Deeds, 1-56]

HAIN, HARRY J., second son of James Hain a publican in Dunfermline, married Nellie, eldest daughter of John Harvey, Belfast Mains, USA, in Boston on 6 July 1891. [DJ]

HALDANE, JAMES, a merchant in Jedburgh, Roxburghshire, a thief, transported from Glasgow to New England in June 1722. [NAS.JC.12.3]

HALKERTON, JAMES, born at Rathillet, Fife, in 1685, educated at St Andrews University, a surgeon in the Royal Navy, settled in Boston during 1716, married Margaret ......, died on 15 June 1721. [Boston g/s] MD, admitted as a member of the Scots Charitable Society of Boston in 1717. [SCS][SA#179]

HALL, DONALD, a farmer in Vermont around 1857, son of Alexander Hall in Dubbs. [NAS.SH.1857]

HALL, JOHN, born in 1729, a farmer in Inchinnan, Renfrewshire, with his wife Jean Allison and children William, John, Janet, Robert, and James, emigrated from Greenock to Salem on the Glasgow Packet master Alexander Porterfield, in April 1775. [PRO.T47/12]

HALL, ROBERT, from Haddington, East Lothian, admitted as a member of the Scots Charitable Society of Boston in 1767. [SCS]

HALLEY, HENRY, admitted as a member of the Scots Charitable Society of Boston in 1729. [SCS]

HALYBURTON, ANDREW, from Edinburgh, admitted as a member of the Scots Charitable Society of Boston in 1722. [SCS]

HALIBURTON, JOHN, born around 1739 in Haddington, East
Lothian, son of Reverend Haliburton, settled in Newport,
Rhode Island, as a physician, with wife Susanna Brenton
and son Brenton {born Newport 3 December 1775}, a
Loyalist in 1776 moved to Halifax, Nova Scotia.
[NENS#47][PRO.AO13.24.241-249]

HAMILTON, ALEXANDER, admitted as a member of the Scots
Charitable Society of Boston in 1692. [SCS]

HAMILTON, ALEXANDER, from Edinburgh, admitted as a
member of the Scots Charitable Society of Boston in 1744.
[SCS]; heir to Daniel
Hamilton, chamberlain of Grange, 1753. [NAS.CS16.1.92]

HAMILTON, ANDREW, admitted as a member of the Scots
Charitable Society of Boston in 1700. [SCS]

HAMILTON, ANDREW, admitted as a member of the Scots
Charitable Society of Boston in 1720. [SCS]

HAMILTON, ANDREW, died in Massachusetts during May 1767.
[SM#29.614]

HAMILTON, ARCHIBALD, admitted as a member of the Scots
Charitable Society of Boston in 1717. [SCS]

HAMILTON, ARCHIBALD, from Glasgow, admitted as a member
of the Scots Charitable Society of Boston in 1748. [SCS]

HAMILTON, ARCHIBALD, [ARTHUR?] a merchant, arrived in
Boston on 7 August 1766 aboard the Lovely Betsy, master
William Hayman, from Greenock. [SG#7.4.15][PAB]

HAMILTON, DAVID, a prisoner of war captured after the Battle of
Dunbar in September 1650, transported to New England on
the Unity from London on 3 November 1650, an indentured
servant at Kittery, Maine, around 1656. [NWI]

HAMILTON, DAVID, a prisoner of war transported to New England
on the John and Sarah of London, master John Greene in
November 1651. [Suffolk Deeds, 1-56]

HAMILTON, GAVIN, a merchant, from Port Glasgow to New England on the Endeavour of Liverpool in September 1684. [NAS.E72.19.9]

HAMILTON GUSTAVUS, admitted as a member of the Scots Charitable Society of Boston in 1690. [SCS]

HAMILTON, GILBERT, admitted as a member of the Scots Charitable Society of Boston in 1687. [SCS]

HAMILTON, HANS, admitted as a member of the Scots Charitable Society of Boston in 1694. [SCS]

HAMILTON, JAMES, a prisoner of war transported to New England on the John and Sarah of London, master John Greene in November 1651. [Suffolk Deeds, 1-56]

HAMILTON, JAMES, from Glasgow, admitted as a member of the Scots Charitable Society of Boston in 1699. [SCS]

HAMILTON, JAMES, from Glasgow, admitted as a member of the Scots Charitable Society of Boston in 1755. [SCS]

HAMILTON, JOHN, settled Charlestown and later Concord, Massachusetts, died during 1681. [CAG#1.135]; a merchant in Boston 1753, heir to Daniel Hamilton, Grange. [NAS.CS16.1.89/92]

HAMILTON, JOHN, Postmaster General, admitted as a member of the Scots Charitable Society of Boston in 1711. [SCS]

HAMILTON, JOHN, possibly the son of Alexander Hamilton in Ayrshire and brother of James Hamilton in the West Indies, emigrated to New England during 1717, settled in Pelham, Massachusetts, then in Shutesbury, Connecticut. [Imm.NE#81]

HAMILTON, JOHN, admitted as a member of the Scots Charitable Society of Boston in 1721. [SCS]

HAMILTON, OTTO, from East Lothian, admitted as a member of the Scots Charitable Society of Boston in 1737. [SCS]

HAMILTON, QUINTEN, admitted as a member of the Scots Charitable Society of Boston in 1700. [SCS]

HAMILTON, ROBERT, from Glasgow, admitted as a member of the Scots Charitable Society of Boston in 1742. [SCS]

HAMILTON, RORY, a prisoner of war transported to New England on the John and Sarah of London, master John Greene in November 1651. [Suffolk Deeds, 1-56]

HAMILTON, WILLIAM, born in 1643 possibly in Glasgow, emigrated to Cape Cod, Massachusetts, in 1668, later moved to Rhode Island, died in 1746. [DAB#8.183][CAG#1.824]

HANNAH, ROBERT, a joiner, admitted as a member of the Scots Charitable Society of Boston in 1695. [SCS]

HANSHALLOT, GEORGE, a merchant, arrived in Boston on 7 August 1766 on the schooner Lovely Betsy, master William Hayman. [SG#7.4.15] [NWI#1/460]

HANNAH, GEORGE, from Barbados admitted as a member of the Scots Charitable Society of Boston in 1691. [SCS]

HANNAH, WILLIAM, admitted as a member of the Scots Charitable Society of Boston in 1693. [SCS]

HANNA, WILLIAM, admitted as a member of the Scots Charitable Society in 1723. [SCS]

HAPPY, FRANCIS, admitted as a member of the Scots Charitable Society of Boston in 1698. [SCS]

HARDCASS, JOHN, of Hardcass, admitted as a member of the Scots Charitable Society of Boston in 1718. [SCS]

HARDY, WILLLIAM FORRESTER, born 1 June 1833, died in Portland, Maine, on 26 April 1898. [Canongate, g/s]

HARKNESS, WILLIAM, arrived in New England in 1710 from Scotland, settled in Pelham, Massachusetts. [Imm.NE#83]

HARLEY, GEORGE, born in Dunfermline, Fife, during 1764, died in Windsor, Connecticut, on 26 November 1858. [FH]

HARPER, WILLIAM, admitted as a member of the Scots Charitable Society of Boston in 1700. [SCS]

HARRIS, JOHN, admitted as a member of the Scots Charitable Society of Boston in 1720. [SCS]

HARRIS, MARGARET, born in 1838, immigrated into Massachusetts aboard the Catherine Rodgers a brig, on 16 July 1849. [LAP]

HARRISON, WILLIAM, a gentleman, arrived in Boston on 28 October 1763 aboard the Douglas, master James Montgomerie, from Scotland. [PAB]

HART, SAMUEL, from Edinburgh, admitted as a member of the Scots Charitable Society of Boston in 1743. [SCS]

HARVIE, ALEXANDER, emigrated from Greenock aboard the brigantine Matty, master Thomas Cochrane, on 19 May 1774 bound for New York, arrived on 22 July 1774, settled Barnet, Vermont. [HBV]

HARVEY, EDWARD, from Campbeltown, Argyll, admitted as a member of the Scots Charitable Society of Boston in 1819. [SCS]

HARVEY, JOHN, admitted as a member of the Scots Charitable Society in 1723. [SCS]

HARVEY, WILLIAM, from Glasgow, admitted as a member of the Scots Charitable Society of Boston in 1751. [SCS]

HASTIE, JAMES, from Greenock, admitted as a member of the Scots Charitable Society of Boston in 1743. [SCS]

HASTY, JOHN, admitted as a member of the Scots Charitable Society of Boston in 1715. [SCS]

HATTRICK, PETER, admitted as an honorary member of the Scots Charitable Society of Boston in 1802. [SCS]

HAWLEY, WILLIAM, in Boston, cnf 1899. [NAS.SC70.1.385]

HAY, JAMES, admitted to the Scots Charitable Society of Boston in 1697. [SCS]

HAY, ROBERT, from Bo'ness, West Lothian, admitted as a member of the Scots Charitable Society of Boston in 1729. [SCS]

HAY, THOMAS, admitted as a member of the Scots Charitable Society of Boston in 1694. [SCS]

HAY, WILLIAM, MD, admitted as a member of the Scots Charitable Society of Boston in 1734. [SCS]; a physician who settled in Massachusetts, died in 1783. [SA#179]

HAYES, GEORGE, emigrated to New England in 1680, settled in Windsor, Connecticut, 1682, to Simsbury, Connecticut. [SSA.46; NY.1917][AncH-NE]

HAYES, THOMAS, admitted as a member of the Scots Charitable Society of Boston in 1713. [SCS]

HAYNMAN, JOHN, admitted as a member of the Scots Charitable Society of Boston in 1694. [SCS]

HEAL, ARTHUR, mariner, admitted as a member of the Scots Charitable Society of Boston in 1684. [SCS]

HEDDRICK, ALEXANDER, born in Kirkcaldy, Fife, during 1825, emigrated to America during 1849, settled in Hartford, Connecticut, a foundry foreman, died there on 16 April 1897. [FFP]

HEDRICK, JAMES, a prisoner of war transported to New England on the John and Sarah of London, master John Greene in November 1651. [Suffolk Deeds, 1-56]

HEDRICK, WILLIAM, a prisoner of war transported to New England on the John and Sarah of London, master John Greene in November 1651. [Suffolk Deeds, 1-56]

HEDDLE, ELIZABETH, from Kirkwall, Orkney, in New England around 1795. [NAS.GD263.167]

HEIGS, JOHN, admitted as a member of the Scots Charitable Society of Boston in 1722. [SCS]

HENDERSON, DAVID, admitted as a member of the Scots Charitable Society of Boston in 1693. [SCS]

HENDERSON, GEORGE, admitted as a member of the Scots Charitable Society of Boston in 1686. [SCS]

HENDERSON, GEORGE, born in Halkirk, Caithness, during 1797, emigrated to Canada in 1817, settled in Boston, Massachusetts, during 1819, naturalised in Rockingham County, New Hampshire, in October 1840. [New Hampshire Naturalisations]

HENDERSON, HUGH, a trader arrived in Boston on 28 November 1768 from Glasgow on the Glasgow, Captain John Dunn. [PAB]

HENDERSON, JAMES, a merchant who arrived in Boston on 7 August 1766 aboard the Lovely Betsy, master William Hayman, from Scotland. [SG#7.4.15][PAB]

HENDERSON, JAMES, a wright from Renfrewshire, emigrated from Greenock to New York on the Matty on 25 March 1773, settled in Ryegate, New Hampshire [now Vermont]. [PRO.T47/12][Whitelaw papers#29, VHS]

HENDERSON, JOHN, admitted as a member of the Scots Charitable Society of Boston in 1691, dead by 6 November 1711. [SCS]

HENDERSON, WILLIAM, emigrated from Glasgow to Dover, New Hampshire, in 1650, a ships carpenter and builder. [Anc.H.NE]

HENDERSON, ..., born 1793, a merchant, arrived in Boston, Charlestown District, on the schooner Cherub, Captain Sheppard, during 1821. [USNA/par]

HENDRY, LOUISA, in Boston, cnf 1893. [NAS.SC70.1.326]

HENRY, WILLIAM, from Greenock, admitted as a member of the Scots Charitable Society of Boston in 1735. [SCS]

HENSHAW, JOHN, admitted as a member of the Scots Charitable Society in 1727. [SCS]

HERRON, PATRICK, a prisoner of war transported to New England on the John and Sarah of London, master John Greene in November 1651. [Suffolk Deeds, 1-56]

HEWETT, JAMES, MD, admitted as a member of the Scots Charitable Society of Boston in 1713. [SCS]

HIGHEN, ROBERT, a prisoner of war transported to New England on the John and Sarah of London, master John Greene in November 1651. [Suffolk Deeds, 1-56]

HILDING, JANE, widow of John Hilding, arrived in America as wife of James McDonald, soldier of the 42nd Regiment, settled in Boston after 1755, Loyalist. [PRO.AO12.102.140]

HILL, GEORGE, in Boston, cnf 1879. [NAS.SC70.1.195]

HILL, MISSALL STODART, in Boston, cnf 1878. [NAS.SC70.1.189]

HILL, THOMAS, admitted as a member of the Scots Charitable Society of Boston in 1686, keykeeper of the poor-box on 4 February 1695. [SCS]

HISLOP, THOMAS, admitted as a member of the Scots Charitable Society of Boston in 1699. [SCS]

HISLOP, WILLIAM, born in Humley parish, east Lothian, emigrated to New England around 1740, a pedlar, died in 1796. [ImmNE#95]

HODGES, JAMES, from Greenock, admitted as a member of the Scots Charitable Society of Boston in 1732. [SCS]

HODGE, JOHN, admitted as a member of the Scots Charitable Society of Boston in 1718. [SCS]

HODGKINS, JOHN, emigrated to New England 1753, settled in Warren, Maine, and later in Boston, Massachusetts. [ImmNE#88]

HODGSON, JOHN, son of William Hodgson a merchant in Glasgow, emigrated to New England 1762, married Cecilia ...., settled in Boston, Massachusetts, as a bookseller, died 1781. [ImmNE#88][NAS.SH.1772]

HOGG, DANIEL, a prisoner of war transported to New England on the John and Sarah of London, master John Greene in November 1651. [Suffolk Deeds, 1-56]

HOGG, JOHN, a prisoner of war transported to New England on the John and Sarah of London, master John Greene in November 1651. [Suffolk Deeds, 1-56]

HOGG, NEIL, a prisoner of war transported to New England on the John and Sarah of London, master John Greene in November 1651. [Suffolk Deeds, 1-56]

HOGG, ROBERT, emigrated to New England in May 1764, settled at Boothbay, Maine. [ImmNE#89]

HOGG, ROBERT, born on 27 February 1832, son of Thomas Hogg and Jane Scoon in Hawick, Roxburghshire, settled in Providence, Rhode Island, died on 26 February 1904. [Trans. of the Hawick. Arch. Soc., 1936, 29]

HOLMES, JOHN J., a dyer in Willimankie, Windham County, Connecticut, cnf 1888. [NAS.SC70.1.268]

HOME, THOMAS, a prisoner of war captured after the Battle of Dunbar in September 1650, transported to New England on the Unity from London on 3 November 1650, an indentured servant at Kittery, Maine, around 1656. [NWI]

HONEY, ..., daughter of Frederick Robertson Honey, was born in Newhaven, Connecticut, on 28 January 1879. [EC#29448]

HONEYMAN, JAMES, born during 1675 in Kinneff, Kincardineshire, son of Reverend James Honeyman, educated at Marischal College, Aberdeen, an Episcopalian clergyman, emigrated in April 1703 on the <u>Portsmouth Galley</u>, arrived in Boston, Massachusetts, on 16 November 1703, settled in Jamaica, Long Island, New York, and in 1708 settled in Rhode Island, married (1) Elizabeth Carr, (2) Elizabeth Brown or Cranston, father of James, Elizabeth and Francis, died in Newport, Rhode Island, on 2 July 1750. [SNQ.1.169][SPG.11.89][SM#12.502][EMA#34]

HONEYMAN, JAMES, born 4 January 1745 in Kinneff, Kincardineshire, son of Reverend James Honeyman and Katherine Allerdyce, educated at Marischal College, Aberdeen, around 1763, a minister in Rhode Island, died in Kinneff on 5 August 1781. [F.5.474][F.7.663][KCA.2.331]

HOOPER, WILLIAM, from Ednam, Berwickshire, an Episcopalian minister, admitted as a member of the Scots Charitable Society of Boston in 1737. [SCS]; emigrated to New England on 7 July 1747, settled in Boston, died on 14 April 1767. [EMA#34][SO#107]

HOPE, JOHN, from Galashiels, admitted as a member of the Scots Charitable Society of Boston in 1819. [SCS]

HOUSTOUN, PATRICK, from Glasgow, admitted as a member of the Scots Charitable Society of Boston in 1750. [SCS]

HOUSTON, WILLIAM, admitted as a member of the Scots Charitable Society of Boston in 1701. [SCS]

HOW, DANIEL, a prisoner of war transported to New England on the <u>John and Sarah of London</u>, master John Greene in November 1651. [Suffolk Deeds, 1-56]

HOW, JAMES, admitted as a member of the Scots Charitable Society of Boston in 1693. [SCS]

HOWNAN, ISABELLA, arrived in Boston from Glasgow aboard the <u>Lesostris</u> on 17 May 1850. [USNA#M277/36]

HUDSON, DANIEL, a prisoner of war transported to New England on the <u>John and Sarah of London</u>, master John Greene in November 1651. [Suffolk Deeds, 1-56]

HUDSON, JOHN, a prisoner of war transported to New England on the <u>John and Sarah of London</u>, master John Greene in November 1651. [Suffolk Deeds, 1-56]

HULBERT, THOMAS, born 1610, a blacksmith, a soldier in the Pequat War 1638, settled in Wetherfield, Connecticut. [AncH-NE]

HUME, ALESTER, a prisoner of war transported to New England on the <u>John and Sarah of London</u>, master John Greene in November 1651. [Suffolk Deeds, 1-56]

HUME, DAVID, a prisoner of war transported to New England on the <u>John and Sarah of London</u>, master John Greene in November 1651. [Suffolk Deeds, 1-56]

HUME, GEORGE, admitted as a member of the Scots Charitable Society of Boston in 1717. [SCS]

HUME, JAMES, from Glasgow, admitted as a member of the Scots Charitable Society of Boston in 1741. [SCS]

HUME, MICHAEL, admitted as a member of the Scots Charitable Society of Boston in 1713. [SCS]

HUMPHREY, M. A., born in 1830, immigrated into Massachusetts aboard the <u>Catherine Rodgers</u>, a brig, on 25 June 1850. [LAP]

HUNTER, ALEXANDER, in Brighton, Massachusetts, around 1878, son of Peter Hunter a mason in Burntisland, Fife. [NAS.SH.1878]

HUNTER, CAMPBELL, born 1870, late of Leslie, Fife, died in St Lawrence, Massachusetts, on 19 May 1891. [PJ]

HUNTER, DANIEL, born 1864, died in Newport, Rhode Island, on 15 December 1894. [Newton-on-Ayr g/s, Ayrshire]

HUNTER, DAVID, from Ayrshire, admitted as a member of the Scots Charitable Society of Boston in 1742. [SCS]

HUNTER, JAMES, from Greenock, admitted as a member of the Scots Charitable Society of Boston in 1738. [SCS]

HUNTER, JAMES, emigrated to New England by 1770, settled in Cornich, New Hampshire. [ImmNE#94]

HUNTER, NATHANIEL, from Irvine, Ayrshire, admitted as a member of the Scots Charitable Society of Boston in 1762. [SCS]

HUNTER, ROBERT, son of Patrick Hunter and Marion Crawford in Hunterstone, Ayrshire, a mariner, settled in Boston, New England, by 1737, admitted as a member of the Scots Charitable Society of Boston in 1739. [Hunter of Hunterstone MSS.53/54, SRS] [SCS][NAS.GD102.2/54]

HUNTER, WILLIAM, settled in Boston, Massachusetts, 1767, auctioneer and Loyalist, privateer officer who drowned at sea. [Loyalists of Mass. p168][PRO.AO12.100.57]

HUNTER, WILLIAM, born 1730, a physician possibly educated at Edinburgh University, settled in Rhode Island, died during 1777. [SA#184]

HUTCHISON, GEORGE, resident in Thomas Heath's house, near the Old Meeting House, Boston, during 1675. [SRA]

HUTCHINS, PARLEY, a soldier from Edinburgh, to New England in 1774,settled in Stratford, New Hampshire, and in Connecticut. [ImmNE#95]

HUTCHINSON, GEORGE, admitted as a member of the Scots Charitable Society of Boston in 1731. [SCS]

HUTCHINSON, WALTER, born in Scotland during 1781, settled in America in 1801, a shoemaker in Norwalk, Connecticut, in 1812. [1812

HUTTON, ALEXANDER, admitted as a member of the Scots Charitable Society of Boston in 1714. [SCS]

HYNDMAN, JOHN, from Greenock, admitted as a member of the Scots Charitable Society of Boston in 1730. [SCS]

HYNDMAN, JOHN, from Kilallen, emigrated with his son John to America in 1771, settled in Baltimore, and in Ryegate, Vermont, in 1773. [Miller and Wells 'History of Ryegate' p.394]

HYSLOP, WILLIAM, in Brooklyn, Suffolk County, Massachusetts, 1772. [NAS.CS16.1.151]

HYSLOP, WILLIAM, born in 1714, a pedlar from Humley, Haddington, East Lothian, admitted as a member of the Scots Charitable Society of Boston in 1746, a resident of Boston in 1787, died during 1796. [SCS][Imm.NE#95]

IMRIE, JAMES, admitted as a member of the Scots Charitable Society of Boston in 1728. [SCS]

INCHES, THOMAS, admitted as a member of the Scots Charitable Society of Boston in 1716. [SCS]

INGLIS, ALEXANDER, from Dunbar, East Lothian, admitted as a member of the Scots Charitable Society of Boston in 1746. [SCS]

INGLIS, ALEXANDER, from Inverness, admitted as a member of the Scots Charitable Society of Boston in 1747. [SCS]

INGLIS, JAMES, admitted as a founder member of the Scots Charitable Society of Boston on 6 January 1657, boxmaster of the Society in July 1663; president of the overseers of the poor-box on 4 February 1695. [SCS]

INGLES, JAMES, jr., admitted as a member of the Scots Charitable Society of Boston in 1702. [SCS]

INGLIS, WEMYSS, born in 1809, son of William Inglis [1780-1843] and Jane Bain [1782-1859], died in Boston on 20 December 1863. [Old Cumnock g/s, Ayrshire]

INNES, ALEXANDER, a minister and schoolmaster from Aberdeenshire, educated at Aberdeen University, emigrated to New England in 1693, died in Elisabethtown, New Jersey, during August 1713. [APB.2.118]

INNES, ALEXANDER, a prisoner of war captured after the Battle of Dunbar in September 1650, transported to New England on the Unity from London on 3 November 1650, an indentured servant at Lynn Ironworks in Massachusetts, settled on Block Island. [NWI]

INNES, LEWIS, admitted as a member of the Scots Charitable Society in 1725. [SCS]

INNES, THOMAS, from Banff, admitted as a member of the Scots Charitable Society of Boston in 1748. [SCS]

INNES, WALTER, MD, admitted as a member of the Scots Charitable Society of Boston in 1700. [SCS]

IRVINE, JOHN, admitted as a member of the Scots Charitable Society in 1724. [SCS]

IRVING, HENRY, from Orkney, admitted as a member of the Scots Charitable Society of Boston in 1750. [SCS]

IRVING, JAMES, admitted as a member of the Scots Charitable Society of Boston in 1723. [SCS]

IRVING, JOHN, admitted as a member of the Scots Charitable Society of Boston in 1720. [SCS]

IRVING, JOHN, admitted as a member of the Scots Charitable Society in 1723. [SCS]

IRVING, JOHN, from Orkney, admitted as a member of the Scots Charitable Society of Boston in 1748. [SCS]

IVER, DAVID, a jeweller, arrived in Boston on 22 January 1766 aboard the snow Peggy, master William Craig, from Scotland. [PAB]

JACK, ANN, born in 1779, immigrated into Massachusetts on board the Mary Ann on 31 August 1849. [LAP]

JACK, WILLIAM, born in 1779, immigrated into Massachusetts on board the Mary Ann on 31 August 1849. [LAP]

JACKSON, JAMES, a prisoner of war captured after the Battle of Dunbar in September 1650, transported to New England on the Unity from London on 3 November 1650, an indentured servant, settled in New Hampshire and later in York, Maine, in the 1650s. [NWI]

JACKSON, JAMES, a prisoner of war transported to New England on the John and Sarah of London, master John Greene in November 1651. [Suffolk Deeds, 1-56]

JACKSON, PATRICK, a prisoner of war transported to New England on the John and Sarah of London, master John Greene in November 1651. [Suffolk Deeds, 1-56]

JACKSON, RICHARD, a prisoner of war transported to New England on the John and Sarah of London, master John Greene in November 1651. [Suffolk Deeds, 1-56]

JACKSON, ROBERT, from Dunbar, East Lothian, admitted as a member of the Scots Charitable Society of Boston in 1746. [SCS]

JACKSON, WALTER, Scots prisoner of war transported from London to Boston on the John and Sarah of London, John Green, May 1652. [NER#I.378]

JACKSON, WILLIAM, a merchant in Boston 1806. [NAS.CS17.1.25/305]

JAIRDEN, WILLIAM, merchant from Dumfries, admitted as a member of the Scots Charitable Society of Boston on 25 October 1684. [SCS]

JAMIESON, ANDREW, a prisoner of war captured after the Battle of Dunbar in September 1650, transported to New England on the Unity from London on 3 November 1650, an indentured servant at the Lynn Ironworks in Massachusetts.

[NWI]; admitted as a founder member of the Scots Charitable Society of Boston on 6 January 1657. [SCS]

JAMIESON, DAVID, a prisoner of war transported to New England on the John and Sarah of London, master John Greene in November 1651. [Suffolk Deeds, 1-56]

JAMIESON, JANE, wife of Thomas McBain, from Leslie, Fife, died in Holyoke, Massachusetts, on 25 September 1894. [FFP]

JAMIESON, NEIL, a prisoner of war transported to New England on the John and Sarah of London, master John Greene in November 1651. [Suffolk Deeds, 1-56]

JAMIESON, PATRICK, a prisoner of war transported to New England on the John and Sarah of London, master John Greene in November 1651. [Suffolk Deeds, 1-56]

JAMIESON, ROBERT, from Gourock, Renfrewshire, admitted as a member of the Scots Charitable Society of Boston in 1759. [SCS]

JAMIESON, WILLIAM, a tailor in Charlestown, admitted as a member of the Scots Charitable Society of Boston in 1684. [SCS]

JAMIESON, WILLIAM, born in Scotland in 1783, settled in America in 1810, a clothier and dyer in Norwalk, Connecticut, in 1812. [1812]

JEFFREY, GEORGE, emigrated to Boston, Massachusetts, in 1676, settled in Portsmouth, New Hampshire, during 1684. [Anc.H-NE]; a merchant in Piscataque, admitted as a member of the Scots Charitable Society of Boston in 1685. [SCS]; a merchant and smuggler in New Hampshire; Member of HM Council of New Hampshire 13 July 1702.[SPAWI]

JEFFREY, JOHN, admitted as a member of the Scots Charitable Society of Boston in 1695. [SCS]

JEFFREYS, WILLIAM, admitted as a member of the Scots Charitable Society in 1725. [SCS]

JELLY, WILLIAM, born around 1770, father of William born 8
September 1794 in Kirkcudbright, also of John, Charles,
Samuel, Elizabeth, and Mary, emigrated to America on the
brig Elizabeth 8 August 1795, landed at Derby Wharf,
Salem, Massachusetts. [SGen.1.1.22]; a cartwright in
Salem, died in November 1813, cnf Commissariat of
Edinburgh 22 November 1821. [NAS.CC8.8.147]

JOHNSON, JOHN R., born in 1834, immigrated into
Massachusetts aboard the Agnes Sophia on 18 July 1850.
[LAP]

JOHNSON, JAMES, Auckley, Scotland, settled in Scarborough,
Maine, around 1732. [ImmNE#97]

JOHNSON, JOHN, admitted as amember of the Scots Charitable
Society of Boston in 1665. [SCS]

JOHNSON, NEIL, a prisoner of war transported to New England
on the John and Sarah of London, master John Greene in
November 1651. [Suffolk Deeds, 1-56]

JOHNSTONE, ADAM, a chapman, admitted as a member of the
Scots Charitable Society of Boston in 1684. [SCS]

JOHNSTONE, ADAM, a doctor who settled in Massachusetts, died
in 1806. [SA#179]

JOHNSTON, ANDREW, a merchant, arrived in Boston on 2 June
1769 from Glasgow on the Glasgow, Captain John Dunn.
[PAB]

JOHNSTON, ANN, born in 1798, wife of William Stewart, died in
Andover, Massachusetts, 1 September 1855. [Farnell g/s,
Angus]

JOHNSTONE, DAVID, a lock maker, admitted as a member of the
Scots Charitable Society of Boston in 1684. [SCS]

JOHNSTOUN, DAVID, a vintner, admitted as a member of the
Scots Charitable Society of Boston in 1695. [SCS]

JOHNSTON, DAVID, a bank clerk in Boston around 1861,
    grandson of David Johnston a shipmaster in East Wemyss,
    Fife. [NAS.SH.1861]

JOHNSTON, EBENEZER, in Boston, deceased by 1846.
    [NAS.SH.1846]

JOHNSTON, JAMES, in Boston, around 1846. [NAS.SH.1846]

JOHNSTON, JANE, born in 1798, wife of William Stewart, died in
    Andover, Massachusetts, on 1 September 1855, [Farnell g/s,
    Angus]

JOHNSTON, JOHN, admitted as a member of the Scots
    Charitable Society of Boston in 1692. [SCS]

JOHNSTON, JOHN, admitted to the Scots Charitable Society of
    Boston in 1696. [SCS]

JOHNSTON, JOSEPH, born in Annan, Dumfries-shire, during
    1841, died in New Bedford, Massachusetts, on 28 March
    1878. [AO]

JOHNSTON, ROBERT, admitted as a member of the Scots
    Charitable Society of Boston in 1702. [SCS]

JOHNSTON, ROBERT HENRY, in Boston around 1846.
    [NAS.SH.1846]

JOHNSTON, THOMAS, admitted as a member of the Scots
    Charitable Society of Boston in 1731. [SCS]

JOHNSTON, THOMAS, emigrated to New England 1735, settled
    in Warren then in Bristol, Maine, died in 1811. [ImmNE#97]

JOHNSTON, WILLIAM, admitted as a member of the Scots
    Charitable Society of Boston in 1699. [SCS]

JONES, HELEN, wife of James Whyte from Kirkcaldy, Fife, a
    painter and decorator in Lenox, Massachusetts, died there
    on 15 July 1897. [FFP]

JONES, PATRICK, a prisoner of war transported to New England on the John and Sarah of London, master John Greene in November 1651. [Suffolk Deeds, 1-56]

JORDAN, WILLIAM, a prisoner of war captured after the Battle of Dunbar in September 1650, transported to New England on the Unity from London on 3 November 1650, an indentured servant at the Lynn Ironworks in Massachusetts. [NWI]

JUNKINS, ROBERT, a prisoner of war captured after the Battle of Dunbar in September 1650, transported to New England on the Unity from London on 3 November 1650, an indentured servant in New Hampshire and later in York, Maine, during the 1650s. [NWI]; in York, York County, Maine, probate 2 January 1699 Maine Probate Office 1/62. [ref. to wife Sarah and my dear children]

KANE, FLORENCE, admitted as a member of the Scots Charitable Society of Boston in 1687. [SCS]

KEIR, WILLIAM, admitted as a member of the Scots Charitable Society of Boston in 1713. [SCS]

KEITH, JAMES, born in 1644, educated at Marischal College, Aberdeen, around 1657, a minister in Aberdeen, emigrated to New England before 1662, settled in Bridgewater, Plymouth County, Massachusetts, married (1) Susanna Edson, father of Josiah, (2) Mary Williams, died in Bridgewater on 23 July 1719. [F.4.664][ANQ#1.73]

KEITH, JAMES, from Aberdeen, admitted as a member of the Scots Charitable Society of Boston in 1743. [SCS]

KEITH, JAMES, a mariner from Aberdeen, settled in Newport, Rhode Island, probate 3 September 1781 Charleston, South Carolina.

KEITH, JAMES, a physician in Rhode Island 17... [SA#184]

KEITH, JEAN, in Rosendale, Boston, cnf 1893. [NAS.SC70.1.322]

KEITH, JOHN, admitted as a member of the Scots Charitable Society of Boston in 1734. [SCS]

KEITH, JOHN, admitted as a member of the Scots Charitable Society of Boston in 1743. [SCS]

KELLY, JAMES, a merchant, arrived in Boston on 18 November 1767 aboard the Glasgow, Captain John Dunn. [PAB]

KELLY, JANE, arrived in Boston on 28 October 1763 aboard the Douglas, master James Montgomerie, from Scotland. [PAB]

KELLY, WILLIAM, a shoemaker, arrived in Boston on 28 October 1763 aboard the Douglas, master James Montgomerie, from Scotland. [PAB]

KELMAN, WILLIAM, born 1832, third son of John Kelman in Keyhead, Aberdeenshire, died at 2 Granite Street, Boston, USA, 16 October 1872. [AJ#6513]

KELSO, ROBERT, from Greenock, admitted as a member of the Scots Charitable Society of Boston in 1732. [SCS]

KELSO, WILLIAM, born in 1652, a surgeon-apothecary in Ayr, a Covenanter who fought at the Battle of Bothwell Bridge, fled to Ireland, emigrated from Belfast to Boston, Massachusetts, on the Anne and Hester, master Francis Branson, in April 1680. [SPC.1682.441][UJA#2.1/274]

KELSO, WILLIAM, a gentleman, arrived in Boston on 3 June 1766 aboard the George and James, master Robert Montgomery, from Scotland. [PAB]

KELT, JAMES, from the Carse of Gowrie, Perthshire, admitted as a member of the Scots Charitable Society of Boston in 1817. [SCS]

KELTON, THOMAS, a prisoner of war captured after the Battle of Dunbar in September 1650, transported to New England on the Unity from London on 3 November 1650, an indentured servant at the Lynn Ironworks in Massachusetts. [NWI]

KEMP, DANIEL, a prisoner of war transported to New England on the <u>John and Sarah of London</u>, master John Greene in November 1651. [Suffolk Deeds, 1-56]

KENNEDY, ADAM, admitted as a member of the Scots Charitable Society of Boston in 1695. [SCS]

KENNEDY, DAVID, admitted as a member of the Scots Charitable Society of Boston in 1693. [SCS]

KENNEDY, HUGH, a physician who settled in Boston by 1720, died 1752. [SA#179]

KENNEDY, RICHARD, (?), {"Veuchteard Kendeidy"}, admitted as a member of the Scots Charitable Society of Boston in 1728. [SCS]

KENNEDY, ROBERT, from Tweeddale, admitted as a member of the Scots Charitable Society of Boston in 1762. [SCS]

KENNEDY, WILLIAM, admitted as a member of the Scots Charitable Society of Boston in 1728. [SCS]

KENNEDY, WILLIAM, in Boston, admitted as a member of the Scots Charitable Society of Boston in 1766, a resident of Boston in 1787. [SCS]

KENNEY, DAVID, from Aberdeen, admitted as a member of the Scots Charitable Society of Boston in 1733. [SCS]

KENNISTON, JOHN, emigrated to New England 1746, settled in Nottingham, New Hampshire. [ImmNE#103]

KENYON, HENRY, in Boston, died on 23 March 1855, cnf 1856. [NAS.SC70.1.90]

KERR, JOHN, admitted as a member of the Scots Charitable Society in 1724. [SCS]

KERR, WILLIAM, admitted as a member of the Scots Charitable Society of Boston in 1799. [SCS]

KILGORE, JOHN, emigrated to New England before 1764,

married Elizabeth Brickett in Berwick, Maine, settled in Kittery, Fryeburg and in Bethel, Maine. [ImmNE#104]

KILLOCH, WILLIAM, from Crawfordyke, Renfrewshire, admitted to the Scots Charitable Society of Boston in 1762. [SCS]

KILPATRICK, DAVID, MD, admitted as a member of the Scots Charitable Society of Boston in 1713. [SCS]

KILPATRICK, SAMUEL, admitted as a member of the Scots Charitable Society of Boston in 1688. [SCS]

KILPATRICK, THOMAS, admitted as a member of the Scots Charitable Society of Boston in 1731. [SCS]

KINCAID, DANIEL, emigrated to New Hampshire 1689. [Anc.H-NE]

KINCAID, DAVID, a servant, admitted as a member of the Scots Charitable Society of Boston in 1684. [SCS]

KINCAID, JOHN, emigrated to New England in 1764, settled in Bothbay, Maine. [ImmNE#105]

KINCAID, PATRICK, born around 1748, emigrated to New England in 1760, married Mary Stanwood, died 27 December 1817 in Brunswick, Maine. [ImmNE#105]

KINLOCH, PATRICK, admitted as a member of the Scots Charitable Society of Boston in 1687. [SCS]

KIRBY, THOMAS ALEXANDER, born in 1692 possibly in Edinburgh, emigrated in 1720, settled in Westmoreland County, Massachusetts, married Elizabeth de Gast, father of Roger, died 1765. [BLG#2779]

KIRK, ABRAHAM, born in Dunfermline, Fife, during 1800, died in Boston Highlands, Massachusetts, on 13 March 1872. [FH]

KIRKPATRICK, JOHN, born 1734 probably son of William and Elizabeth Kirkpatrick in Stirling, a cooper, emigrated in June or July 1753 on the brig Dolphin (possibly) from Glasgow to Massachusetts, arrived there 1 September 1753, settled in

Stirling, Maine. [SG.37.1.29][Imm.NE#106]

KIRKPATRICK, SAMUEL, from Londonderry, admitted as a member of the Scots Charitable Society of Boston in 1694. [SCS]

KIRKPATRICK, SAMUEL, from Dumfries, admitted as a member of the Scots Charitable Society of Boston in 1769. [SCS]

KIRKWOOD, ALEXANDER, from Dunbar, East Lothian, admitted as a member of the Scots Charitable Society of Boston in 1750. [SCS]

KIRKWOOD, JAMES, from Dunbar, East Lothian, admitted as a member of the Scots Charitable Society of Boston in 1751. [SCS]

KIRKWOOD, JOHN, emigrated to Boston, Massachusetts, in 1736. [NAS.GD110]

KIRKWOOD, WILLIAM, a pedlar, from Glasgow to Boston, Massachusetts, on the snow Amity, master Nathaniel Breed, 14 May 1716. [NWI.1.459]

KIRKWOOD, WILLIAM, emigrated to Boston, Massachusetts, in 1736; admitted as a member of the Scots Charitable Society of Boston in 1735. [SCS] [NAS.GD110]

KITCHEN, ROBERT, admitted as a member of the Scots Charitable Society of Boston in 1828. [SCS]

KITCHEN, W., admitted as a member of the Scots Charitable Society of Boston in 1830. [SCS]

KNEELAND, EDWARD, born around 1580, emigrated to New England in 1630. [Anc.H-NE]

KNEELAND, JOHN, admitted as a founder member of the Scots Charitable Society of Boston on 6 January 1657. [SCS]

KNEELAND, JOHN, admitted as a member of the Scots Charitable Society of Boston in 1699. [SCS]

KNEELAND, SOLOMON, admitted as a member of the Scots Charitable Society of Boston in 1699. [SCS]

KNOWLES, LUKE, born 1788, a cooper, arrived in Boston, Charlestown District, during late 1821 on the sloop <u>Katy Ann</u>, Captain Fisher. [USNA/par]

KNOX, ANDREW, born in 1864, from Anstruther, Fife, died in Providence, Rhode Island, on 6 September 1889. [EFR]

KNOX, THOMAS, from Saltcoats, Ayrshire, admitted as a member of the Scots Charitable Society of Boston in 1756. [SCS]

KYE, ROBERT, emigrated to New England in 1753, settled in Warren, Maine, killed by Indians at Mill River. [ImmNE#107]

LAING, DAVID, born in 1849, son of Robert Laing and Margaret Miller, died in Hartford, USA, on 18 December 1870. [Alyth g/s, Perthshire]

LAING, WILLIAM, a bookseller in Boston possibly from Glasgow, dead by 1765, husband of Margaret Tod or Grier. [NAS.CS16.1.122]

LAIRD, JAMES, emigrated from Greenock aboard the brigantine <u>Matty</u>, master Thomas Cochrane, on 19 May 1774 bound for New York, arrived there on 22 July 1774, settled Barnet, Vermont. [HBV]

LAMB, JAMES, from Teviotdale, admitted as a member of the Scots Charitable Society of Boston in 1750. [SCS]; settled in Boston by 1754. [NER#x/ii.319]

LAMB, WILLIAM, admitted as a member of the Scots Charitable Society of Boston in 1799. [SCS]

LAMB, WILLIAM, born in Ceres, Fife, during 1789, a music teacher who died at his brother-in-law's house at 26, 7th Street, Fall River, Massachusetts, on 30 April 1872. [EFR, 24.5.1872]

LAMBERT, SAMUEL, admitted as a member of the Scots Charitable Society of Boston in 1715. [SCS]

LAMONT, BARBARA, possibly from Aberdeen, widow of Dwight Bishop in Stratford, Connecticut, by 1878. [NAS.SH.1878]

LAMONT, HELEN, possibly from Aberdeen, wife of William McGrath, in Bridgeport, Connecticut, around 1878. [NAS.SH.1878]

LAMONT, NEIL, MD, from Fife, admitted to the Scots Charitable Society of Boston in 1758. [SCS]

LANG, JOHN, a carpenter, arrived in Boston on 22 January 1766 aboard the snow Peggy, master William Craig, from Scotland. [PAB]

LANG, WILLIAM, from Glasgow, admitted to the Scots Charitable Society of Boston in 1759, [SCS]; a bookseller in Boston, husband of Margaret Tod or Grier, father of William, 1766. [NAS.CS16.1.125/128][Imm.NE#108]

LANG, WILLIAM, born in Glasgow during 1771, married Maria Bailey in New York during 1796, a merchant in New York, died in Wyoming, Massachusetts, on 27 August 1849. [ANY

LAPLEY, GEORGE, a joiner, emigrated from Greenock to Boston on the Douglas, master R. Manderston, arrived there on 26 July 1764. [NWI][PAB]

LAPLEY, PATRICK, a joiner, emigrated from Greenock to Boston on the Douglas, master R. Manderston, arrived there on 26 July 1764. [NWI][PAB]

LATTA, WILLIAM, a joiner, arrived in Boston on 29 August 1768 aboard the snow Catherine, master Hugh Morris, from Scotland. [PAB]

LATTA, WILLIAM, a Scot in Massachusetts, Loyalist, moved to Nova Scotia 1783, returned to U.S. [Loyalists in Nova Scotia, p156]

LAUGHLAND, THOMAS, a merchant in Boston, 1751. [NAS.CS16.1.85]

LAURANCE, JOHN, admitted as a member of the Scots Charitable Society of Boston in 1803. [SCS]

LAURIE, MARGARET S., daughter of George Laurie in Miramachi, New Brunswick, died in Cambridge, Boston, Massachusetts, 15 May 1850. [AJ#5348]

LAURIE, PETER, late of Urrall, Wigtonshire, died in Stamford, Connecticut, on 13 December 1858. [CM#21614]

LAW, DAVID, from Innerleithen, Peeblesshire, admitted as a member of the Scots Charitable Society of Boston in 1734. [SCS]

LAWRIE, JAMES, born 1851, son of John Lawrie from Dunfermline, Fife, died in Danvers, Massachusetts, on 1 December 1858. [FH]

LAWRIE, JOHN, born in Dunfermline during 1813, emigrated to Massachusetts by 1858, died in West Lynn, Massachusetts, on 20 March 1904. [FFP]

LAWSON, JOHN admitted as a member of the Scots Charitable Society of Boston in 1691. [SCS]

LAWSON, JOHN, admitted as a member of the Scots Charitable Society of Boston in 1734. [SCS]

LAWSON, ROGER, admitted as a member of the Scots Charitable Society of Boston in 1702. [SCS]

LEACH, ANDREW, admitted as a member of the Scots Charitable Society of Boston in 1799. [SCS]

LEACH, JAMES, admitted as a member of the Scots Charitable Society of Boston in 1829. [SCS]

LEACH, THOMAS, admitted as a member of the Scots Charitable Society of Boston in 1814. [SCS]

LEES, JOHN, born in 1803, son of John Lees a manufacturer and Jean Young in Galashiels, Selkirkshire, died in Chelsea,

Boston, Massachusetts, on 4 March 1878. [Galashiels g/s]

LEES, ROBERT, from Glasgow, admitted as a member of the Scots Charitable Society of Boston in 1740. [SCS]

LEIGHTON, MATTHEW, born in 1818, son of Miles Leighton and Elizabeth Ridley, settled in Boston, died on 26 July 1854. [St Michael's g/s, Dumfries]

LEISHMAN, JAMES, admitted as a member of the Scots Charitable Society of Boston in 1717. [SCS]

LEISHMAN, JOHN, born in Falkirk, Stirlingshire, in 1739, married Sarah McCulloch in 1760, emigrated to New England in 1764, settled in Boothbay, Maine, died in 1780. [ImmNE#110]

LEISHMAN, JOHN, admitted as a member of the Scots Charitable Society of Boston in 1830. [SCS]

LENNEY, WILLIAM, from Orkney, admitted as a member of the Scots Charitable Society of Boston in 1750. [SCS]

LENNOX, DAVID, admitted as a member of the Scots Charitable Society of Boston in 1753; servitor of the Society. [SCS]

LENNOX, JAMES, admitted as a member of the Scots Charitable Society of Boston in 1735. [SCS]

LENNOX, PATRICK, born in Portpatrick during April 1750, emigrated to New England, married Margaret McNear in Newcastle, Maine, in 1785, father of Robert, Thomas and Patrick, died on 17 April 1831. [Imm.NE#111]

LESSLY, ANDREW, admitted as a member of the Scots Charitable Society of Boston in 1719. [SCS]

LESSLY, ANDREW, from Fife, admitted as a member of the Scots Charitable Society of Boston in 1752. [SCS]

LESTON, CHARLES, a prisoner of war transported to New England on the John and Sarah of London, master John Greene in November 1651. [Suffolk Deeds, 1-56]

LEWIS, JOHN, from Edinburgh, admitted as a member of the
Scots Charitable Society of Boston in 1762. [SCS]

LEWIS, JOHN, a merchant, arrived in Boston on 20 August 1764
aboard the sloop Ann, master Joshua Aitken, from Scotland.
[PAB]

LEWIS, JOHN, a merchant, arrived in Boston on 30 May 1767
aboard the snow Mary, master William Welchman, from
Glasgow. [PAB]

LIDDLE, JAMES, a prisoner of war captured after the Battle of
Dunbar in September 1650, transported from London on 3
November 1650 on the Unity to New England, an indentured
servant at the Lynn Ironworks in Massachusetts. [NWI]

LIMEBURNER, ANDREW, a farmer, arrived in Boston on 1 May
1769 from Glasgow on the Nancy, Captain James Moody.
[PAB]

LIMBURNER, MATTHEW, a farmer, and his wife, arrived in
Boston on 1 June 1768 aboard the snow Jenny, master
Hector Orr, from Glasgow. [PAB]

LINDSAY, ALEXANDER, from Forfar, Angus, settled in Portland,
New Hampshire, married Lydia Crossman 3 December
1719. [Imm.N.E.#113]

LINDSAY, CHRISTOPHER, son of Christopher Lindsay and
Christina Scott, grandson of Robert Lindsay of Pitscottie, to
America 1629, settled in Lynn, Massachusetts, married
Margaret ..., died 10 April 1669. [Col.Fams.VI.324]

LINDSAY, GEORGE, from North Leith, admitted as a member of
the Scots Charitable Society of Boston in 1762. [SCS]

LINDSAY, GEORGE, a merchant, arrived in Boston on 20 August
1764 aboard the sloop Ann, master Joshua Aitken, from
Scotland.[PAB]

LINN, WILLIAM, admitted as a member of the Scots Charitable
Society of Boston in 1732. [SCS]

LINKLETTER, ALEXANDER, trader in Boston, Loyalist, settled in Halifax, Nova Scotia, by 1783. [PRO.AO13.91.35]

LITTLEJOHN, DAVID, from Edinburgh, admitted as a member of the Scots Charitable Society of Boston in 1748. [SCS]

LISK, JOHN, from Orkney, admitted as a member of the Scots Charitable Society of Boston in 1755. [SCS]

LISTER, CHRISTINA, born in Leslie, Fife, during 1831,wife of Thomas Rae, died in Holyoke, Massachusetts, on 15 November 1893. [FFP]

LIVESTON, ROBERT, admitted as a member of the Scots Charitable Society of Boston in 1690. [SCS]

LIVINGSTON, JOHN, admitted as a member of the Scots Charitable Society of Boston in 1659. [SCS]

LIVINGSTON, JOHN, from New London, admitted as a member of the Scots Charitable Society of Boston in 1711. [SCS]

LIVINGSTON, ROBERT, born in Ancrum, Roxburghshire, on 13 December 1654, son of Reverend John Livingston and Janet Fleming, emigrated to America in 1673, settled in Charlestown, Massachusetts, and later in Albany, New York, a merchant and civil servant, died on 1 October 1728. [Col.Fams.#6.334]; possibly admitted as a member of the Scots Charitable Society of Boston in 1690. [SCS]

LIVINGSTONE, WILLIAM, admitted as a member of the Scots Charitable Society of Boston in 1715. [SCS]

LOCKHART, GEORGE, admitted as a member of the Scots Charitable Society of Boston in 1735. [SCS]

LOGAN, ALEXANDER, a fisherman, admitted as a member of the Scots Charitable Society of Boston in 1684. [SCS]

LOGAN, GEORGE, a sailor in New England, 1758. [NAS.CS16.1.100]

LOGAN, JAMES, grandson of James Logan [1778-1860] and Margaret Thompson [1783-1825] in Howwood, Renfrewshire, settled in Worcester, Massachusetts. [Lochwinnoch g/s, Renfrewshire]

LOGAN, ROBERT admitted as a member of the Scots Charitable Society of Boston in 1691. [SCS]

LOGAN, WALTER, from New Kilpatrick, Dunbartonshire, admitted as a member of the Scots Charitable Society of Boston in 1762. [SCS]

LONG, WILLIAM, in Boston 9 June 1685. [SCS]

LORIMER, DAVID, from Glasgow, admitted as a member of the Scots Charitable Society of Boston in 1749. [SCS]

LORIMER, THOMAS, admitted to the Scots Charitable Society of Boston in 1696. [SCS]

LORRAIN, W., from the south of Scotland, settled in Barnet, New Hampshire, around 1775. [HGP]

LOTHIAN, JOHN, from Caledonia {Darien}, admitted as a member of the Scots Charitable Society of Boston in 1699. [SCS]

LOTHIAN, THOMAS, a physician who settled in Massachusetts, died in 1749. [SA]

LOUDON, JOHN, admitted as a member of the Scots Charitable Society of Boston in 1803. [SCS]

LOUDON, ROBERT, in Boston around 1875, possibly from Lanarkshire. [NAS.SH.1875]

LOVELL, EBENEZER, a merchant in Boston, father of John Lovell in Greenock, 1752. [NAS.RD4.239.1061; RD4.178/1.566]

LOVELL, JOHN, admitted as a member of the Scots Charitable Society of Boston in 1718. [SCS]

LOVELL, JOHN, admitted as a member of the Scots Charitable Society of Boston in 1735. [SCS]

LOVELL, JOHN, in Boston, 1752, son of Ebenezer Lovell. [NAS.RD4.178/506,553,884]

LOVEL, JOHN, son of Thomas Lovel, a merchant in Boston, 1755. [NAS.CS16.1.95]

LOWE, DAVID, born in Pathhead, Fife, on 6 May 1796, a hat manufacturer who emigrated to New York in 1822, settled in Norwalk, Connecticut, during September 1872, died there during March 1885. [FFP,11.4.1885]

LOW, JAMES, possibly from Kirkcaldy, Fife, a wright in Boston, New England, 1773. [NAS.B41.7.8.205]

LOWRIE, JAMES, from Irvine, Ayrshire, admitted as a member of the Scots Charitable Society of Boston in 1771. [SCS]

LOWTHAIN, THOMAS, a physician in Massachusetts, died 1749. [SA#179]

LUDLOW, ARCHIBALD, admitted as a member of the Scots Charitable Society of Boston in 1826. [SCS]

LUKE, HUMPHREY, admitted as a member of the Scots Charitable Society of Boston in 1711. [SCS]

LUSK, JOHN, born in 1702, settled in Wethersfield, Connecticut, died in 1788. [CAG#1.547][DAB.xi.510]

LYALL, JOHN, from Dunbar, East Lothian, admitted as a member of the Scots Charitable Society of Boston in 1761. [SCS]

LYALL, WILLIAM DAVID, in Boston, cnf 1891. [NAS.SC70.1.291]

LYON, HENRY, born in 1625, settled in Milford, Connecticut, during 1648, later in Newark, New Jersey, died in 1703. [CAG#1/593]

LYON, JOHN, from Greenock, admitted as a member of the Scots Charitable Society of Boston in 1740. [SCS]

LYON, THOMAS, admitted as a member of the Scots Charitable Society of Boston in 1732. [SCS]

MCADAM, ARCHIBALD, a Covenanter, transported from Leith to New England in July 1685. [RPCS.11.94]

MCADAM, WILLIAM, son of James McAdam and Margaret Reid in Beith, emigrated to New England by 1750. [HA.1/309]

MACALESTER, DANIEL, a prisoner of war transported to New England on the John and Sarah of London, master John Greene in November 1651. [Suffolk Deeds, 1-56]

MACALESTER, JOHN, a prisoner of war transported to New England on the John and Sarah of London, master John Greene in November 1651. [Suffolk Deeds, 1-56]

MACALESTER, Reverend JOHN, from Arran, admitted as a member of the Scots Charitable Society of Boston in 1737. [SCS]

MCALISTER, RANDAL, born 1744, married Mary Blair {1749-1833}, British Army deserter, settled in Peterborough, New Hampshire, died 1819. [ImmNE.117]

MACKALISTEN, ALISTER, a prisoner of war transported to New England on the John and Sarah of London, master John Greene in November 1651. [Suffolk Deeds, 1-56]

MCALPINE, DONALD, born in Scotland around 1730, an officer of the 78 th Highlanders during the French and Indian War who settled in Exeter, New Hampshire, a Loyalist in 1776, a Lieutenant of the North Carolina Highlanders, 1777-1783, died in London 25 January 1789. [PRO.CO5.III][PRO.AO12.101.39]

MCALPINE, WALTER, emigrated to New England in 1743, settled in Boston. [ImmNE.118]; admitted to the Scots Charitable Society of Boston in 1744. [SCS]

MCALPINE, WILLIAM, from Greenock, a printer and stationer in Boston by 1753, admitted as a member of the Scots Charitable Society of Boston in 1755, Loyalist in 1776, married Ann Crawford, died in Greenock on 3 August 1788. [SCS][Imm.NE#118] [DGC:11.10.1788][PRO.AO12.82.1]

MCALPINE, WILLIAM, emigrated from Greenock aboard the brigantine Matty, master Thomas Cochrane, on 19 May 1774 bound for New York, arrived there on 22 July 1774, settled Barnet, Vermont. [HBV]

MACANDREW, WILLIAM, a prisoner of war transported to New England on the John and Sarah of London, master John Greene in November 1651. [Suffolk Deeds, 1-56]

MCARTHUR, DUNCAN, a passenger on the Glasgow Packet, master Alexander Porterfield, bound for Boston, was recruited into the 84th [Royal Highland Emigrant] Regiment on 23 October 1775. [NAS.GD174/2093]

MCARTHUR, JOHN, from Perth, emigrated to New England in 1735, settled in Limington, Maine, died in 1816. [ImmNE#118]

MCARTHUR, JOHN, from Dunoon, Argyll, admitted as a member of the Scots Charitable Society of Boston in 1743. [SCS]

MACAULAY, ALEXANDER, from Gareloch, Ross-shire, a member of the Scots Charitable Society of Boston in 1740. [SCS]

MACAULAY, JAMES, a prisoner of war transported to New England on the John and Sarah of London, master John Greene in November 1651. [Suffolk Deeds, 1-56]

MACAULAY, JOHN, admitted as a member of the Scots Charitable Society of Boston in 1713. [SCS]

MCAUSLINE, DUNCAN, from Greenock, admitted as a member of the Scots Charitable Society of Boston in 1748. [SCS]

MCBEAN, ANGUS, settled at Otter Creek, Vermont, a Loyalist in 1776, moved to Isle aux Noix, Montreal, by 1786. [PRO.AO13.59.249]

MCBRIDE, JOHN, a Covenanter from Argyll, transported from Leith to New England on 6 July 1685. [RPCS.11.119]

MCCALL, DUNCAN, indentured servant of John Hardy in Salem, Massachusetts ca.1652. [see John Hardy's inventory 30 January 1652, Essex County Probate Records]

MCCALL, JAMES, admitted as a member of the Scots Charitable Society of Boston in 1734. [SCS]

MCCALL, ..., son of William McCall jr., was born in Taunton, Massachusetts, on 12 December 1875. [EC#28482]

MCCALLUM, JOHN, born 1767, married Mary Miller, settled in Warren, Maine, died 23 September 1837. [ImmNE.119]

MCCALLUM, DUNCAN, a Covenanter from Argyll, transported from Leith to New England in July 1685. [RPCS.9.94]

MCCALLUM, MALCOLM, a prisoner of war captured after the Battle of Dunbar in September 1650, transported from London on 3 November 1650 on the Unity to New England, an indentured servant at the Lynn Ironworks in Massachusetts. [NWI]; admitted as a founder member of the Scots Charitable Society of Boston on 6 January 1657. [SCS]

MCCARA, JAMES, settled in Banff, Vermont, in 1774, a Loyalist in 1776, later in Halifax, Nova Scotia, by 1786. [PRO.AO12.99.12]

MCCARNEY, MICHAEL, arrived in Boston on 28 October 1763 aboard the Douglas, master James Montgomerie, from Scotland. [PAB]

MCCARTER, JOHN, a flax dresser, arrived in Boston on 16 April 1766 aboard the Stirling Castle, master John Cockburn, from Greenock. [PAB]

MACCAUL, ROBERT, admitted as a member of the Scots Charitable Society of Boston in 1713. [SCS]

MCCLELLAN, COLIN, a Highland prisoner of war in Worcester, Massachusetts, 1776, married Elizabeth ... from Inverness-shire. [ImmNE121]

MCCLINTOCK, WILLIAM, emigrated via Ireland to New England 1730, settled in Medford, Massachusetts, died on 28 May 1770. [ImmNE123]

MCCLINTOCK, WILLIAM, from Glasgow, admitted as a member of the Scots Charitable Society of Boston in 1758. [SCS]

MCCLURE, GILBERT, merchant in Falmouth, Maine, a Loyalist in 1776, later in Ayr. [PRO.AO13.95.377]

MCCOLL, JAMES, a prisoner of war captured after the Battle of Dunbar in September 1650, transported from London on 3 November 1650 on the Unity to New England, an indentured servant at the Lynn Ironworks in Massachusetts. [NWI]

MCCOLM, DAVID a prisoner of war transported to New England on the John and Sarah of London, master John Greene in November 1651. [Suffolk Deeds, 1-56]

MCCOLM, JOHN a prisoner of war transported to New England on the John and Sarah of London, master John Greene in November 1651. [Suffolk Deeds, 1-56]

MCCOLM, QUINTIN, son of John McColm and Elizabeth Kennedy in Maybole, Ayrshire, a merchant who settled in New England before 1745, died there on 3 August 1746. Cnf 1752 Commissariat of Edinburgh. [NAS.CC8.8.114]

MCCOMIE, DAVID, born around 1635, prisoner after the Battle of Dunbar 1650, shipped to New England on the John and Sara 1652 as an indentured servant; settled in Woburn, Massachusetts, married Elizabeth ..., father of John 1665-1723. [SG.XLIV.2.89][CAG.1/564]

MCCONNELL, CANA, a prisoner of war transported to New England on the John and Sarah of London, master John Greene in November 1651. [Suffolk Deeds, 1-56]

MCCONNELL, DANIEL, a prisoner of war transported to New England on the John and Sarah of London, master John Greene in November 1651. [Suffolk Deeds, 1-56]

MCCONNELL, SANDER, a prisoner of war transported to New England on the <u>John and Sarah of London</u>, master John Greene in November 1651. [Suffolk Deeds, 1-56]

MCCONNELL, WILLIAM, a prisoner of war transported to New England on the <u>John and Sarah of London</u>, master John Greene in November 1651. [Suffolk Deeds, 1-56]

MCCOWAN, PATRICK, a laborer, arrived in Boston on 26 July 1764 aboard the snow <u>Douglas</u>, master Robert Manderston, from Greenock. [PAB]

MACCOWMES, ALEXANDER, member of the Scots Charitable Society of Boston 1659. [SCS]

MCCOY, ALEXANDER, emigrated from the Highlands to New England in 1721, settled in Windham, Massachusetts. [ImmNE#125]

MCCRACKAN, JOHN, son of Andrew McCrackan in Old Glenluce, Galloway, died in Newhaven, New England, probate 1769 PCC

MCCRACKEN, WILLIAM, merchant in Newhaven, Connecticut, Loyalist in 1776. [PRO.AO13.80.278-280]

MACKREITH, JAMES, a prisoner of war transported to New England on the <u>John and Sarah of London</u>, master John Greene in November 1651. [Suffolk Deeds, 1-56]

MACKRETH, PATRICK, a prisoner of war transported to New England on the <u>John and Sarah of London</u>, master John Greene in November 1651. [Suffolk Deeds, 1-56]

MCCULLIE, JAMES, admitted as a member of the Scots Charitable Society of Boston in 1692. [SCS]

MCCULLOCH, ADAM, born during 1742 in Dornoch, Cromarty, emigrated to Maine in 1766, settled in Kennebunk Port, married Louisa Browne on 8 February 1769, died during 1812. [AA.8.122][DAB.12/6][ImmNE#126]

MCCULLOCH, ALEXANDER, from Ayr, in Boston on 25 October 1684; admitted as a member of the Scots Charitable Society of Boston in 1691. [SCS]

MCCULLOCH, HUGH, son of Adam McCulloch, to New England by 1768, married Abiel Perkins 10 April 1790, a merchant in Kennebunk, Maine. [ImmNE#126]

MCCULLOCH, JAMES, from Dumfries, admitted as a member of the Scots Charitable Society of Boston in 1747. [SCS]

MCCULLOCH, JOHN, from Glasgow, admitted as a member of the Scots Charitable Society of Boston in 1727. [SCS]

MCCULLOCH, THOMAS, son of Alexander McCulloch from Ayr, in Boston on 25 October 1684; admitted as a member of the Scots Charitable Society of Boston in 1691. [SCS]

MCCULLOCH, THOMAS, admitted as a member of the Scots Charitable Society of Boston in 1736. [SCS]

MCCUN, ARCHIBALD, from Greenock, admitted as a member of the Scots Charitable Society of Boston in 1748. [SCS]

MCCUN, JOHN, from Greenock, admitted as a member of the Scots Charitable Society of Boston in 1747. [SCS]

MCCUNN, WILLIAM, from Glasgow, admitted as a member of the Scots Charitable Society of Boston in 1743. [SCS]

MCCURDY, LAUCHLIN, a Loyalist in Maine 1776, settled in St Andrew's, New Brunswick, by 1786. [PRO.AO13.22.160]

MCDERNEL, TIMOTHY, a Highlander, settled in Portland, Maine, married Mary Winslow. [ImmNE#128]

MCDONAGH, THOMAS, British Consul in Massachusetts, died in Boston on 26 June 1804. [CM#13035]; probate December 1805 PCC

MCDONALD, CHARLES, a granite quarryman from Dyce, Aberdeenshire, emigrated to Barre, Vermont, returned to Aberdeen in 1877. [APL]

MCDONALD, DANIEL, of the Olive of Glasgow, admitted to the Scots Charitable Society of Boston in 1726. [SCS]

MCDONALD, DONALD, born 1722, soldier at Siege of Quebec, settled in Lynn, Massachusetts, died on 3 October 1830. [ImmNE#128]

MCDONALD, KATE, from Alness, Ross and Cromarty, wife of William Husband jr., late of Kingsbarns, died in Worcester, Massachusetts, on 2 April 1887. [PJ]

MCDONALD, HUMPHREY, a gentleman, arrived in Boston on 22 January 1766 aboard the snow Peggy, master William Craig, from Scotland. [PAB]

MCDONALD, JAMES, (1), a husbandman, arrived in Boston on 22 January 1766 aboard the snow Peggy, master William Craig, from Scotland. [PAB]

MCDONALD, JAMES, (2), a husbandman, arrived in Boston on 22 January 1766 aboard the snow Peggy, master William Craig, from Scotland. [PAB]

MCDONALD, JAMES, born in 1836, immigrated into Massachusetts aboard the Agnes Sophia on 18 June 1850. [LAP]

MCDONALD, JOHN, admitted as a founder member of the Scots Charitable Society of Boston on 6 January 1657. [SCS]

MCDONALD, JOHN, from Glencoe, Argyll, emigrated to New England by 1726, settled in Wells and in Gorham, Maine, died on 9 May 1768.[ImmNE#128]

MCDONALD, JOHN, a husbandman, arrived in Boston on 22 January 1766 aboard the snow Peggy, master William Craig, from Scotland. [PAB]

MCDONNELL, JOHN, born 1798, a mechanic who arrived in Plymouth [Massachusetts?] during 1821 on the schooner Albion. [USNA/par]

MCDONOUGH, MARY, born in 1810, with John McDonough born in 1834, James McDonough born 1837, and Catherine McDonough born in 1841, aboard the brig Lydia on 20 May 1850. [LAP]

MCDOUGALL, ALISTAIR, admitted as a member of the Scots Charitable Society of Boston in 1658. [SCS]

MCDOUGALL, DUNCAN, a passenger on the Glasgow Packet, Captain Porterfield, bound for Boston, was recruited into the 84 th [Royal Highland Emigrant] Regiment on 23 October 1775. [NAS.GD174/2093]

MCDOUGALL, JAMES, admitted as a member of the Scots Charitable Society of Boston in 1736. [SCS]

MCDOUGALL, JAMES, emigrated to New England, married Mary Patrick, settled in Stroudwater, Maine, died there. [ImmNE#129]

MACDOWALL, DAVID, admitted as a member of the Scots Charitable Society of Boston in 1717. [SCS]

MCDOWELL, FERGUS, admitted as a member of the Scots Charitable Society of Boston in 1684. [SCS]

MACDOWELL, JAMES, a mason in Boston 1808. [NAS.CS17.1.28/200]

MACDOWELL, SANDER, a prisoner of war transported to New England on the John and Sarah of London, master John Greene in November 1651. [Suffolk Deeds, 1-56]

MCDOWAL, WILLIAM, a bookbinder from Greenock, arrived in Boston on 30 May 1767 aboard the snow Mary, master William Welchman, from Glasgow. [PAB]; admitted as a member of the Scots Charitable Society of Boston in 1767. [SCS]

MCDUFFIE, ALEXANDER, arrived in Boston on 31 October 1766 aboard the snow Jenny, master Archibald Orr, from Scotland. [PAB]

MCEWAN, DAVID, son of James McEwan in Dunfermline, died in
Greendale, Connecticut, on 6 December 1869. [DP]

MCEUAN, JAMES, emigrated from Islay, Argyll, in November
1740 aboard the Happy Return bound for New York and
Wood Creek on the Hudson River, believed to have settled
in Boston by 1763. [HSPC][NY.Col.MS#72/170]

MCEWEN, JAMES, from Thortorwald, Nithsdale, Dumfries-shire,
admitted as a member of the Scots Charitable Society of
Boston in 1767. [SCS]

MCEWEN, JAMES, admitted as a member of the Scots Charitable
Society of Boston in 1772. [SCS]

MCEWAN, JAMES, in New Milford, Connecticut, Loyalist in 1776,
soldier in De Lancey's Regiment 1776-1783, settled in Nova
Scotia. [PRO.AO13.26.263]

MCEWAN, ROBERT, a tailor in Stratford, Connecticut, 1685.
[AncH-NE]

MCFADYEN, alias McFadyean, JOHN, in Boston, probate
December 1805 PCC

MCFARLIN, Lord, and his son, arrived in Boston on 2 June 1769
from Glasgow on the Glasgow, Captain John Dunn. [PAB]

MCFARLAND, DUNCAN, admitted as a member of the Scots
Charitable Society of Boston in 1692. [SCS]

MCFARLANE, JOHN, born in Paisley, Renfrewshire, during 1762,
emigrated with his wife Helen Barr to Boston in 1795,
admitted as a member of the Scots Charitable Society of
Boston in 1799, later settled in Germantown, Pennsylvania,
died on 24 December 1820. [CMF][SCS]

MCFEE, ANGUS, soldier in the Westchester Loyalists, settled in
Nova Scotia 1786. [PRO.AO.13.26.264-265]

MCFEE, JOHN, arrived in Boston on 31 October 1766 aboard the
snow Jenny, master Archibald Orr, from Scotland. [PAB]

MCGILCHRIST, WILLIAM, born in Inchinnan, Renfrewshire, during 1707, son of James McGilchrist, educated at Balliol College, Oxford, around 1735, a clergyman in Charleston, South Carolina, from 1741 to 1745, and in Salem, New England, from 1747 to 1780, died on 19 April 1780. [CCNE]

MCGILL, CATHERINE, alias Norrie, a widow in Portsmouth, New England, probate February 1804 PCC

MCGILL, DONALD, late of Little White Creek, Rupert, Vermont, a Loyalist in 1776, later in New Carlisle, Bay of Chaleur. [PRO.AO13.81.231]

MACGOMERY, PETER, from Glasgow, admitted as a member of the Scots Charitable Society of Boston in 1748. [SCS]

MCGOWAN, JOHN, born 1625, settled in Higham, Massachusetts, in 1655, later in Scituate, Massachusetts,1662. [AncH-NE] [CAG.1#200/712]

MCGOWAN, JOHN, admitted as a member of the Scots Charitable Society of Boston in 1695. [SCS]; a merchant in Boston, New England, 1699. [NAS.RD3.92.2]

MCGOWAN, PATRICK, a laborer, emigrated from Greenock to Boston on the Douglas, Captain R. Manderston, in July 1764. [NWI#I.459]

MCGRAW, ..., emigrated from Scotland to New England, settled in Dublin, New Hampshire, and in Billingham, Vermont. [ImmNE#132]

MACHALE, ALESTER a prisoner of war transported to New England on the John and Sarah of London, master John Greene in November 1651. [Suffolk Deeds, 1-56]

MACHALE, JAMES a prisoner of war transported to New England on the John and Sarah of London, master John Greene in November 1651. [Suffolk Deeds, 1-56]

MCHATTON, NEIL, a Covenanter from Argyll, transported from Leith to New England in July 1685. [RPCS.11.94]

MACHAWTHERN, PATRICK a prisoner of war transported to New England on the John and Sarah of London, master John Greene in November 1651. [Suffolk Deeds, 1-56]

MACHELLIN, DANIEL a prisoner of war transported to New England on the John and Sarah of London, master John Greene in November 1651. [Suffolk Deeds, 1-56]

MACHELLIN, JOHN a prisoner of war transported to New England on the John and Sarah of London, master John Greene in November 1651. [Suffolk Deeds, 1-56]

MCIAN, WILLIAM, admitted as a member of the Scots Charitable Society in 1725. [SCS]

MACINTOSH, DANIEL a prisoner of war transported to New England on the John and Sarah of London, master John Greene in November 1651. [Suffolk Deeds, 1-56]

MCINTOSH, DONALD, born in 1788, British Consul in Maine, died in Inverness on 29 December 1845. [AJ#5116]

MCINTOSH, ELIZABETH, daughter of Lachlan McIntosh of Borlum, wife of Isaac Ryall, settled in New England before 1773. [NAS.CS.GMB8/73]

MACKINTOSH, HENRY, admitted as a member of the Scots Charitable Society of Boston in 1702. [SCS]

MCINTOSH, JOHN, settled in Dedham, Massachusetts, pre 1659. [Anc.H-NE]

MCINTOSH, JOHN, a house carpenter, arrived in Boston on 17 August 1767 aboard the snow Jenny, master Hector Orr, from Glasgow. [PAB]

MCINTOSH, LACHLAN, of Borlum, Inverness-shire, settled in Bristol, Rhode Island, before 1721, married Elizabeth, father of Elizabeth and Mary, died in June 1723. ["Genealogical Gleanings in England", p.1288, Baltimore, 1969]

MACINTOSH, LAUCHLAN, admitted as a member of the Scots Charitable Society of Boston in 1702. [SCS]

MCINTOSH, MARY, daughter of Lachlan McIntosh of Borlum, wife of .... Palmer, settled in New England before 1773. [NAS.CS.GMB8/73]

MCINTOSH, WILLIAM, a prisoner of war transported to New England on the John and Sarah 1652, an iron worker in Braintree, Block Island, by 1660, died 1685. [EAF]

MCINTYRE, MALCOLM, a prisoner of war captured after the Battle of Dunbar in September 1650, transported on 3 November 1650 from London to New England on Unity, in Lynn, Massachusetts, 1653, in Kittery, New Hampshire, 1662, in Ready, New Hampshire, 1665, died in North Reading, New Hampshire, buried 2 October 1705. [EAF][NWI]; son of Pierce, husband of Sarah ..., father of John, Daniel and Malcolm, probate 2 October 1705 Maine Probate Office 1/62:PO1.111.

MCINTYRE, PHILIP, from Argyll, settled in Reading, Essex County, Massachusetts, around 1650. [CAG.1/490]

MCISAAK, MURDOCH, a Covenanter from Machrimore, Kintyre, Argyll, transported from Leith to New England in July 1685. [RPCS.11.94]

MCIVAR, ANGUS, a Covenanter from Glassary, Argyll, transported from Leith to New England in July 1685. [RPCS.11.94]

MCIVOR, EDWARD, from Edinburgh, admitted as a member of the Scots Charitable Society of Boston in 1734. [SCS]

MACJEROW, JAMES, admitted as a member of the Scots Charitable Society of Boston in 1715. [SCS]

MACK, HENRY, a prisoner of war transported to New England on the John and Sarah of London, master John Greene in November 1651. [Suffolk Deeds, 1-56]

MACKAIN, DANIEL, a prisoner of war transported to New England on the John and Sarah of London, master John Greene in November 1651. [Suffolk Deeds, 1-56]

MACKAINE, NEIL, a prisoner of war transported to New England on the <u>John and Sarah of London</u>, master John Greene in November 1651. [Suffolk Deeds, 1-56]

MACKANE, JOHN, a prisoner of war transported to New England on the <u>John and Sarah of London</u>, master John Greene in November 1651. [Suffolk Deeds, 1-56]

MACKANE, PATRICK, a prisoner of war transported to New England on the <u>John and Sarah of London</u>, master John Greene in November 1651. [Suffolk Deeds, 1-56]

MACKANE, ROBERT, a prisoner of war transported to New England on the <u>John and Sarah of London</u>, master John Greene in November 1651. [Suffolk Deeds, 1-56]

MACKANE, SAMUEL, a prisoner of war transported to New England on the <u>John and Sarah of London</u>, master John Greene in November 1651. [Suffolk Deeds, 1-56]

MACKAINE, WILLIAM, a prisoner of war transported to New England on the <u>John and Sarah of London</u>, master John Greene in November 1651. [Suffolk Deeds, 1-56]

MCKARRELL, ROBERT admitted as a member of the Scots Charitable Society of Boston in 1691. [SCS]

MACKARTER, JOHN, admitted as a member of the Scots Charitable Society of Boston in 1717. [SCS]

MACKAY, AENEAS, a merchant from Inverness, settled in Boston, Massachusetts, before 1745, admitted as a member of the Scots Charitable Society of Boston; in Greenock during 1752. [NAS.RD4.178.566/553][SCS][NLS.CH3816]

MACKAY, DANIEL, settled in Newton, Massachusetts, by 1673. [AncH-NE]

MACKAY, DANIEL, from Caledonia {Darien}, admitted as a member of the Scots Charitable Society of Boston in 1699. [SCS]

MCKAY, HUGH, a prisoner of war transported to New England on the <u>John and Sarah of London</u>, master John Greene in November 1651. [Suffolk Deeds, 1-56]

MCKAY, HUGH, from Inverness, admitted as a member of the Scots Charitable Society of Boston in 1750. [SCS]

MACKAY, JAMES, from Durness, Sutherland, admitted as a member of the Scots Charitable Society of Boston in 1817. [SCS]

MCKAY, JOHN, a prisoner of war transported to New England on the <u>John and Sarah of London</u>, master John Greene in November 1651. [Suffolk Deeds, 1-56]

MACKAY, JOHN, admitted as a member of the Scots Charitable Society of Boston in 1717. [SCS]

MACKAY, JOHN, from Kilmarnock, Ayrshire, admitted as a member of the Scots Charitable Society of Boston in 1774. [SCS]

MCKAY, JOHN, born in Scotland in 1764, settled in America in 1784, a farmer in Woodbury, Connecticut, in 1812. [1812]

MACKAY, MARGARET, in Edinburgh, widow of James Murray in Boston, cnf 4 May 1789 Commissariat of Edinburgh

MCKAY, NEIL, a prisoner of war transported to New England on the <u>John and Sarah of London</u>, master John Greene in November 1651. [Suffolk Deeds, 1-56]

MACHY, RORY, a prisoner of war transported to New England on the <u>John and Sarah of London</u>, master John Greene in November 1651. [Suffolk Deeds, 1-56]

MCKAY, SANDER a prisoner of war transported to New England on the <u>John and Sarah of London</u>, master John Greene in November 1651. [Suffolk Deeds, 1-56]

MACKAY, WILLIAM FREDERICK, a merchant, arrived in Boston on 24 November 1764 aboard the brigantine <u>Mermaid</u>, master Ebenezer Graham, from Kirkwall, Orkney. [PAB]

MCKAY, WILLIAM, born 1741, a farmer from Dundee, with his wife Helen Boyd and daughter Helen, emigrated from Greenock to Salem on the <u>Glasgow Packet</u> in April 1775.[PRO.T47.12]

MCKEAN, Reverend JOSEPH, admitted as an honorary member of the Scots Charitable Society of Boston in 1811. [SCS]

MCKEAN, WILLIAM, a tobacconist from Glasgow then at Charles Wharf, North End, Boston in 1764, [BosGaz.8.10.1764]; admitted as a member of the Scots Charitable Society of Boston in 1767, a resident of Boston in 1787. [SCS]

MACKELL, JAMES a prisoner of war transported to New England on the <u>John and Sarah of London</u>, master John Greene in November 1651. [Suffolk Deeds, 1-56]

MACKEN, WILLIAM a prisoner of war transported to New England on the <u>John and Sarah of London</u>, master John Greene in November 1651. [Suffolk Deeds, 1-56]

MACKENTHOW, JOHN a prisoner of war transported to New England on the <u>John and Sarah of London</u>, master John Greene in November 1651. [Suffolk Deeds, 1-56]

MCKECHNIE, JOHN, born in 1703, educated in Aberdeen or in Edinburgh, emigrated to America during 1755, settled in Boston and later in Maine, died in 1783. [SA]

MCKEES, JAMES, born in Scotland in 1762, a bricklayer in Washington, Connecticut, in 1812. [1812]

MCKEICHIE, THOMAS, admitted as a member of the Scots Charitable Society of Boston in 1803. [SCS]

MCKELLAR, ANGUS, a Covenanter from Argyll, transported from Leith to New England in July 1685. [RPCS.11.94]

MCKENLEY, WILLIAM, admitted as a member of the Scots Charitable Society in 1724. [SCS]

MACKENRY, JOHN, admitted as a member of the Scots Charitable Society of Boston in 1698. [SCS]

MCKENZIE, ALEXANDER, MD, admitted as a member of the
   Scots Charitable Society of Boston in 1716. [SCS]

MCKENZIE, ANDREW, a merchant in Boston, 1755.
   [NAS.CS16.1.95]

MCKENZIE, DANIEL, born in 1746, a farmer from Dundee,
   emigrated from Greenock to Salem on the Glasgow Packet,
   master Alexander Porterfield, in April 1775. [PRO.T47.12]

MCKENZIE, DONALD, born 1778, late British Consul in Maine,
   died in Inverness on 29 December 1845. [AJ#5116]

MCKENZIE, FRANK S., woollen manufacturer in Woodstock,
   Vermont, 1875. [NAS.GD71.409]

MCKENZIE, GORDON, granite polisher from Huntly,
   Aberdeenshire, emigrated to America in 1869, settled in
   Quincy, Massachusetts, during 1869. [AJ:29.9.1885]

MCKENZIE, JOHN, admitted as a member of the Scots Charitable
   Society of Boston in 1732. [SCS]

MCKENZIE, PETER, from Cromarty, son of the Earl of Cromarty,
   admitted as a member of the Scots Charitable Society of
   Boston in 1739. [SCS]

MCKENZIE, WILLIAM, born in 1680 son of William McKenzie, the
   Commissary of Orkney, and Margaret Stewart, emigrated to
   New England in 1714. [HGM]

MCKENZIE, WILLIAM, from Inverness, admitted as a member of
   the Scots Charitable Society of Boston in 1749. [SCS]

MCKENZIE, WILLIAM, from Wigtownshire, married Elizabeth
   Sloane from Wigtownshire, in Wakefield, Massachusetts, on
   24 December 1872. [EC#27554]

MACKHENE, ALESTER, a prisoner of war transported to New
   England on the John and Sarah of London, master John
   Greene in November 1651. [Suffolk Deeds, 1-56]

MACKETH, DAVID a prisoner of war transported to New England
on the John and Sarah of London, master John Greene in
November 1651. [Suffolk Deeds, 1-56]

MACKETH, NEIL a prisoner of war transported to New England on
the John and Sarah of London, master John Greene in
November 1651. [Suffolk Deeds, 1-56]

MACKEY, WILLIAM, admitted as a member of the Scots
Charitable Society in 1725. [SCS]

MACKIE, JOHN FLETCHER, born in Aberdeen during April 1806,
son of John Mackie and Mary Fletcher, emigrated to New
York in 1822, agent and later manager of the Jersey City
Rolling Mills from 1836 to 1851, admitted as a member of
the St Andrews Society of New York in 1831, died in
Saugatuck, Connecticut, in April 1851. [ANY]

MCKINLAY, ARCHIBALD, admitted as a member of the Scots
Charitable Society of Boston in 1695. [SCS]

MCKINNON, JOHN, prisoner of war captured after the Battle of
Dunbar 1650, transported to New England. [SG.35.3.136]

MCKISSON, THOMAS, born 1753, a shoemaker from Perth,
emigrated from Greenock to Salem on the Glasgow Packet
in May 1775. [PRO.T47.12]

MCKNIGHT, JOHN, born around 1702, emigrated to New England
in 1718, married Jerusha Crane about 1720, settled in
Ellington, Connecticut, died 16 March 1785. [ImmNE#136]

MCKNOW, THOMAS, admitted as a member of the Scots
Charitable Society of Boston in 1802. [SCS]

MCLACHLIN, ROBERT, a prisoner of war transported to New
England in 1651, settled in Brookfield, Massachusetts.
[AncH-NE]

MCLAFLIN, ROBERT, in Wenham, probate April 1691 Salem,
Massachusetts

MACLAINE, MURDOCH, a passenger on the Glasgow Packet, Captain A. Porterfield, bound for Boston was enrolled into the 84 [Royal Highland Emigrants] Regiment on 23 October 1775, [NAS.GD174/2093]; later commissioned as a Captain in the Royal Highland Emigrants Regiment in Boston in 1776. [NAS.GD174.2405/1]

MCLANE, ROBERT, admitted as a member of the Scots Charitable Society of Boston in 1736. [SCS]

MCLAREN, JANET, possibly from Stirlingshire, settled in Lincoln Center, Maine, before 1881. [NAS.SH.20.8.1881]

MCLAREN, JOHN, settled in Barnet, New Hampshire, around 1775. [HGP]

MCLAREN, PATRICK, in Middletown, Hartford, Connecticut, husband of Dorothy ...., probate 4 April 1732 Connecticut

MCLAREN, PATRICK, a laborer, and his wife, arrived in Boston on 26 July 1764 aboard the snow Douglas, master Robert Manderston, from Greenock. [PAB][NWI#1.459]

MCLAUGHLIN, ANGUS, born in 1830, immigrated into Massachusetts on the Alexander a brig, on 9 October 1850. [LAP]

MCLAUCHLIN, THOMAS, from Burntisland, Fife, father of a daughter born on 18 September 1883 and a son Thomas who died on 23 September 1882, both in Ansonia, Connecticut. [FFP]

MACLEAN, ALLAN, born in Kilbride, Isle of Coll, Argyll, on 1 August 1715, fourth son of Allan MacLean of Grishipol, emigrated to America during 1740, a merchant in Hartford, Connecticut, married Mary Loomis in 1744, father of Mary, Alexander, Jabez, and Susanna, a British officer around 1760, then a farmer in Vernon after 1763, died in 1786. [CG]

MCLEAN, ALLAN, born in Skye, Inverness-shire, educated at King's College, Aberdeen, in 1762, a physician and minister in Bristol, Maine, from 1773 to 1795, died there during 1805. [CCNE][KCA]

MCLEAN, HECTOR, a passenger on the <u>Glasgow Packet</u>, Captain Porterfield, bound for Boston, was recruited into the 84 th [Royal Highland Emigrant] Regiment on 23 October 1775. [NAS.GD174/2093]

MCLEAN, HUGH, admitted as a member of the Scots Charitable Society of Boston in 1728. [SCS]

MCLEAN, Mrs IRVING, born in 1787, relict of David McLean in Powfoot, died at the residence of her son-in-law John Irving in Norfolk, Connecticut, during 1866. [AO]

MACLEAN, JOHN, born in August 1707, son of Neil MacLean of Balliphetrish, Tiree, to America on 20 May 1757 as an officer of the 42nd Highlanders [the Black Watch], arrived there on 14 August 1757, later settled in Danbury, Connecticut, as a merchant, married Deborah Adams in Fairfield, Connecticut, on 12 October 1759, father of Mary, Anne, Deborah, Alexander, Lilly, John, Lany, Sally, and Hugh or Ewan, died on 7 April 1805. [CG] [MB#82]

MCLEAN, JOHN, a mariner from the parish of Learside, Argyllshire, admitted as a member of the Scots Charitable Society of Boston in 1767. [SCS]

MCLEAN, LACHLAN, a passenger on the <u>Glasgow Packet</u>, master Alexander Porterfield, bound for Boston, was recruited into the 84th [Royal Highland Emigrants] Regiment on 23 October 1775. [NAS.GD174/2093]

MCLEAN, MALCOLM, probably from Mull, Inverness-shire, arrived in Boston on 30 October 1773, settled in New Boston 60 miles away on 20 December 1773. [NAS.GD174.1294]

MCLEAN, MARGARET, born in 1745, from Paisley, Renfrewshire, emigrated from Greenock to Salem on the <u>Glasgow Packet,</u> master Alexander Porterfield, in April 1775. [PRO.T47/12]

MCLEHOSE, JOHN HOZIER, second son of James McLehose of Nellands, died in New London, North America, on 16 January 1786. [GM#IX.435.174]

MCLEISH, ISABELLA, daughter of David McLeish a cooper in Edinburgh, wife of T. E. Sharpe in Boston, 1875. [NAS.SH.8.1.1875]

MACLELLAN, HENRY B., died in Boston on 5 September 1833. [DPCA, 8.11.1833]

MCLELLEN, JAMES, emigrated from Ayr to America before 1726, settled in Taunton, Massachusetts, married Margaret Fleming. [SG.7.2.55]

MCLELLAN, WILLIAM, settled in Worcester, Massachusetts, during 1718, married Jeannie Calhoun. [CAG.1/175]

MCLEOD, DAVID, from Fife, admitted to the Scots Charitable Society of Boston in 1738. [SCS]

MCLEOD, JOHN a prisoner of war transported to New England on the John and Sarah of London, master John Greene in November 1651. [Suffolk Deeds, 1-56]

MCLEOD, MURTLE a prisoner of war transported to New England on the John and Sarah of London, master John Greene in November 1651. [Suffolk Deeds, 1-56]

MCLEOD, NORMAN, a merchant in Boston from 1761 to 1765, died in 1767. [NAS.NRAS.O623, T-MJ377/C]

MCLEOD, WILLIAM, born in 1825, from Crocketford, Kirkcudbrightshire, died in Millville, Providence, Rhode Island, on 24 January 1856. [DGH: 4.3.1856]

MACLURE, ANTHONY, admitted as a member of the Scots Charitable Society in 1724. [SCS]

MCMASTER, JAMES, a merchant, arrived in Boston on 11 November 1766 aboard the George and James, master Robert Montgomery, from Glasgow, [PAB]; from Old Glenluce, Galloway, admitted as a member of the Scots Charitable Society of Boston in 1767, [SCS]; merchant in Boston and Portsmouth, Loyalist, settled in Nova Scotia 1783. [Loyalists in Nova Scotia, p155][NAS.CS16.1.173] [PRO.AO12.12.23]

MCMASTER, JOHN, a merchant, arrived in Boston on 22 August 1765 aboard the Jamieson and Peggy, master John Aitken, from Leith. [PAB] arrived in Boston on 29 August 1768 aboard the snow Catherine, master Hugh Morris, from Scotland. [PAB]; Loyalist, from Galloway, claim. [PRO.AO12.12.23]

MCMASTER, JOHN, Wiscassett, Lincoln County, Maine, probate December 1824 PCC

MCMASTER, PATRICK, a merchant, arrived in Boston on 17 August 1767 aboard the snow Jenny, master Hector Orr, from Glasgow. [PAB]from Glen Luce, Galloway, admitted as a member of the Scots Charitable Society of Boston in 1774; a Scots merchant in Boston and Portsmouth, Loyalist, settled in Nova Scotia 1783. [Loyalists in Nova Scotia, p155] [SCS][PRO.AO12.12.23]

MCMASTER, WILLIAM, from Galloway, settled in Boston during 1765, a merchant and a Loyalist, settled in Shelborne, Nova Scotia, after 1783. [Loyalists of Massachusetts, p.209]

MCMASTER, WILLIAM, Augusta, Kennebee County, Massachusetts, probate May 1815 PCC

MCMATH, JOHN, a mariner in New England, 1741. [NAS.CS16.1.69]

MCMILLAN, ALISTER, born in Scotland 1631, settled in Salem, Massachusetts, by 1661. [Essex County Quarterly Court Files, Vol.7, 38] [AncH-NE]

MCMILLAN, JOHN, a Covenanter from Argyll, transported from Leith to New England in July 1685. [RPCS.11.94]

MCMILLAN, JOHN, a prisoner of war captured after the Battle of Dunbar in September 1650, transported from London on 3 November 1650 on the Unity to New England, an indentured servant at the Lynn Ironworks in Massachusetts. [NWI]

MCMILLAN, ROBERT, from Glasgow, emigrated via Belfast to Boston on 4 August 1718. [CMM]

MCMIN, GEORGE, admitted as a member of the Scots Charitable Society in 1727. [SCS]

MACMITH, JOHN, admitted as a member of the Scots Charitable Society of Boston in 1711. [SCS]

MCMORAN, JOHN, admitted as a member of the Scots Charitable Society of Boston in 1693. [SCS]

MCNACHTEN, NEIL, a shoemaker, settled in Boston around 1729, sought by his brother Alexander who had come from Islay, Argyll, to find him. [NYGaz., 4.12.1738]

MACNAIR, ALEXANDER, a prisoner of war captured after the Battle of Dunbar in September 1650, transported from London on 3 November 1650 on the Unity to New England, an indentured servant in New Hampshire and in York, Maine. [NWI]

MCNAIR, ALLISON SHEPHERD, born 1840, daughter of James McNair from Dysart and Dunfermline, Fife, then in Bridgeport, Connecticut, wife of Richard Hinchcliffe, died in Bridgeport on 18 May 1874. [FFP]

MCNAUGHT, WILLIAM, from Glasgow, settled in Norwood, Massachusetts, by 1855. [MNS.1/298]

MCNAUGHTON, ALEXANDER, settled in Wolfsboro, New Hampshire, before 1776, a Loyalist soldier in the 84th Regiment, settled in Halifax, Nova Scotia, 1784. [PRO.AO26.277.279]

MCNEILL, CHARLES, admitted as a member of the Scots Charitable Society of Boston in 1735. [SCS]

MCNEILL, JOHN, admitted as a member of the Scots Charitable Society of Boston in 1735. [SCS]

MACKNESTER, ALESTER a prisoner of war transported to New England on the John and Sarah of London, master John Greene in November 1651. [Suffolk Deeds, 1-56]

MACKNITH, DANIEL a prisoner of war transported to New England on the <u>John and Sarah of London</u>, master John Greene in November 1651. [Suffolk Deeds, 1-56]

MACKNITH, PATRICK, a prisoner of war transported to New England on the <u>John and Sarah of London</u>, master John Greene in November 1651. [Suffolk Deeds, 1-56]

MCNUTT, ALEXANDER, born in 1656, settled in Palmer, Massachusetts, around 1720, wife Sarah ..., father of Barnard. [CAG.1/199]

MCNUTT, JOHN, arrived in Boston on 31 October 1766 aboard the snow <u>Jenny</u>, master Archibald Orr, from Scotland. [PAB]

MCPHEADRIS, ARCHIBALD, admitted as a member of the Scots Charitable Society of Boston in 1709. [SCS]

MCPHERSON, C., admitted as a member of the Scots Charitable Society of Boston in 1826. [SCS]

MCPHERSON, JOHN a prisoner of war transported to New England on the <u>John and Sarah of London</u>, master John Greene in November 1651. [Suffolk Deeds, 1-56]

MCPHERSON, JOHN, from Strathspey, admitted as a member of the Scots Charitable Society of Boston in 1758. [SCS]

MCPHERSON, JOHN, in Boston, cnf 1873. [NAS.SC70.1.163]

MACPHERSON, ORIGLAIS a prisoner of war transported to New England on the <u>John and Sarah of London</u>, master John Greene in November 1651. [Suffolk Deeds, 1-56]

MACPHERSON, ROBERT a prisoner of war transported to New England on the <u>John and Sarah of London</u>, master John Greene in November 1651. [Suffolk Deeds, 1-56]

MACPHERSON, ROLAND, reference to in will of Archibald Anderson, 25 September 1662. [Essex County Quarterly Court Files, Vol.7,fo38]

MACPHERSON, RUTH, daughter of John Pickworth, referred to in his will probate September 1663 Salem, Massachusetts

MCQUARIE, HECTOR, a passenger on the Glasgow Packet, master Alexander Porterfield, bound for Boston, was recruited into the 84 th [Royal Highland Emigrant] Regiment on 23 October 1775. [NAS.GD174/2093]

MCQUEEN, ARCHIBALD, born in Applecross, Wester Ross, in 1786, arrived in America via Halifax, Nova Scotia, on 25 September 1813, settled in Worcester, Massachusetts, by 9 October 1813. [1812]

MCQUEEN, GEORGE, admitted as a member of the Scots Charitable Society in 1727. [SCS]

MCQUEEN, JOHN, admitted as a member of the Scots Charitable Society of Boston in 1731. [SCS]

MCRAE, COLIN, born in Scotland 1776, formerly in Demerara, arrived with his wife and four children in 1812, a merchant in New Haven, Connecticut. [1812]

MCSHANE, JOHN, a prisoner of war captured after the Battle of Dunbar in September 1650, transported from London on 3 November 1650 on the Unity to New England, an indentured servant in the Lynn Ironworks in Massachusetts. [NWI]

MCSPARRAN, JAMES, an Episcopalian minister who was educated at Glasgow and Oxford universities, to New England on 17 November 1720, settled in Narragansett, Connecticut, died on 14 April 1767. [SCHR#14.145][EMA#43][FPA#1/221]

MCTAGARD, JOHN, from Irvine, Ayrshire, admitted as a member of the Scots Charitable Society in 1725. [SCS]

MACKRORE, ALESTER, a prisoner of war transported to New England on the John and Sarah of London, master John Greene in November 1651. [Suffolk Deeds, 1-56]

MACTENNETH, SENNEL, a prisoner of war transported to New England on the <u>John and Sarah of London</u>, master John Greene in November 1651. [Suffolk Deeds, 1-56]

MACKTENTHA, CANA, a prisoner of war transported to New England on the <u>John and Sarah of London</u>, master John Greene in November 1651. [Suffolk Deeds, 1-56]

MACTHOMAS, ALESTER, a prisoner of war transported to New England on the <u>John and Sarah of London</u>, master John Greene in November 1651. [Suffolk Deeds, 1-56]

MCURICH, ARCHIBALD, a herd and a Covenanter from Argyll, transported from Leith to New England in July 1685. [RPCS.11.330]

MCVICAR, DUNCAN, a Covenanter, son of baillie McVicar in Campbelltown, Argyll, transported from Leith to New England in July 1685. [RPCS.11.330]

MCVICAR, JOHN, admitted as a member of the Scots Charitable Society of Boston in 1718. [SCS]

MCVURRIE, ARCHIBALD, admitted as a member of the Scots Charitable Society of Boston in 1693. [SCS]

MACWALTER, WILLIAM, a prisoner of war captured after the Battle of Dunbar in September 1650, transported from London on 3 November 1650 on the <u>Unity</u> to New England, an indentured servant in the Lynn Ironworks in Massachusetts. [NWI]

MCWHORTER, JOHN, from the parish of Strathearn, Ayrshire, admitted as a member of the Scots Charitable Society of Boston in 1770 [SCS]

MCWILLIAM, GELLUST, a prisoner of war transported to New England on the <u>John and Sarah of London</u>, master John Greene in November 1651. [Suffolk Deeds, 1-56]

MCWILLIAM, JAMES, from Kirkcowan, Wigtownshire, died in Boston during 1844. [DGH:18.7.1844]

MAIR, PETER, from Edinburgh, admitted as a member of the
Scots Charitable Society of Boston in 1806, a housewright in
Boston, and his wife Mary, 1809. [NAS.RD4.293.814][SCS]

MAITLAND or PYOTT, JAMES, son of James Pyett a merchant in
Montrose, Angus, a merchant in New York in 1797.
[NAS.RD4.263.1084]

MALCOLM, ALEXANDER, a minister, emigrated to New England
on 3 April 1740, settled in Marblehead, Massachusetts.
[EMA#43][SPG#3.20][FPA#5/305]

MALCOLM, ANDREW, from Ayr, in Boston on 25 October 1684;
admitted as a member of the Scots Charitable Society of
Boston in 1693. [SCS]

MALCOLM, Reverend ARCHIBALD, in Marblehead,
Massachusetts, during 1741. [EUL.Laing MS#II/91]

MALCOLM, DUNCAN, admitted as a member of the Scots
Charitable Society of Boston in 1694. [SCS]

MALCOLM, JAMES, admitted as a member of the Scots
Charitable Society of Boston in 1694. [SCS]

MALCOLM, JAMES, from Kirkcaldy, Fife, admitted as a member of
the Scots Charitable Society of Boston in 1766. [SCS]

MALCOLM, JOHN, emigrated to North Carolina after 1745, an
Aide to Governor Tryon in 1771, later a Customs House
officer in Portland, Maine, and in Boston, Massachusetts.
[TSA]; Customs Surveyor for American Ports, resident in
Boston, a Loyalist in 1776, in London 1782.
[PRO.AO12.105.141]

MALCOLM, QUINTIN, from Maybole, Ayrshire, a merchant in New
England, cnf 4 May 1752 Commisariat of Edinburgh.
[NAS.CC8.8.114]

MALLOCH, JOHN, admitted as a member of the Scots Charitable
Society of Boston in 1706. [SCS]

MALTMAN, JAMES, from Dunblane, Perthshire, admitted as a member of the Scots Charitable Society of Boston in 1765, a resident of Boston in 1787. [SCS]

MAN, DANIEL, a prisoner of war transported to New England on the John and Sarah of London, master John Greene in November 1651. [Suffolk Deeds, 1-56]

MANN, JAMES, born in Elgin, Morayshire, on 15 December 1795, son of John Mann and Janet Laing, a husbandman who emigrated to Philadelphia, later settled in New England during 1812, settled in Hampstead, New Hampshire, naturalised in Rockingham County, New Hampshire, on 11 March 1833. [N. H. Naturalisation Records]

MANN, JOHN, a prisoner of war transported to New England on the John and Sarah of London, master John Greene in November 1651. [Suffolk Deeds, 1-56]

MANN, PATRICK, a prisoner of war transported to New England on the John and Sarah of London, master John Greene in November 1651. [Suffolk Deeds, 1-56]

MANN, WILLIAM, born in Elgin, Morayshire, during 1777, son of John Mann and Janet Laing, a ship's carpenter on an East India Company vessel which was wrecked on the coast of Africa, rescued and landed at Salem, Massachusetts, in 1803, settled in Essex County. [H]

MANSON, ALEXANDER, admitted as a member of the Scots Charitable Society in 1724. [SCS]

MANSON, WILLIAM, admitted as a member of the Scots Charitable Society in 1724. [SCS]

MARCH, JAMES, born in Edinburgh, settled in Boston, died in New York on 19 November 1841. [EEC#20297]

MARCHANT, Mrs JANET, born in Luss, Dunbartonshire, during 1824, settled in Edgarstown, Massachusetts, by 1850. [C]

MARR, ANDREW, admitted as a member of the Scots Charitable Society of Boston in 1800. [SCS]

MARSHALL, ALEXANDER, admitted to the Scots Charitable Society of Boston in 1696. [SCS]

MARSHALL, PATRICK, from Springfield, admitted as a member of the Scots Charitable Society of Boston in 1716. [SCS]

MARTIN, ALEXANDER, a clerk in Boston around 1883, son of Robert Martin, a mason in Dunblane, Perthshire, and Helen Millar. [NAS.SH.1873]

MARTIN, ANN, born 1772, landed, with a child, in Barnstable [Massachusetts?] during 1821 from the schooner Alert, Captain Pease. [USNA/par]

MARTIN, DANIEL, a prisoner of war transported to New England on the John and Sarah of London, master John Greene in November 1651. [Suffolk Deeds, 1-56]

MARTIN, DAVID, admitted as a member of the Scots Charitable Society of Boston in 1686. [SCS]

MARTIN, JOHN, from Inverness, Captain of the Royal Marines, admitted as a member of the Scots Charitable Society of Boston in 1762. [SCS]

MARTYN, WILLIAM, admitted as a member of the Scots Charitable Society of Boston in 1749. [SCS]

MASON, JAMES, a prisoner of war captured after the Battle of Dunbar in September 1650, transported from London on 3 November 1650 on the Unity to New England, an indentured servant in the Lynn Ironworks in Massachusetts. [NWI]

MASON, JOHN, admitted as a founder member of the Scots Charitable Society of Boston on 6 January 1657. [SCS]

MATHESON, ALEXANDER, from Anstruther, Fife, admitted as a member of the Scots Charitable Society of Boston in 1736. [SCS]

MATTHEWS, JOHN, emigrated from Greenock aboard the brigantine Matty, master Thomas Cochrane, on 19 May 1774 bound for New York, arrived there on 22 July 1774, settled Barnet, Vermont. [HBV]

MATTHEWS, WILLIAM, emigrated from Greenock aboard the brigantine Matty, master Thomas Cochrane, on 19 May 1774 bound for New York, arrived there on 22 July 1774, settled Barnet, Vermont. [HBV]

MAXWELL, ALEXANDER, a prisoner of war captured after the Battle of Dunbar in September 1650, transported from London on 3 November 1650 on the Unity to New England, an indentured servant in the Lynn Ironworks in Massachusetts. [NWI]; a planter in York, York County, Maine, husband of Sarah ..., probate 8 October 1707 Maine Probate Office 2/12

MAXWELL, GILBERT, baptised 13 August 1736, son of Edward Maxwell and Margaret Allan in Holm & Paplay, Orkney, admitted as a member of the Scots Charitable Society of Boston in 1764. [SCS]

MAXWELL, HENRY, admitted as a member of the Scots Charitable Society in 1723. [SCS]

MAXWELL, JAMES, a shoemaker, admitted as a member of the Scots Charitable Society of Boston in 1684. [SCS]

MAXWELL, JOHN, admitted as a member of the Scots Charitable Society of Boston in 1686. [SCS]

MAXWELL, JOHN, a merchant from Glasgow, in Boston 1688, co-owner of the 40 ton Two Brothers of Boston. [RPCS#15.307]

MAXWELL, JOHN, jr., admitted as a member of the Scots Charitable Society of Boston in 1705. [SCS]

MAXWELL, ROBERT admitted as a member of the Scots Charitable Society of Boston in 1691. [SCS]

MAXWELL, WILLIAM, admitted as a member of the Scots Charitable Society of Boston in 1717. [SCS]

MEEME,(?), RICHARD, a prisoner of war captured after the Battle of Dunbar in September 1650, transported from London on

3 November 1650 on the <u>Unity</u> to New England, an indentured servant in the Lynn Ironworks in Mass. [NWI]

MEEN, PATRICK, admitted as a member of the Scots Charitable Society of Boston in 1686. [SCS]

MEIN, BENJAMIN, admitted as a member of the Scots Charitable Society of Boston in 1830. [SCS]

MEIN, JOHN, son of John Mein a slater burgess of Edinburgh, a bookseller who settled in Boston, Massachusetts, admitted as a member of the Scots Charitable Society of Boston in 1765. [REB.1765.138][SCS]

MELDRUM, ALEXANDER, admitted as a member of the Scots Charitable Society of Boston in 1827. [SCS]

MELROSE, WILLIAM, admitted as a member of the Scots Charitable Society of Boston in 1699. [SCS]

MELVILL, ALAN, born 7 December 1727, a merchant from Leven, son of Reverend Thomas Melvill and Ann Lamont in Scoonie, Fife, admitted to the Scots Charitable Society of Boston in 1749, died on 2 January 1760. [SCS][ANY.II.79][F#5.118]

MELVILLE, DAVID, from Glasgow, emigrated to New England in the 1690s, a merchant in Boston, admitted as a burgess and guildsbrother of Glasgow on 12 August 1717. [GBR][SO#44]

MELVILLE, JAMES, admitted as a member of the Scots Charitable Society of Boston in 1718. [SCS]

MELVILLE, JOHN, born in Scotland during 1803, a gardener, emigrated from Scotland to Boston on the <u>Cherub</u> a schooner, Captain Shepperd, during late 1821. [USNA/par]

MELVILLE, THOMAS, in Boston, admitted as a burgess of St Andrews 13 September 1772. [StABR]; admitted as a member of the Scots Charitable Society of Boston in 1788. [SCS]; in Boston 1810. [NAS.CS17.1.30/67]

MELVIN, DAVID, admitted as a member of the Scots Charitable Society of Boston in 1692. [SCS]

MELVIN, JAMES, from Pittenweem, Fife, admitted as a member of the Scots Charitable Society of Boston in 1730. [SCS]

MELVIN, JOHN, born in Fife during 1651, emigrated to Boston, a tailor in Charlestown, Massachusetts, admitted as a member of the Scots Charitable Society of Boston in 1684, married (1) Hannah Lewis (1655-1696) in Charlestown; (2) Margaret Shamesbury, he died on 21 August 1726 in Concord, Massachusetts. [SCS][Concord g/s]

MELVIN, ROBERT, a carpenter in Charlestown, admitted as a member of the Scots Charitable Society of Boston in 1684. [SCS]

MENZIES, JAMES, admitted as a member of the Scots Charitable Society of Boston in 1695. [SCS]

MENZIES, JAMES, admitted as a member of the Scots Charitable Society of Boston in 1711. [SCS]

MENZIES, JAMES, admitted as a member of the Scots Charitable Society of Boston in 1800. [SCS]

MENZIES, JOHN, of Cammo, born 1650, son of Alexander Menzies of Cultermains, an advocate and judge in Boston, Massachusetts, married (1) Rachel Wilkie, (2) Janet Bruce, and (3) Isobel Winram. [FAS#417]; Judge of the Admiralty, admitted as a member of the Scots Charitable Society of Boston in 1716. [SCS]

MENZIES, JOHN, admitted as a member of the Scots Charitable Society of Boston in 1713. [SCS]

MENZIES, RICHARD, MD, admitted as a member of the Scots Charitable Society of Boston in 1737. [SCS]

MERRY, HENRY, a prisoner of war transported to America 1651, settled in Reading, Massachusetts, 1661, died there 5 November 1685. [EAF]

MESSER, ALEXANDER, born 185-, son of Alexander Messer an architect and Jane Messer, died in Andover, Massachusetts, 1861. [St Clement's, Dingwall, g/s, Ross & Cromarty]

MESSER, ELIZABETH REID PEARSON, born 1852, daughter of Alexander Messer an architect and Jane Messer, died in Andover, Massachusetts. [St Clement's, Dingwall, g/s, Ross & Cromarty]

MESSER, JAMES, born 18.., son of Alexander Messer an architect and Jane Messer, died in Andover, Massachusetts 189-. [St Clement's, Dingwall, g/s, Ross & Cromarty]

MESSER, JANE, wife of Alexander Messer {1810-1857} an architect, died in Andover, Massachusetts, aged 76. [St Clement's, Dingwall, g/s, Ross & Cromarty]

MIDDLETON, ALEXANDER, baptised on 3 September 1709, third son of Alexander (or George Middleton?) {1676-1751} and Elspet Burnet (or Janet Gordon?), emigrated to America, admitted as a member of the Scots Charitable Society of Boston in 1736, a merchant in Boston by 1738, admitted as a burgess of Old Aberdeen on 20 May 1738, married Ann Todd in Boston, died on 21 August 1750. [SCS] [NAS.AC7.43.493][SP#6.177][OABR][SP#VI][NEHGR.52/13]

MIDDLETON, JANET, born 1762, wife of Peter Smith (1772-1810) from Brechin, Angus, died in Andover, Massachusetts, during 1839. [Brechin Cathedral g/s, Angus]

MILL, JAMES, a joiner, arrived in Boston on 3 June 1766 aboard the George and James, master Robert Montgomery, from Scotland. [PAB]

MILLER, ALEXANDER, admitted as a member of the Scots Charitable Society of Boston in 1713. [SCS]

MILLER, Reverend ALEXANDER, settled in Plainfield, Connecticut, around 1750, in Volumton, Connecticut, in 1751, a Separist minister. [AA#5/104]

MILLER, ANN, wife of ... Harris, possibly from Leith, settled in Portsmouth, New Hampshire, 1830. [NAS.SH.29.11.1830]

MILLER, JAMES, from Kirkwall, Orkney, admitted as a member of the Scots Charitable Society of Boston in 1758. [SCS]

MILLER, JAMES W., admitted as a member of the Scots Charitable Society of Boston in 1828. [SCS]

MILLER, JOHN admitted as a member of the Scots Charitable Society of Boston in 1691. [SCS]

MILLER, JOHN, admitted as a member of the Scots Charitable Society of Boston in 1718. [SCS]

MILLER, JOHN, from Lanark, admitted as a member of the Scots Charitable Society of Boston in 1733. [SCS]

MILLER, JOHN, a merchant, arrived in Boston on 31 October 1766 aboard the snow Jenny, master Archibald Orr, from Scotland. [PAB]

MILLER, JOHN, admitted as a member of the Scots Charitable Society of Boston in 1805. [SCS]

MILLER, JOHN, from Clunie, Perthshire, admitted as a member of the Scots Charitable Society of Boston in 1817. [SCS]

MILLER, JOHN L, admitted as a member of the Scots Charitable Society of Boston in 1831. [SCS]

MILLER, JOHN, born in Kinghorn, Fife, during 1824, died in Andover, Massachusetts, in March 1900. [PJ]

MILLER, JOSEPH, from Glasgow, admitted as a member of the Scots Charitable Society of Boston in 1739. [SCS]

MILLER, SANDER, a prisoner of war transported to New England on the John and Sarah of London, master John Greene in November 1651. [Suffolk Deeds, 1-56]

MILLER, THOMAS, admitted as a member of the Scots Charitable Society of Boston in 1720. [SCS]

MILLER, WILLIAM, from Glasgow, admitted as a member of the Scots Charitable Society of Boston in 1758. [SCS]

MILLER, WILLIAM, from Edinburgh, admitted as a member of the Scots Charitable Society of Boston in 1762. [SCS]

MILLER, WILLIAM, from Glasgow, admitted as a member of the Scots Charitable Society of Boston in 1765. [SCS]

MILLER, WILLIAM, emigrated to New England in May 1771, Deputy Controller of Customs at Newberry, Pitscataqua, a Loyalist in 1776, then in Glasgow, 1786. [NAS.CS17.1.5/278] [PRO.AO12.81.44]

MILLER, WILLIAM, admitted as a member of the Scots Charitable Society of Boston in 1828. [SCS]

MILLER, WILLIAM FORRESTER HARDY, born 1 June 1833, died in Portland, Maine, 26 April 1898. [Old Calton g/s, Edinburgh]

MILLESON, SANDER, a prisoner of war transported to New England on the John and Sarah of London, master John Greene in November 1651. [Suffolk Deeds, 1-56]

MILLIKEN, HUGH, emigrated to Massachusetts in 1650. [CAG#1/615]

MILLIKEN, JAMES, admitted as a member of the Scots Charitable Society of Boston in 1698. [SCS]

MILLS, GEORGE, from Kirkwall, Orkney, a member of the Scots Charitable Society of Boston in 1739. [SCS]

MILNE, ALEXANDER, in Stanford, Connecticut, cnf 1899. [NAS.SC70.1.372]

MILNE, ANDREW, admitted as a member of the Scots Charitable Society of Boston in 1799. [SCS]

MILNE, GEORGE, in Cincinatti, Ohio, married Helen Eliza, eldest daughter of Hon. Hugh Grinnell, in Greenfield, Massachusetts, on 6 September 1847. [AJ#5205]

MILNE, JANE MENMUIR, born 1856, daughter of William Milne a

gardener in Stitchill, died in East Milton, Massachusetts, on 17 August 1888. [Stitchill g/s, Roxburghshire]

MILNE, JOHN, admitted as a member of the Scots Charitable Society of Boston in 1693. [SCS]

MILNE, JOHN, born in Huntly, Aberdeenshire, during 1775, died at Fall River, Massachusetts, on 4 April 1857. [AJ:13.5.1857]

MILWARD, DAVID, a prisoner of war transported to New England on the John and Sarah of London, master John Greene in November 1651. [Suffolk Deeds, 1-56]

MILWARD, JAMES, a prisoner of war transported to New England on the John and Sarah of London, master John Greene in November 1651. [Suffolk Deeds, 1-56]

MITCHELL, ALEXANDER, from Aberdeen, admitted as a member of the Scots Charitable Society of Boston in 1694. [SCS]

MITCHELL, ANDREW, admitted to the Scots Charitable Society of Boston in 1696. [SCS]

MITCHELL, DAVID, born in 1793, son of David Mitchell a manufacturer and Agnes Kilpatrick in Kilmarnock, Ayrshire, settled in New Haven, Connecticut, by 1835. [Glasgow Necropolis g/s]

MITCHELL, JAMES, a prisoner of war transported to New England on the John and Sarah of London, master John Greene in November 1651. [Suffolk Deeds, 1-56]

MITCHELL, JAMES, born in Paisley or Glasgow during 1705, emigrated to New England in 1730, settled in Weathersfield, Connecticut, as a merchant, died there in 1800. [NAS.RD4.178/2.198] [NNQ.7.89] [NAS.RD4.178.198][AA#3/161][DAB#13/65]

MITCHELL, JAMES, son of Elizabeth Mitchell in Montrose, Angus, quarter gunner of HMS Renown, died in Rhode Island, pro. April 1781 PCC

MITCHELL, JOHN, admitted as a member of the Scots Charitable Society of Boston in 1713. [SCS]

MITCHELL, JOHN, a sailor from Irvine, Ayrshire, later in New England, May 1755. [NAS.CS16.1.95/255]

MITCHELL, JOHN, emigrated from Greenock aboard the brigantine Matty, master Thomas Cochrane, on 19 May 1774 bound for New York, arrived there on 22 July 1774, settled Barnet, Vermont. [HBV]

MITCHELL, ROBERT, from Bo'ness, West Lothian, admitted as a member of the Scots Charitable Society of Boston in 1731. [SCS]

MITCHELL, ROBERT, born in Scotland during 1803, a butcher, landed in Boston in late 1821 from the brig Missionary, Captain Sears. [USNA/par]

MITCHELL, THOMAS, in Irvine, Ayrshire, then in New England, 1755. [NAS.CS16.1.95]; admitted as a member of the Scots Charitable Society of Boston in 1750. [SCS]

MITCHELL, WILLIAM, admitted as a member of the Scots Charitable Society of Boston in 1716. [SCS]

MITCHELL, WILLIAM, born in Glasgow during 1703, son of John Mitchell and Janet McLauchlan, father of William born 1735, emigrated to New England in 1755, settled in Weatherfield and Chester, Connecticut. [NNQ.VII.89]

MITCHELL, WILLIAM, born on 16 September 1803 son of David Mitchell a manufacturer and Agnes Kilpatrick in Kilmarnock, Ayrshire, settled in New Haven, Connecticut. [Glasgow Necropolis g/s]

MITCHELL, WILLIAM ALEXANDER, youngest son of Archibald Mitchell late in Kemback and Largo, Fife, died in Norwich, Connecticut, on 23 November 1893. [FH]

MITCHELSON, DAVID, born in Kirriemuir, Angus, on 26 January 1732,admitted as a member of the Scots Charitable Society of Boston, in 1767, "late of New York", died at Fyfe Place, Leith Walk, Edinburgh, on 24 October 1802. [SCS/NEHGS] [Canongate g/s, Edinburgh]

MOFFAT, JOHN, admitted as a member of the Scots Charitable Society of Boston in 1722. [SCS]

MOFFAT, JOHN, admitted as a member of the Scots Charitable Society of Boston in 1738. [SCS]; died in August 1777, probate 21 November 1777 Boston, [NLS.CH3824]

MOFFAT, MARGARET, born in 1814, daughter of William Moffat and Sarah Corrie in Torthorwald, Dumfriesshire, settled in Boston, died there on 15 July 1844. [Torthorwald g/s, Dumfries-shire]

MOFFAT, THOMAS, MD, from Edinburgh, admitted as a member of the Scots Charitable Society of Boston in 1739, [SCS]; a Scottish physician educated at Rheims, France, settled in Rhode Island, died during 1787. [SA#184]; educated at Edinburgh University 1732, a physician in Newport, Rhode Island, a Loyalist in 1776, died in London on 14 March 1787. [PRO.AO12.82.1]; Customs Controller of New London 1768. [NLS.CH3824]

MOFFAT, WILLIAM, White Creek, Charlotte County, Vermont, Loyalist in 1776. [PRO.AO13.81.291]

MOIR, JOHN, MD, from Aberdeen, admitted as a member of the Scots Charitable Society of Boston in 1703. [SCS]

MONCRIEFF, ARCHIBALD, admitted as a member of the Scots Charitable Society of Boston in 1736. [SCS]

MONCRIEFF, ARTHUR, admitted as a member of the Scots Charitable Society of Boston in 1695. [SCS]

MONCRIEFF, GEORGE, admitted as a member of the Scots Charitable Society of Boston in 1737. [SCS]; a shipbuilder in Boston around 1738. [NAS.AC10/283]

MONCUR, THOMAS, from Dundee, admitted as a member of the Scots Charitable Society of Boston in 1739. [SCS]

MONTGOMERY, ADAM, admitted as a member of the Scots Charitable Society of Boston in 1694. [SCS]

MONTGOMERY, ADAM, admitted as a member of the Scots Charitable Society of Boston in 1734. [SCS]

MONTGOMERY, ALEXANDER, admitted as a member of the Scots Charitable Society of Boston in 1758. [SCS]

MONTGOMERY, JAMES, admitted as a member of the Scots Charitable Society of Boston in 1689. [SCS]

MONTGOMERY, JAMES, admitted as a member of the Scots Charitable Society of Boston in 1706. [SCS]

MONTGOMERY, JAMES, from Glasgow, admitted as a member of the Scots Charitable Society of Boston in 1733. [SCS]

MONTGOMERY, JAMES, from Saltcoats, Ayrshire, admitted as a member of the Scots Charitable Society of Boston in 1748. [SCS]

MONTGOMERY, JOHN, from Glasgow, admitted as a member of the Scots Charitable Society of Boston in 1758. [SCS]

MONTGOMERY, ROBERT, from West Kirkbride, admitted as a member of the Scots Charitable Society of Boston in 1734. [SCS]

MONTGOMERY, WILLIAM, from Irvine, Ayrshire, admitted as a member of the Scots Charitable Society of Boston in 1738. [SCS]

MONTGOMERY, WILLIAM, born at Blantyre Mills on 3 March 1820, son of James Montgomery, settled in Maine during 1837, died in Wakefield, Massachusetts, on 15 September 1905. [ANY.2.302]

MONTIER, JAMES, from Glasgow, admitted as a member of the Scots Charitable Society of Boston in 1739. [SCS]

MONTROSE, LAUGHRELL, a prisoner of war transported to New
England on the John and Sarah of London, master John
Greene in November 1651. [Suffolk Deeds, 1-56]

MONWILLIAM, DANIEL, a prisoner of war transported to New
England on the John and Sarah of London, master John
Greene in November 1651. [Suffolk Deeds, 1-56]

MONWILLIAM, DAVID, a prisoner of war transported to New
England on the John and Sarah of London, master John
Greene in November 1651. [Suffolk Deeds, 1-56]

MOODY, HUGH, from Glasgow, admitted as a member of the
Scots Charitable Society of Boston in 1758. [SCS]

MOODY, HUGH, from Glasgow, admitted as a member of the
Scots Charitable Society of Boston in 1764. [SCS]

MOODIE, INGRAM, born 1619, a prisoner of war captured after
the Battle of Dunbar in September 1650, transported from
London on 3 November 1650 on the Unity to New England,
an indentured servant in the Lynn Ironworks in
Massachusetts. [NWI]; probate 1693 Essex County, #7168

MOODIE, JAMES, born 1829, son of James Moodie and Mary
Pearson, died in Quincy, Massachusetts, 3 April 1900.
[Monigaff g/s]

MOODY, ROBERT, a merchant, arrived in Boston on 25 January
1766 aboard the snow Peggy, master William Craig, from
Glasgow. [PAB]

MOODIE, ROBERT, from Lanark, admitted as a member of the
Scots Charitable Society of Boston in 1766. [SCS]

MOODIE, THOMAS, a sailor, admitted as a member of the Scots
Charitable Society of Boston in 1684. [SCS]

MOODIE, WILLIAM, admitted as a member of the Scots
Charitable Society of Boston in 1685. [SCS]

MOORE, ANNE, arrived in Boston on 28 October 1763 aboard the

Douglas, master James Montgomerie, from Scotland. [PAB]

MOORE, JACOB, admitted as a member of the Scots Charitable Society of Boston in 1711. [SCS]

MOORE, JAMES, possibly a prisoner of war transported on the John and Sarah of London master John Greene, November 1651, in Boston, Massachusetts, 1657, co-founder of Scots Charitable Society of Boston 6 January 1657. [AncH-NE][SCS][Suffolk Deeds.I.5-6]

MOORE, JOHN, admitted as a member of the Scots Charitable Society of Boston in 1735. [SCS]

MOOR, ..., admitted as a member of the Scots Charitable Society in 1723. [SCS]

MOOR, ..., a cooper, arrived in Boston on 28 October 1763 aboard the Douglas, master James Montgomerie, from Scotland. [PAB]

MORAN, THOMAS, born 1791, arrived in Barnstable [Massachusetts?] during 1821 on the schooner Alert, Captain Pease. [USNA/par]

MORCOT, SANDER, a prisoner of war transported to New England on the John and Sarah of London, master John Greene in November 1651. [Suffolk Deeds, 1-56]

MORDOE, JOHN, admitted as a member of the Scots Charitable Society of Boston in 1707. [SCS]

MORLAND, WILLIAM, from Stranraer, Wigtonshire, admitted as a member of the Scots Charitable Society of Boston in 1762. [SCS]

MORRE, JOHN, a prisoner of war transported to New England on the John and Sarah of London, master John Greene in November 1651. [Suffolk Deeds, 1-56]

MORRE, JOHN, a prisoner of war transported to New England on the John and Sarah of London, master John Greene in November 1651. [Suffolk Deeds, 1-56]

MORRIS, JAMES, admitted as a member of the Scots Charitable Society of Boston in 1717. [SCS]

MORRIS, JANE, third daughter of James Morris in Balridgeburn, Fife, married David Clark, a baker, in Marlboro, Boston, on 23 July 1890. [DJ]

MORRIS, ROBERT, admitted as a member of the Scots Charitable Society of Boston in 1800. [SCS]

MORRISON, ALEXANDER, merchant in Penobscot, Maine, a Loyalist, settled in St Andrews, New Brunswick, by 1786. [PRO.AO.13.22.183]

MORRISON, ALEXANDER, from Sutherland, admitted as a member of the Scots Charitable Society of Boston in 1805. [SCS]

MORRISON, ARCHIBALD, admitted as a member of the Scots Charitable Society of Boston in 1685. [SCS]

MORRISON, DANIEL, born around 1668 possibly in Glasgow, settled in Newbury, New England, married (1) Hannah Griffin, (2) Mary Foulson, in Exeter, New Hampshire, (3) Mary ... [GH]

MORRISON, DANIEL, a house carpenter, and his wife, arrived in Boston on 17 August 1767 aboard the snow Jenny, master Hector Orr, from Glasgow. [PAB]

MORRISON, DONALD, a merchant, arrived in Boston on 17 August 1767 aboard the snow Jenny, master Hector Orr, from Glasgow. [PAB]

MORRISON, HECTOR, from Sutherland, admitted as a member of the Scots Charitable Society of Boston in 1805. [SCS]

MORISON, JOHN, born in Aberdeenshire, emigrated via Ireland to New England in 1720, settled in Windham, New Hampshire, died in 1736.[ImmNE#140]

MORRISON, JOHN, admitted as a member of the Scots

Charitable Society of Boston in 1815. [SCS]

MORRISON, ROBERT, from Inverkip, Renfrewshire, admitted as a
member of the Scots Charitable Society of Boston in 1766.
[SCS]

MORRISON, RODERICK, from Sutherland, admitted as a member
of the Scots Charitable Society of Boston in 1805. [SCS]

MORRISON, Reverend JOHN, born 1743, graduated from
Edinburgh University 1765, emigrated from Pathfoot to New
England, first minister in Peterborough, New Hampshire,
died in Charleston, South Carolina, 1782. [ImmNE#142]

MORRISON, JOHN, admitted as a member of the Scots
Charitable Society of Boston in 1815. [SCS]

MORRISON, JOHN, born in Lanark on 29 July 1805, emigrated to
Boston in 1819, settled in New York in 1820, died 23
November 1876. [ANY]

MORRISON, ROBERT, emigrated to New England in 1719,
married Elizabeth ..., settled in Londonderry, New
Hampshire. [ImmNE.142]

MORRISON, WILLIAM, born ca.1684, emigrated via Portrush to
New England 7 August 1726, married Mary Henry, died
during 1758 in Nottingham, New Hampshire. [ImmNE#142]

MORRISON, WILLIAM, from Kilwinning, Ayrshire, admitted as a
member of the Scots Charitable Society of Boston in 1748.
[SCS]

MORRISON, WILLIAM, from Greenock, admitted as a member of
the Scots Charitable Society of Boston in 1757. [SCS]

MORRISON, WILLIAM, arrived in Boston on 28 October 1763
aboard the Douglas, master James Montgomerie, from
Scotland. [PAB]

MORRISON, WILLIAM, born in Auchlines, Perthshire, during
1748, a minister in Londonderry, NH, from 1783, husband of
Jean Fullarton, died in September 1829. [Imm.NE#140]

MORRISON, WILLIAM, in Fall River, Bristol, Massachusetts, cnf 1889. [NAS.SC70.1.276]

MORROW, DUNCAN, admitted as a member of the Scots Charitable Society of Boston in 1731. [SCS]

MORSMAN, JAMES, born in 1626, settled in Massachusetts by 1667. [CAG.1.945]

MORSON, ANDREW, member of the Scots Charitable Society of Boston 1690. [SCS]

MORTON, JOHN, born in Kelso, Roxburghshire, during 1798, a baker in Boston from 1817 to 1820, later a merchant in New York, died there on 15 May 1891. [ANY]

MORTON, PATRICK, a prisoner of war transported to New England on the John and Sarah of London, master John Greene in November 1651. [Suffolk Deeds, 1-56]

MORTON, ..., born in Newhaven, Connecticut, on 25 May 1891, son of John Morton from Dunfermline, Fife. [DJ]

MOSES, JOHN, settled in Sagamore Creek, New Hampshire, by 1658. [AA#7/143]

MOTERFIELD, THOMAS, born in Scotland during 1793, an engineer, arrived in Boston on the Missionary, a brig, Captain Sears, in late 1821. [USNA/par]

MOTTLE, ANN, wife of William Douglas, settled in Boston during 1640. [AA#4/67]

MOWAT, GEORGE, from Orkney, admitted as a member of the Scots Charitable Society of Boston in 1744. [SCS]

MOWAT, JOHN, from Burrow, Orkney, admitted as a member of the Scots Charitable Society of Boston in 1770. [SCS]

MOWATT, MAGNUS, baptised 11 January 1733 in Evie and Randall, Stromness, Orkney, son of George Mowatt, settled in New England before 1767, married Anna Pickman in

Salem on 22 March 1767. [Imm.NE#143]

MUCKLEWEE, JOHN, emigrated to New England 1753, settled in Warren, Maine. [ImmNE#140]

MUCKSTORE, NEIL, a prisoner of war transported to New England on the John and Sarah of London, master John Greene in November 1651. [Suffolk Deeds, 1-56]

MUIR, JAMES, admitted as a member of the Scots Charitable Society in 1724. [SCS]

MUIR, JOHN arrived in Boston on 31 October 1766 aboard the snow Jenny, master Archibald Orr, from Scotland. [PAB]

MUIR, ROBERT, born in 1757, a weaver from Paisley, Renfrewshire, emigrated from Greenock to Salem on the Glasgow Packet, master Alexander Porterfield, in April 1775. [PRO.T47/12]

MUIRHEAD, EBENEZER, eldest son of William Muirhead of Crochmore and Janet Richardson, in Dumfries-shire, a physician in Providence, Rhode Island, 11 October 1754. [NAS.RS23.17.17]

MUIRHEAD, GEORGE, admitted as a member of the Scots Charitable Society of Boston in 1686. [SCS]

MUIRHEAD, JOHN, in Lubec, Washington County, Maine, around 1874, grandson of John Muirhead in Denny, Stirlingshire. [NAS.SH.1874]

MULLIGAN, HUGH, a smith, admitted as a member of the Scots Charitable Society of Boston in 1684. [SCS]

MULLIGAN, JOHN, admitted as a member of the Scots Charitable Society of Boston in 1685. [SCS]

MUNCKRELL, WILLIAM, a prisoner of war transported to New England on the John and Sarah of London, master John Greene in November 1651. [Suffolk Deeds, 1-56]

MUNDELL, JOHN, from Dumfries, admitted as a member of the
Scots Charitable Society of Boston in 1694. [SCS]

MUNDEN, PATRICK, born 1695, emigrated via Ireland to New
England, runaway indentured servant from John Menzies in
Leicester, Massachusetts, 11 September 1719.
[ImmNE#143]

MUNN, ALEXANDER, admitted as a member of the Scots
Charitable Society of Boston in 1713. [SCS]

MUNROE, ALEXANDER, a printer from Inverness, admitted as a
member of the Scots Charitable Society of Boston in 1767.
[SCS]

MONROW, DANIEL, a prisoner of war transported to New
England on the John and Sarah of London, master John
Greene in November 1651. [Suffolk Deeds, 1-56]

MUNRO, DONALD, a merchant, arrived in Boston on 1 June 1768
aboard the snow Jenny, master Hector Orr, from Glasgow.
[PAB]

MUNROW, JOHN, a prisoner of war transported to New England
on the John and Sarah of London, master John Greene in
November 1651. [Suffolk Deeds, 1-56]

MUNRO, JOHN, a merchant, arrived in Boston on 1 June 1768
aboard the snow Jenny, master Hector Orr, from Glasgow.
[PAB]

MUNRO, JOHN, emigrated to New England during 1769, married
Elizabeth Larrabee? 1770, settled in Salem, Massachusetts
[ImmNE.#143]

MUNRO, JOHN PEARSON, graduated from Glasgow University
MB, CM, in 1894, a ships surgeon who died in Boston on 6
May 1897. [MAGU#461]

MUNRO, WILLIAM, born 1625, possibly son of Robert Munro of
Foulis, banished to New England after the Battle of
Worcester 3 September 1651, died in 1717 in Lexington,
Massachusetts. [Munro Tree, 1734, 1978][SG]

MURDOCH, JAMES, possibly from Springs Coylton, resident in Massachusetts around 1842. [NAS.SH.1842]

MURDOCH, JOHN, settled in Plymouth, Massachusetts, around 1688. [AA#8/162]; possibly, admitted as a member of the Scots Charitable Society of Boston in 1691. [SCS]

MURDOCH, JOHN, admitted as a member of the Scots Charitable Society of Boston in 1713. [SCS]

MURDOCH, JOHN, from Plymouth, admitted as a member of the Scots Charitable Society of Boston in 1717. [SCS]

MURDOCH, ROBERT, born in 1665, settled in Plymouth and later Roxbury, Massachusetts. [DAB#13/342][AA#9/162]

MURDOCH, JOHN, emigrated from Greenock aboard the brigantine Matty, master Thomas Cochrane, on 19 May 1774 bound for New York, arrived there on 22 July 1774, settled Barnet, Vermont. [HBV]

MURISON, GEORGE, born in 1675, educated at King's College, Aberdeen, around 1701, emigrated to America, a schoolmaster in Albany, New York, during 1703, a minister in New York and Connecticut from 1705 to 1708, died in Rye, Connecticut, on 12 October 1708. [SNQ.1.59][SPG.11.86][CCMC][ANQ]

MURRAY, ALEXANDER, in Cumberland County, Providence, Rhode Island, cnf 1880. [NAS.SC70.1.203]

MURRAY, DANIEL, with his wife and three children, emigrated from Greenock aboard the brigantine Matty, master Thomas Cochrane, on 19 May 1774 bound for New York, arrived there on 22 July 1774, settled Barnet, Vermont. [HBV]

MURRAY, DOROTHY, born in 1743, wife of Reverend John Forbes, died in Milton, Massachusetts, in June 1811. [House of Forbes, Aberdeen, 1937]

MURRAY, ELIZABETH, born 7 July 1726, daughter of John Murray and Ann Bennet in Unthank, Roxburghshire, settled in North Carolina in 1749 and later in Boston by 1755, married (1) Thomas Campbell in Wilmington, (2) James Smith in Brush Hill, Massachusetts, (3) Ralph Inman in Cambridge, Massachusetts, during September 1771, died 22 May 1785. [NEHGS#112/273][LJM]

MURRAY, JAMES, born on 9 August 1713, son of John Murray and Ann Bennet in Unthank, Roxburghshire, emigrated to the Carolinas, later settled in Boston, admitted as a member of the Scots Charitable Society of Boston in 1754, a merchant and a Loyalist, died in 1781. [SCS] [NNQ#6/141][NEHGS#112/273]; husband of Margaret Mackey in Edinburgh cnf 4 May 1786 Commissariat of Edinburgh

MURRAY, JOHN B., born around 1755, a merchant in Virginia and New York, died in Eastport, Maine, 7 October 1828. [ANY

MURRAY, JOHN, a merchant, arrived in Boston on 31 October 1766 on the snow Jenny, master Archibald Orr, from Scotland. [PAB]

MURRAY, JOHN, son of John Murray and Ann Bennet in Unthank, Roxburghshire, settled in Norwich, Connecticut, by 1772, a Loyalist. [NEHGS#112/273]

MURRAY, JULIA A., born in 1840, wife of James Murrie from Dunfermline, Fife, died in Lowell, Massachusetts, on 29 January 1875. [FA]

MURRAY, WILLIAM, born in 1690, settled in Londonderry, New Hampshire, in 1720. [AA#9/118]

MURRAY, WILLIAM, emigrated to New England in 1720, settled in Hadley, Massachusetts. [ImmNE#144]

MURROW, JAMES, a prisoner of war transported to New England on the John and Sarah of London, master John Greene in November 1651. [Suffolk Deeds, 1-56]

MURROW, JOHN, a prisoner of war transported to New England on the John and Sarah of London, master John Greene in November 1651. [Suffolk Deeds, 1-56]

MURROW, JONAS, a prisoner of war transported to New England on the John and Sarah of London, master John Greene in November 1651. [Suffolk Deeds, 1-56]

MURROW, NEIL, a prisoner of war transported to New England on the John and Sarah of London, master John Greene in November 1651. [Suffolk Deeds, 1-56]

NAIRN, JAMES, a gentleman arrived in Boston on 29 May 1712 aboard the Expedition, master David Preshaw. [PTA#131]

NAIRN, JAMES, of Jamaica, admitted as a member of the Scots Charitable Society in 1727. [SCS]

NEAL, JOHN, probate April 1691 Salem, Massachusetts

NEAN, JANE, arrived in Boston on 28 October 1763 aboard the Douglas, master James Montgomerie, from Scotland. [PAB]

NEILL, ANDREW, admitted as a member of the Scots Charitable Society of Boston in 1659. [SCS]

NEILL, JOHN, a prisoner of war captured after the Battle of Dunbar in September 1650, transported from London on 3 November 1650 on the Unity to New England, an indentured servant in Kittery, Maine, around 1656. [NWI]

NEIL, Mrs, a widow, admitted as a member of the Scots Charitable Society of Boston in 1684. [SCS]

NEILSON, JAMES, from Dunbar, East Lothian, admitted as a member of the Scots Charitable Society of Boston in 1738. [SCS]

NEILSON, JAMES, settled in Ryegate, Vermont, before 1780. [VHS]

NEILSON, JAMES, admitted as a member of the Scots Charitable Society of Boston in 1803. [SCS]

NEILSON, JAMES, from Haddington, East Lothian, a member of the Scots Charitable Society of Boston in 1817. [SCS]

NEILSON, WILLIAM, settled in Ryegate, Vermont, before 1780. [VHS]

NELSON, CHARLES, admitted as a member of the Scots Charitable Society of Boston in 1693. [SCS]

NESBIT, ARCHIBALD, emigrated from Greenock aboard the brigantine Matty, master Thomas Cochrane, on 19 May 1774 bound for New York, arrived there on 22 July 1774, settled Barnet, Vermont. [HBV]

NESBETT, SAMUEL, a physician educated at Edinburgh University, settled in New Haven, Connecticut, during 17... [SA#176]

NEWGAR, PETER, from Orkney, admitted as a member of the Scots Charitable Society of Boston in 1749. [SCS]

NICHOLLS, DAVID, admitted to the Scots Charitable Society of Boston in 1726. [SCS]

NICHOLLS, JAMES, from Glasgow, admitted as a member of the Scots Charitable Society of Boston in 1733. [SCS]

NICHOLLS, JOHN, admitted as a member of the Scots Charitable Society of Boston in 1823. [SCS]

NICHOLSON, JOHN, admitted as a member of the Scots Charitable Society of Boston in 1829. [SCS]

NICHOLSON, ROBERT, from Weetra, Orkney, admitted as a member of the Scots Charitable Society of Boston in 1767. [SCS]

NICOL, JAMES, a merchant in Newport, Rhode Island, then in Leicester, Worcester County, New England, 1766. [NAS.CS16.1.125]

NICOLLS, JOHN, surgeon, arrived in Boston on the Expedition, master David Preshaw on 29 May 1712. [PTA#131]

NICOLLS, JOHN, from Glasgow, admitted as a member of the Scots Charitable Society of Boston in 1748. [SCS]

NICOLS, WILLIAM, admitted as a member of the Scots Charitable Society of Boston in 1718. [SCS]

NICOLSON, ANGUS, admitted as a member of the Scots Charitable Society of Boston in 1711. [SCS]

NICOLSON, FRANCIS, admitted as a member of the Scots Charitable Society of Boston in 1710. [SCS]

NICOLSON, JAMES, admitted as a member of the Scots Charitable Society of Boston in 1733. [SCS]

NICOLSON, JOHN, admitted as a member of the Scots Charitable Society of Boston in 1690. [SCS]

NISBET, JAMES, admitted as a member of the Scots Charitable Society of Boston in 1686. [SCS]

NISBET, JAMES, admitted as a member of the Scots Charitable Society of Boston in 1720. [SCS]

NISBET, MUNGO, admitted as a member of the Scots Charitable Society of Boston in 1695. [SCS]

NISBET, ROBERT, a laborer, arrived in Boston on 22 August 1765 aboard the Jamieson and Peggy, master John Aitken, from Leith. [PAB]

NISBET, WILLIAM, admitted as a member of the Scots Charitable Society of Boston in 1737. [SCS]

NOBLE, WILLIAM, from Dunbarton, admitted as a member of the Scots Charitable Society of Boston in 1757. [SCS]

NORMAND, JOSEPH, possibly from Edinburgh, settled in Worcester, Massachusetts, by 1871. [NAS.SH.1871]

NOTT, WILLIAM, born 1793, arrived, with a child, in Barnstable [Massachusetts] in 1821 on the Alert, Captain Pease. [USNA/par]

OCHTERLONY, DAVID, from Montrose, Angus, a mariner in
Boston, husband of Catherine .., probate 1 July 1767 NY

O'DONAL, RALPH, arrived in Boston on 28 October 1763 aboard
the Douglas, Captain Montgomerie, from Scotland. [PAB]

OGILVIE, DAVID, from Arbroath, admitted as a member of the
Scots Charitable Society of Boston in 1742. [SCS]

OGILVY, PATRICK, admitted as a member of the Scots Charitable
Society of Boston in 1712. [SCS]

OGILVIE, PATRICK, arrived in Boston on 30 June 1716 aboard
the Patience and Judith, from London. [BSPL]

O'HARA, DANIEL, born in Glasgow 1 September 1822, a laborer,
settled in Edgarstown, Dukes County, Massachusetts, by
1850. [C]

O'HARA, MARY, born in Ayrshire, during 1829, settled in
Chilmark, Dukes County, Massachusetts, by 1850. [C]

OLIPHANT, ANDREW, emigrated to New England in 1762, settled
in Providence, Rhode Island, later in Charleston, South
Carolina. [ImmNE#148]

OLIPHANT, DAVID, a physician and surgeon, settled in
Charleston, South Carolina, before 1755, later in Newport,
Rhode Island. [CAG.1/520]

OLIVER, ANDREW, with his wife Elizabeth Halliburton, emigrated
to America during 1735, settled in Boston. ["Memoirs of the
Haliburtons", Edinburgh, 1824]; admitted as a member of the
Scots Charitable Society of Boston in 1736. [SCS]

OMAND, HENRY, from Orkney, admitted as a member of the
Scots Charitable Society of Boston in 1766. [SCS]

O'NEILL, CHARLES HENRY, a sailmaker in Portsmouth around
1861, grandson of Charles O'Neill and Elizabeth Lovie in St
Quivox, Ayrshire. [NAS.SH.1861]

O'NEALE, DANIEL, a prisoner of war transported to New England on the <u>John and Sarah of London</u>, master John Greene in November 1651. [Suffolk Deeds, 1-56]

O'NEILL, JOHN, in Roxbury, Boston, around 1851, possibly from Edinburgh. [NAS.SH.1851]

OREM, JAMES, to New England on 19 October 1721. [EMA#48]

ORR, HUGH, born on 2 January 1715, son of Robert Orr in Lochwinnoch, Renfrewshire, arrived in Boston on 7 June 1740, settled in Bridgewater, Massachusetts, a firearms inventor and edgeware tool manufacturer, died in December 1798. [NAS.SH.1795][SG][WA][SN.3/266]

ORR, JAMES, a Scots settler in Wells, York County, New England, around 1675. [York Deeds, Book II, folio 167]

ORR, JAMES, from Greenock, admitted as a member of the Scots Charitable Society of Boston in 1761. [SCS]

ORR, JOHN, from Renfrewshire, emigrated to America in April 1774, settled in Ryegate, Vermont, before 1780. [VHS]

ORR, ROBERT, from Renfrewshire, emigrated to America in April 1774, settled in Ryegate, Vermont, before 1780. [VHS]

ORR, WILLIAM, admitted as a member of the Scots Charitable Society of Boston in 1692. [SCS]

OUCHTERLONIE, DAVID, from Montrose, Angus, a mariner in Boston, probate 7 March 1766 Boston [reference to wife Catharine, witnesses Sam Minot, Miriam Taylor and Mary Tyler]

OWLER, CHARLES B., born in Cupar, Fife, during 1826, son of William Owler a postmaster, died in Boston, Massachusetts, on 3 December 1890. [FH, 31.12.1890]

PAGAN, ROBERT, settled at Casco Bay, Maine, in 1748, later a merchant and factor in Falmouth, Loyalist, [PRO.AO.212.81.45]

PARDEE, JOHN, a prisoner of war captured after the Battle of
Dunbar in September 1650, transported from London on 3
November 1650 on the Unity to New England, an indentured
servant at the Lynn Ironworks in Massachusetts. [NWI]

PARK, ALEXANDER, born in Scotland in 1688, emigrated via
Ireland to New England in 1729, settled in Windham, New
Hampshire. [ImmNE#151]

PARK, JAMES, from Kilwinning, Ayrshire, admitted as a member
of the Scots Charitable Society of Boston in 1747. [SCS]

PARK, JOHN, in Newark, Glasgow, apprenticed to Robert
Glenfield, master of the Benjamin of New England in 1683.
[NAS.RD4.52.892]

PARK, JOHN, a mason, his wife and three children, arrived in
Boston on 17 August 1767 aboard the snow Jenny, master
Hector Orr, from Glasgow. [PAB]

PARK, RICHARD, admitted as a member of the Scots Charitable
Society of Boston in 1737. [SCS]

PARK, ROBERT, from Ayr, admitted as a member of the Scots
Charitable Society of Boston in 1771. [SCS]

PARK, WILLIAM, born in Glasgow on 7 October 1704, son of
James Park and Lilias Liddle, married Anna Law in Glasgow
on 6 May 1730, emigrated to Boston in 1756, father of
Margaret and Janet, died in Groton, Massachusetts, on 17
June 1788. [ImmNE#151]

PARKER, ALEXANDER, admitted as a member of the Scots
Charitable Society of Boston in 1734. [SCS]

PARKER, GEORGE, in Clam Cove, Deer Isle, Maine, dead by
1836. [NAS.SH.31.12.1836]

PARKER, JOHN R., in Clam Cove, Deer Isle, Maine, around 1836.
[NAS.SH.31.12.1836]

PARKER, WILLIAM, a soldier, guilty of forgery, transported to
Boston, Massachusetts, in June 1751. [AJ#251]

PARNELL, FRANCIS, admitted as a member of the Scots Charitable Society in 1724. [SCS]

PARTRIDGE, WILLIAM, from Berwickshire, settled in Hartford, Connecticut, in 1644, later in Hadley, Massachusetts, married Mary Smith on 12 December 1644. [AA.9/168]

PATTERSON, ANDREW, born in Hamilton, Lanarkshire, during 1659, settled in Stratford, Connecticut, in 1685. [AA.10/104]

PATERSON, DAVID, a prisoner of war transported to New England on the John and Sarah of London, master John Greene in November 1651. [Suffolk Deeds, 1-56]

PATTERSON, GEORGE, emigrated to New England, settled in Boston, married Susanna Copstick on 7 November 1713. [ImmNE#153]

PATERSON, GEORGE, from Edinburgh, admitted as a member of the Scots Charitable Society of Boston in 1736. [SCS]

PATTERSON, GEORGE, granite polisher from Huntly, Aberdeenshire, emigrated to America in 1869, settled in Quincy, Massachusetts. [AJ:29.9.1885]

PATTERSON, HUGH, from Irvine, Ayrshire, admitted as a member of the Scots Charitable Society of Boston in 1745. [SCS]

PATERSON, JAMES, born 1633, emigrated to New England by 1670, died in 1701. [CAG.1/347]

PATERSON, JAMES, admitted as a member of the Scots Charitable Society of Boston in 1699. [SCS]

PATERSON, JAMES, admitted as a member of the Scots Charitable Society in 1725. [SCS]

PATERSON, JAMES, admitted as a member of the Scots Charitable Society of Boston in 1734. [SCS]

PATTERSON, JOHN, a merchant skipper from Glasgow, settled in Boston before 1690. [PC.15.307]

PATERSON, JOHN, admitted as a member of the Scots Charitable Society of Boston in 1738. [SCS]

PATTERSON, LILLIAS, wife of J. B. Laurie in Boston, Massachusetts, died at 26 Findlay Street, Glasgow, on 19 October 1849. [SG#1866]

PATTERSON, ROBERT, from Old Meldrum, Aberdeenshire, admitted as a member of the Scots Charitable Society of Boston in 1774. [SCS]

PATTERSON, T. H., born 1791, arrived in Boston during 1821 on the Jasper, Captain Crocker. [USNA/par]

PATTISON, JAMES, a prisoner of war transported to New England on the John and Sarah of London, master John Greene in November 1651. [Suffolk Deeds, 1-56]

PATTOUN, ROBERT, admitted to the Scots Charitable Society of Boston in 1696. [SCS]

PAUL, MARY, emigrated from Greenock aboard the brigantine Matty, master Thomas Cochrane, on 19 May 1774 bound for New York, arrived there on 22 July 1774, settled Barnet, Vermont. [HBV]

PAUL, ROBERT, emigrated from Greenock aboard the brigantine Matty, master Thomas Cochrane, on 19 May 1774 bound for New York, arrived there on 22 July 1774, settled Barnet, Vermont. [HBV]

PAUL, WILLIAM, admitted as a member of the Scots Charitable Society of Boston in 1804. [SCS]

PAUL, Mrs, emigrated from Greenock aboard the brigantine Matty, master Thomas Cochrane, on 19 May 1774 bound for New York, arrived there on 22 July 1774, settled Barnet, Vermont. [HBV]

PEADY, JOHN, from Glasgow, admitted as a member of the Scots Charitable Society of Boston in 1699. [SCS]

PEASLY, ROBERT, from Glasgow, admitted as a member of the Scots Charitable Society of Boston in 1737. [SCS]

PEAT, ..., born in Scotland during 1789, a merchant who landed in Boston during late 1821 from the schooner Cherub, Captain Sheppard. [USNA/par]

PECK, THOMAS HANDYSIDE, admitted as a member of the Scots Charitable Society of Boston in 1735. [SCS]

PEACOCK, ROBERT, admitted as a member of the Scots Charitable Society in 1724. [SCS]

PEACOCK, ..., a cordwainer, arrived in Boston from Glasgow aboard the Success, a brigantine, master Andrew Gibson, on 12 April 1712. [PTA#129]

PEDIE, JAMES, from Glasgow, admitted as a member of the Scots Charitable Society of Boston in 1743. [SCS]

PEDDY, JOHN, admitted as a member of the Scots Charitable Society of Boston in 1731. [SCS]

PEDDY, ..., admitted as a member of the Scots Charitable Society of Boston in 1721. [SCS]

PERRY, GEORGE, a prisoner of war transported to New England on the John and Sarah of London, master John Greene in November 1651. [Suffolk Deeds, 1-56]

PERRY, JAMES, admitted as a member of the Scots Charitable Society of Boston in 1712. [SCS]

PERRY, WILLIAM, admitted as a member of the Scots Charitable Society of Boston in 1708. [SCS]

PETERS, THOMAS, a merchant from Glasgow, emigrated from Port Glasgow to New England on the Boston Merchant on 24 October 1685, [NAS.E72.19.8]; admitted as a member of the Scots Charitable Society of Boston 1700. [SCS]

PETTIGREW, WILLIAM, a physician from Crawforddykes, Renfrewshire, admitted as a member of the Scots Charitable

Society of Boston in 1766. [SCS]

PETTIGREW, WILLIAM, a surgeon, arrived in Boston on 17 August 1767 aboard the snow Jenny, master Hector Orr, from Glasgow. [PAB]

PETTIGREW, ..., a boy, arrived in Boston on 17 August 1767 aboard the snow Jenny, master Hector Orr, from Glasgow. [PAB]

PHILIP, MARGARET, from Aberdeen, married James Sievewright, in Stonington, Connecticut, on 22 September 1847. [AJ#5208]

PHILLIPS, PATRICK, admitted as a member of the Scots Charitable Society of Boston in 1799. [SCS]

PIGGAN, ALEXANDER, from New London, admitted as a member of the Scots Charitable Society of Boston in 1695. [SCS]

PITBLADDO, CHARLES BRUCE, in Portsmouth, New Hampshire, around 1881, son of Colin Pitbladdo in Garalands, Dunfermline, Fife. [NAS.SH.1881]

PITCAIRN, JOHN, son of Reverend David Pitcairn and Catherine Hamilton in Dysart, Fife, a Major of the Royal Marines, died at Bunker Hill, New England, on 19 April 1775. [F#5.87]

PITT, WILLIAM, of Wiscassett, admitted as an honorary member of the Scots Charitable Society of Boston in 1817. [SCS]

PLAYFAIR, LYON, married Edith Russell, eldest daughter of Samuel H. Russell of boston, in Boston on 3 October 1878. [EC#29338]

PLUDDER (?), ROBERT, arrived in Boston on 7 August 1766 aboard the schooner Lovely Betsy, master William Hayman, from Scotland. [PAB]

POLLOCK, DAVID, born in Scotland during 1788, a physician who landed in Boston during late 1821 from the sloop Katy Ann, Captain Fisher. [USNA/par]

POLLOCK, JOHN, admitted as a member of the Scots Charitable Society of Boston in 1694. [SCS]

POLLOCK, THOMAS, eldest son of George Pollock a manufacturer in Paisley, sometime a manufacturer in Paisley, then in Boston, husband of late Elizabeth McKellar, 1816, [NAS.CS17.1.35/630; CS17.1.25/30]; from Paisley, Renfrewshire, a merchant, father of George and Thomas in Boston, USA, probate November 1838 PCC

POLSON, THOMAS, founder member of the Scots Charitable Society of Boston on 6 January 1657. [SCS]

PORTEOUS, CHRISTINA, born 1856, daughter of John Porteous (1824-1902), died in New York 30 May 1901, buried in Yantic Cemetery, Norwich, Connecticut. [West Linton g/s]

PORTEOUS, JOHN, born 1824, husband of Annie Gray, died in Norwich, USA, 21 November 1902. [West Linton g/s]

PORTEOUS, ROBERT, admitted as a founder member of the Scots Charitable Society of Boston on 6 January 1657, first boxmaster of the Society. [SCS]

PORTERFIELD, JOHN, a merchant skipper who settled in Bristol, New England, before 1699. [SPC.1700.195]; admitted as a member of the Scots Charitable Society of Boston in 1701. [SCS]

POTTER, EDWARD, admitted as a member of the Scots Charitable Society of Boston in 1734. [SCS]

PRATT, JOHN, admitted as a member of the Scots Charitable Society of Boston in 1694. [SCS]

PRESHAW, DAVID, admitted as a member of the Scots Charitable Society of Boston in 1712. [SCS]

PRINGLE, ANDREW, from Edinburgh, admitted as a member of the Scots Charitable Society of Boston in 1734. [SCS]

PRINGLE, JAMES, from Teviotdale, admitted as a member of the Scots Charitable Society of Boston in 1753. [SCS]

PRINGLE, JOHN, from the Merse, Berwickshire, admitted as a member of the Scots Charitable Society in 1739. [SCS]

PRINGLE, SARAH I., born in 1848, immigrated into Massachusetts aboard the Isabel Stewart, a bark, on 16 July 1849. [LAP]

PRINGLE, WILLIAM, born in Perth 1790, son of Reverend Alexander Pringle and Jean Moncrieff, emigrated to America in 1829, minister of the Associate congregation of Ryegate, Vermont, 1830-1852, married Margaret Bullions, father of Alexander, William, Mary and Jennie, died 14 December 1858. [Lyons of Cossins and Wester Ogil, p.75, A.Ross, Edinburgh, 1901][AUPC#663]

PRINGLE, ..., born 1785, a merchant, with his wife born 1794, and two children, arrived in Boston during 1821 on the schooner Albion, Captain Ward. [USNA/par]

PROVAN, JOHN, from Aberlady, East Lothian, admitted as a member of the Scots Charitable Society of Boston in 1746. [SCS]

PROUDFOOT, JAMES, born in Perth during 1732, emigrated to Boston in 1754, an Associate Presbyterian minister in Pennsylvania and in New York from 1757 to 1799, died in Salem, New York, on 22 October 1802. [CCMC]

PROVINCE, JOHN, admitted as a member of the Scots Charitable Society of Boston in 1767, a resident of Boston in 1787. [SCS]

PULLAR, THOMAS, born 1833, died in New Britain, Connecticut, 3 March 1901. [Little Dunkeld g/s, Perthshire]

PURDIE, HUGH, from Glasgow, admitted as a member of the Scots Charitable Society of Boston in 1750. [SCS]

PURDIE, ROBERT, admitted as a member of the Scots Charitable Society of Boston in 1689. [SCS]

QUARK, MARGARET, arrived in Boston on 28 October 1763 on the Douglas, Captain Montgomerie, from Scotland. [PAB]

RAE, JOHN, from Glasgow, admitted as a member of the Scots Charitable Society of Boston in 1747. [SCS]

RAE, ROBERT, admitted as a member of the Scots Charitable Society of Boston in 1734. [SCS]

RAE, TINA J., eldest daughter of Thomas Rae, late in Leslie, Fife, died in Holyoke, Massachusetts, on 11 January 1895. [PJ]

RAEBURN, Mrs ANNE, born in 1847, wife of Alexander Raeburn from Cartlehaugh, Old Deer, Aberdeenshire, died in Stamford, Connecticut, on 22 February 1869. [AJ:17.3.1869]

RAESIDE, ROBERT, arrived in Boston on 31 October 1766 aboard the snow Jenny, master Archibald Orr, from Scotland. [PAB]

RAIT, ALEXANDER, from Bervie, Kincardineshire, admitted as a member of the Scots Charitable Society of Boston in 1746. [SCS]

RAITT, ALEXANDER, born 1722, settled in Kittery, Maine, died 1776. [CAG#1/211]

RAIT, ALEXANDER, in New England, 1783; a merchant in Boston 1799. [NAS.CS17.1.2/144; CS17.1.18/80; CS17.1.17/219]

RAITT, ALEXANDER, formerly of Kittery, Maine, probate May 1825 PCC

RALSTON, ALEXANDER, born in Falkirk, Stirlingshire, during 1755, emigrated to New England in 1773, settled in New Hampshire, died in Keene, New Hampshire, during 1810. [ImmNE#161]

RALSTON, ALEXANDER, in Bethel, Vermont, around 1821. [NAS.SH.1821]

RALSTON, JAMES, admitted as an honorary member of the Scots Charitable Society of Boston in 1805. [SCS]

RALSTON, WILLIAM, admitted as a member of the Scots Charitable Society of Boston in 1698. [SCS]

RAMAGE, ALEXANDER, from Linlithgow, West Lothian, admitted as a member of the Scots Charitable Society of Boston in 1765. [SCS]

RAMSAY, ALEXANDER, admitted as a member of the Scots Charitable Society of Boston in 1659. [SCS]

RAMSAY, ARCHIBALD, MD, from Linlithgow, West Lothian, admitted as a member of the Scots Charitable Society of Boston in 1736. [SCS]

RAMSAY, JOHN, possibly from Stewarton, Ayrshire, resident in Massachusetts by 1800. [NAS.SH.1800]

RAMSAY, Dr., died in New Hampshire during November 1824. [AJ#4026]

RANKIN, ALEXANDER, a carpenter, arrived in Boston on 26 July 1764 aboard the snow Douglas, master Robert Manderston, from Greenock. [PAB]

RANKIN, ANDREW, a prisoner of war captured after the Battle of Dunbar in September 1650, transported from London on 3 November 1650 on the Unity to New England, an indentured servant in New Hampshire, and in York, Maine, during 1650s. [NWI]

RANKINE, ANDREW, admitted as a member of the Scots Charitable Society of Boston in 1692. [SCS]

RANKINE, GEORGE, from Kirkbride, admitted as a member of the Scots Charitable Society of Boston in 1734. [SCS]

RANKINE, JOHN, emigrated from Glasgow to New England before 1719, married Sarah Clark in Boston during 1719. [Imm.NE]

RANKINE, ROBERT, from Lothian, admitted as a member of the Scots Charitable Society of Boston in 1744. [SCS]

RANKIN, THOMAS, possibly from Auchtermuchty, Fife, resident in Smithfield, Rhode Island, during 1867. [NAS.SH.1867]

RANNEY, THOMAS, born around 1616, settled in Middleton, Connecticut, in 1657, died during 1713. [CAG#1/204]

REDLAND, MAGNUS, born in 1674, son of Thomas Redland and Barbara Laughton in Orkney, settled in York, later in Saco, Maine, died in 1772. [AA#3/98]

REID, ANDREW, admitted as a member of the Scots Charitable Society of Boston in 1799. [SCS]

REID, Mrs BARBARA, daughter of Alexander Barrack in Ellon, Aberdeenshire, died in Gloucester, Massachusetts, on 13 July 1877. [AJ:13.7.1877]

REID, DAVID, settled in Ryegate, Vermont, before 1780. [VHS]

REID, JOHN, from Edinburgh, admitted as a member of the Scots Charitable Society of Boston in 1734. [SCS]

REID, JOHN, from Aberdeen, admitted as a member of the Scots Charitable Society of Boston in 1747. [SCS]

REID, JOHN, emigrated from Greenock aboard the brigantine Matty, master Thomas Cochrane, on 19 May 1774 bound for New York, arrived there on 22 July 1774, settled Barnet, Vermont. [HBV]

REID, ROBERT, in New London, Connecticut, cnf 1876. [NAS.SC70.1.181]

REID, WILLIAM, from Ayr, admitted as a member of the Scots Charitable Society of Boston in 1734. [SCS]

REID, WILLIAM, a millwright, and his wife, arrived in Boston on 26 July 1764 aboard the snow <u>Douglas</u>, master Robert Manderston, from Greenock. [PAB]

RENTON, ALEXANDER, of Greenhill, Lanarkshire, a surveyor in Largs, Ayrshire, settled in Boston, Massachusetts, before 1729, married Mary Young, father of Alexander, Janet, Jean, John, Mary, and William. [NAS.RS42.13/14]

RENTON, JOHN, from Prestonpans, Midlothian, admitted as a member of the Scots Charitable Society of Boston in 1754. [SCS]

RENTOUL, ROBERT, a sailor in Massachusetts, eldest son of Robert Rentoul a mason in Middleton and Mary Preston, 1797. [NAS.CS17.1.16/25]

REOCH, ROBERT, a colormaker in Riverpoint, Rhode Island, around 1875, possibly from Grahamston, Renfrewshire. [NAS.SH.1875]

REYNOLDS, DAVID, a chapman in New England, admitted as a member of the Scots Charitable Society of Boston in 1685.[SCS]

RICH, HENRY, admitted as a member of the Scots Charitable Society of Boston in 1731. [SCS]

RICHARDS, JOHN, emigrated to New England, settled in Boston, married Priscilla Bass on 23 November 1720. [ImmNE#164]

RICHARDSON, COLIN, from Perthshire, admitted as a member of the Scots Charitable Society of Boston in 1818. [SCS]

RICHARDSON, ROBERT, admitted as a member of the Scots Charitable Society of Boston in 1799. [SCS]

RICHIE, ALEXANDER, emigrated to New England in 1736, settled in Windham, New Hampshire. [ImmNE#164]

RICHIE, JOHN, MD, admitted as a member of the Scots Charitable Society of Boston in 1731. [SCS]

RIDDOCH, ALEXANDER, admitted as a member of the Scots Charitable Society of Boston in 1690. [SCS]

RIDDOCH, SAMUEL, admitted as a member of the Scots Charitable Society of Boston in 1690. [SCS]

RIDLON, MAGNUS, born 1674 in Orkney, settled in York, Saco, Maine, married (1) Susannah Young, (2) Maisie Townsend, father of Mathias, died 1771. [Imm.NE#165]

RILLEY, HUGH, from Irvine, Ayrshire, admitted as a member of the Scots Charitable Society of Boston in 1772. [SCS]

RINTOUL, ROBERT, born in 1753, from Middleton, Kinross-shire, emigrated to New England in1769, settled in Salem, Massachusetts, died on 17 July 1816. [ImmNE#161]

RIOCH, KENNETH, in Boston, New England, probate October 1802 PCC

RITCHIE, ANDREW, a merchant in Boston, 1769.
[NAS.CS16.1.134/250]; a Loyalist in Boston 1776, with wife Margaret MacNeish and daughter Ann moved to Annapolis, Nova Scotia, by 1784. [NENS#127] [PRO.AO12.10.157] admitted as a member of the Scots Charitable Society of Boston in 1799. [SCS]

RITCHIE, ANDREW, jr., admitted as an member of the Scots Charitable Society of Boston in 1806. [SCS]

RITCHIE, ARCHIBALD, possibly from Port Glasgow, settled in Reigate before 1861. [NAS.SH.11.3.1861]

RITCHIE, JOHN, from Aberdeen, admitted as a member of the Scots Charitable Society of Boston in 1729. [SCS]

RITCHIE, JOHN, from Glasgow, admitted as a member of the Scots Charitable Society of Boston in 1732. [SCS]

RITCHIE, JOHN, from Irvine, Ayrshire, admitted as a member of the Scots Charitable Society of Boston in 1766. [SCS]

RITCHIE, JOHN, born in Glasgow around 1745, married (1) Janet ..., emigrated to America, a merchant and office holder in Boston, married (2) Maria Le Cain, settled in Annapolis Royal, Nova Scotia, around 1775, died 20 July 1790. [DCB]

RITCHIE, ROBERT, from Glasgow, admitted as a member of the Scots Charitable Society of Boston in 1758. [SCS]

RITCHIE, WILLIAM, admitted as a member of the Scots Charitable Society of Boston in 1805. [SCS]

ROBB, JAMES admitted as a member of the Scots Charitable Society of Boston in 1691. [SCS]

ROBB, JAMES, from Whithorn, Galloway, admitted as a member of the Scots Charitable Society of Boston in 1756. [SCS]

ROBB, JOHN, settled in Ackworth, New Hampshire, died in 1799. [ImmNE#166]

ROBERTON, JOHN, admitted as a member of the Scots Charitable Society of Boston in 1713. [SCS]

ROBERTSON, ALEXANDER, emigrated to New England by 1773, settled in Norwich, Connecticut, died in Shelbourne, Nova Scotia, in 1784. [ImmNE#166]

ROBERTSON, ARCHIBALD, a merchant in New London, New England, 1742, 1743, 1744. [NAS.CS16.1.71/72/75]

ROBERTSON, ARCHIBALD, born in 1708, emigrated to New England in 1754, settled in Chesterfield, New Hampshire. [ImmNE#166]

ROBERTSON, DONALD, born in 1831, immigrated into Massachusetts on 15 August 1850 aboard the bark Eclipse. [LAP]

ROBERTSON, JAMES, from Kirkcudbright, admitted as a member of the Scots Charitable Society of Boston in 1759. [SCS]

ROBERTSON, JAMES, a printer and bookseller in Edinburgh, later a newspaper publisher in Charleston, South Carolina, a printer in Boston and in New York, settled in Nova Scotia during 1783. [NAS.CS236.R12/3]

ROBERTSON, JAMES, settled in Norwich, Connecticut, by 1773, moved to Edinburgh. [ImmNE#167]

ROBERTSON, JANET, or CROOM, in Boston, 26 May 1854. [NAS.RS.Edinburgh#65/117]

ROBERTSON, JOHN, a shipmaster from Campbeltown, admitted as a member of the Scots Charitable Society of Boston in 1767. [SCS]

ROBERTSON, JOHN, a house carpenter, arrived in Boston on 17 August 1767 aboard the snow Jenny, master Hector Orr, from Glasgow. [PAB]

ROBERTSON, JOHN, a printer from Stonehaven, Kincardineshire, admitted as a member of the Scots Charitable Society of Boston in 1767. [SCS]

ROBERTSON, MARGARET, emigrated from Greenock aboard the brigantine Matty, master Thomas Cochrane, on 19 May 1774 bound for New York, arrived there on 22 July 1774, settled Barnet, Vermont. [HBV]

ROBERTSON, METHVEN, in Millbury, Worcester, [New England?] 1856. [NAS.SH.6.11.1856]

ROBERTSON, PATRICK, a prisoner of war transported to New England on the John and Sarah of London, master John Greene in November 1651. [Suffolk Deeds, 1-56]

ROBERTSON, PATRICK, son of William Robertson and Agnes Fleming, a merchant baillie of Edinburgh, settled in New London, New England, by 1742. [NAS.RD4.211.547][NAS.CS16.1.70/71/75]

ROBERTSON, ROBERT, from Edmonstone, Midlothian, admitted as a member of the Scots Charitable Society of Boston in 1767. [SCS]

ROBERTSON, ROBERT, with his wife and child, emigrated from Greenock aboard the brigantine Matty, master Thomas Cochrane, on 19 May 1774 bound for New York, arrived there on 22 July 1774, settled Barnet, Vermont. [HBV]

ROBERTSON, SAMUEL admitted as a member of the Scots Charitable Society of Boston in 1829. [SCS]

ROBERTSON, WILLIAM, admitted as a member of the Scots Charitable Society of Boston in 1802. [SCS]

ROBERTSON, WILLIAM, in Carlisle Street, Newhaven, Connecticut, cnf 1898. [NAS.SC70.1.368]

ROBINSON, ALESTER, a prisoner of war transported to New England on the John and Sarah of London, master John Greene in November 1651. [Suffolk Deeds, 1-56]

ROBINSON, CHARLES, a prisoner of war transported to New England on the John and Sarah of London, master John Greene in November 1651. [Suffolk Deeds, 1-56]

ROBINSON, DANIEL, a prisoner of war transported to New England on the John and Sarah of London, master John Greene in November 1651. [Suffolk Deeds, 1-56]

ROBINSON, GEORGE, a merchant, arrived in Boston on 30 May 1767 on the Mary, master William Welchman, from Glasgow. [PAB]

ROBINSON, JAMES, a prisoner of war transported to New England on the John and Sarah of London, master John Greene in November 1651. [Suffolk Deeds, 1-56]

ROBINSON, JOHN, a prisoner of war transported to New England on the John and Sarah of London, master John Greene in November 1651. [Suffolk Deeds, 1-56]

ROBINSON, JOHN, born in Edinburgh during 1817, a barber, settled in Edgarstown, Massachussetts, by 1850. [C]

ROBINSON, JAMES, admitted as a member of the Scots Charitable Society of Boston in 1698. [SCS]

ROBINSON, JOHN, born in Edinburgh 16 September 1816, a barber, settled in Edgarstown, Dukes County, Massachusetts, by 1850. [C]

ROBISON, DAVID, admitted as a member of the Scots Charitable Society of Boston in 1695. [SCS]

ROBISON, JOHN, admitted to the Scots Charitable Society of Boston in 1726. [SCS]

ROBISON, JOHN, a carpenter, arrived in Boston on 26 July 1764 aboard the snow Douglas, master Robert Manderston, from Greenock. [PAB]

ROBISON, PATRICK, admitted as a member of the Scots Charitable Society of Boston in 1731. [SCS]

ROCHEAD, JOHN, from Jamaica, admitted as a member of the Scots Charitable Society of Boston in 1716. [SCS]

RODGERS, MENEVITH, from Greenock, admitted as a member of the Scots Charitable Society of Boston in 1748. [SCS]

ROLAND, WILLIAM, admitted as a member of the Scots Charitable Society in 1725. [SCS]

ROLLO, MARGARET, wife of George Lumsden from Cupar, Fife, died in Norwich, Connecticut, on 10 July 1886. [PJ]

ROLLO, WILLIAM, from Edinburgh, admitted as a member of the Scots Charitable Society of Boston in 1766. [SCS]

ROME, GEORGE, a merchant in Newport, Rhode Island, a Loyalist in 1776, later in London. [PRO.AO12.72.93]

ROSE, DERMOT, a prisoner of war captured after the Battle of Dunbar in September 1650, transported from London on 3 November 1650 on the Unity to New England, an indentured servant, settled on Block Island. [NWI]

ROSS, ALESTER, a prisoner of war transported to New England on the John and Sarah of London, master John Greene in

November 1651. [Suffolk Deeds, 1-56]

ROSS, ALEXANDER, born in Stroma, Orkney, on 19 October 1717, married Elizabeth ..... in Portland, Maine, died in Falmouth, Maine, on 24 November 1768. [Imm.NE#169][PRO.AO12.11.42]

ROSS, ALEXANDER, admitted as a member of the Scots Charitable Society of Boston in 1802. [SCS]; in Boston, Suffolk County, Massachusetts, 1809. [NAS.RD4.293.814]

ROSS, CATHERINE, eldest daughter of William Ross from Kirkcaldy, Fife, married James Milne Smith from Edinburgh, in Boston on 2 July 1857. [FJ]

ROSS, DANIEL, a prisoner of war transported to New England on the John and Sarah of London, master John Greene in November 1651. [Suffolk Deeds, 1-56]

ROSS, DANIEL, admitted as a member of the Scots Charitable Society of Boston in 1714. [SCS]

ROSS, DAVID, a prisoner of war transported to New England on the John and Sarah of London, master John Greene in November 1651. [Suffolk Deeds, 1-56]

ROSS, Mrs ELIZABETH, born 1 January 1721 in South Ronaldsay, Orkney, married Alexander Ross, died in Gorham, Maine, on 1 March 1798. [Imm.NE#169]

ROSS, JAMES, a prisoner of war transported to New England on the John and Sarah of London, master John Greene in November 1651. [Suffolk Deeds, 1-56]

ROSS, JAMES, from Galloway, admitted as a member of the Scots Charitable Society of Boston in 1732. [SCS]

ROSS, JAMES, settled in Gorham, Maine, by 1758, died in 1780. [ImmNE#170]

ROSS, JOHN, a prisoner of war transported to New England on the John and Sarah of London, master John Greene in November 1651. [Suffolk Deeds, 1-56]

ROSS, JOHN, a prisoner of war captured after the Battle of Dunbar in September 1650, transported from London on 3 November 1650 on the Unity to New England, an indentured servant in Kittery, Maine, around 1656. [NWI]

ROSS, JOHN, admitted as a member of the Scots Charitable Society of Boston in 1803. [SCS]

ROSS, JONAS, a prisoner of war transported to New England on the John and Sarah of London, master John Greene in November 1651. [Suffolk Deeds, 1-56]

ROSS, MARTHA, fifth daughter of Alexander Ross in Williamston, Aberdeenshire, married John Bruce, a stonecutter, in Boston on 24 September 1872. [AJ#6511]

ROSS, WILLIAM, in Westerly, Rhode Island, died during 1712, probate 12 June 1712 Rhode Island

ROSS, WILLIAM, admitted as a member of the Scots Charitable Society of Boston in 1720. [SCS]

ROSS, WILLIAM, from Ross-shire, admitted as a member of the Scots Charitable Society of Boston in 1748. [SCS]

ROSS, WILLIAM, from "Tain near Aberdeen", admitted as a member of the Scots Charitable Society of Boston in 1755. [SCS]

ROSS, WILLIAM, a stonecutter in Quincy, cnf 1893. [NAS.SC70.1.322]

ROW, JAMES, a prisoner of war transported to New England on the John and Sarah of London, master John Greene in November 1651. [Suffolk Deeds, 1-56]

ROWAN, ANDREW, MD, admitted as a member of the Scots Charitable Society of Boston in 1717. [SCS]

ROWANS, ARCHIBALD, emigrated from Scotland via Nova Scotia to Boston. Sought by his brother William Rowans in Fitchburg, Massachusetts, during 1842. [BP: 21.5.1842]

ROXBURGH, WILLIAM, admitted as a member of the Scots Charitable Society in 1723. [SCS]

ROY, ALEXANDER, admitted as a member of the Scots Charitable Society of Boston in 1832. [SCS]

ROYE, DONALD, Scots prisoner of war transported from London to Boston on the John and Sarah of London, master John Green, in May 1652. [Suffolk Deeds, I, 5-6]

ROY, JOHN, a mariner, admitted as a member of the Scots Charitable Society of Boston in 1685. [SCS]

ROY, PETER, born in 1812, son of Joh Roy and Mary Davidson in Balquhairn, Logie, Stirlingshire, settled in Pittsfield, Massachusetts, died there on 24 December 1840. [Logie g/s, Stirlingshire]

RULE, HENRY, born 1765, arrived in America in 1802, a farmer in Sunderland, Bennington County, Vermont, in 1812. [1812]

RULE, JAMES, admitted as a member of the Scots Charitable Society of Boston in 1800. [SCS]

RUNCIMAN, ROBERT INGLIS, son of Reverend David Runciman in Glasgow, married Mary Spring, third daughter of Andrew Spring of Portland, Maine, in Buenos Ayres on 24 April 1876. [EC#288576]

RUSSELL, ALEXANDER, from Tweeddale, Berwickshire, admitted as a member of the Scots Charitable Society of Boston in 1749. [SCS]

RUSSELL, DAVID, born during 1749, a cooper, emigrated via London to Boston on the Success in February 1774. [PRO.T47/9-11]

RUSSELL, JAMES, from Edinburgh, admitted as a member of the Scots Charitable Society of Boston in 1745. [SCS]

RUSSELL, JOHN, from Glasgow, admitted as a member of the Scots Charitable Society of Boston in 1755, [SCS]; in

Boston, New England, cnf 29 September 1777
Commissariat of Edinburgh. [NAS.CC8.8.122]

RUSSELL, JOHN, admitted as a member of the Scots Charitable
Society of Boston in 1801. [SCS]

RUSSELL, ROBERT, admitted as a member of the Scots
Charitable Society in 1727. [SCS]

RUSSELL, ROBERT, born 1842, late of Kinghorn and of Lanark,
died in Gilbertville, Massachusetts, on 28 December 1900.
[FFP]

RUSSELL, SAMUEL, a merchant in Marblehead, Essex County,
Massachusetts Bay, 1722. [NAS.GD155.705]

RUSSELL, SIMON, a prisoner of war transported to New England
on the John and Sarah of London, master John Greene in
November 1651. [Suffolk Deeds, 1-56]

RUSSELL, THOMAS, admitted to the Scots Charitable Society of
Boston in 1696. [SCS]

RUSSELL, THOMAS C., a baker, son of James Russell in
Freuchie, Fife, married Charlotte, second daughter of John
Sutherland from Helmsdale, in Hudson, Massachusetts, on
16 October 1889, their infant son died there on 12 August
1891. [PJ]

RUSSELL, WILLIAM, a mason, arrived in Boston on 18 November
1767 from Glasgow on the Glasgow, Captain John Dunn.
[PAB]

RUSSELL, WILLIAM, born 1751, a farmer from Cupar, Fife,
emigrated via Greenock to Salem on the Glasgow Packet,
master Alexander Porterfield, in April 1775. [PRO.T47/12]

RUSSELL, WILLIAM, born 28 April 1798 son of Alexander Russell
and Janet Jamieson in Glasgow, educated at Glasgow
University 1811, emigrated to Savannah, Georgia, 1819,
Head Teacher of Chatham Academy, a teacher in
Massachusetts, died in Lancaster, Massachusetts, 17 May
1873. [MAGU#259]

RUTHERFORD, WALTER, admitted as a member of the Scots Charitable Society of Boston in 1742. [SCS]

RUTHERFORD, WILLIAM, from Teviotdale, admitted as a member of the Scots Charitable Society in 1748. [SCS]

RUTHVEN, JAMES, born in Edinburgh during 1783, son of John Ruthven and Elizabeth Irvin, a horner and cutler in New York and in Bridgeport, Connecticut, died 25 November 1855. [ANY.2.111]

RUXTON, JOHN, a prisoner of war captured after the Battle of Dunbar in September 1650, transported from London on 3 November 1650 on the Unity to New England, an indentured servant at the Lynn Ironworks in Massachusetts. [NWI]

RYND, WILLIAM, from Stirling, surgeon on HMS Rose, admitted as a member of the Scots Charitable Society of Boston in 1743. [SCS]

ST CLAIR, JOHN, from Lybster, Caithness, settled in Exeter, New Hampshire, during 1656. [AA#10/23]

SANDELAND, JAMES, admitted as a member of the Scots Charitable Society of Boston in 1687. [SCS]

SANDEMAN, ROBERT, born in Perth during 1718, educated at Edinburgh University, a linen merchant then a minister, married a daughter of the Reverend John Glass of Tealing, Angus, emigrated to Boston in 1764, landed on 18 October 1764, settled in Danbury, Massachusetts, died on 2 April 1771. [TSA][SN#3/401][ImmNE#172][Pa.Chron:22.4.1771]

SANGSTER, WILLIAM, born 1787, arrived from Scotland in 1809, a dyer in Norwalk, Connecticut, in 1812. [1812]

SAVAGE, EDWARD, born in Loudoun, Ayrshire, emigrated via Ireland to New England before 1727. [Imm.NE#173]

SCOBIE, JAMES, admitted as a member of the Scots Charitable Society of Boston in 1801. [SCS]

SCOBIE, JAMES G., admitted as a member of the Scots
Charitable Society of Boston in 1827. [SCS]

SCOBIE, JOHN, admitted as a member of the Scots Charitable
Society of Boston in 1826. [SCS]

SCOBIE, WILLIAM, in Boston around 1830, grandson of Catherine
Tainsh or Scobie in Auchterarder, Perthshire.
[NAS.SH.1830]

SCOLLAY, JAMES, admitted as a member of the Scots Charitable
Society of Boston in 1713. [SCS]

SCOLLAY, JAMES, jr., admitted as a member of the Scots
Charitable Society of Boston in 1716. [SCS]

SCOLLAY, JOHN, admitted as a member of the Scots Charitable
Society of Boston in 1731. [SCS]

SCOLLAY, JOHN, admitted as a member of the Scots Charitable
Society of Boston in 1737, a resident of Boston in 1787.
[SCS]

SCOTLAND, LAWRENCE, born 1678, emigrated from Liverpool to
New England on the Virginia Merchant in March 1699.
[LRO.HQ.3252.Fre]

SCOTT, ANDREW, admitted as a member of the Scots Charitable
Society of Boston in 1687. [SCS]

SCOTT, ANDREW, admitted to the Scots Charitable Society of
Boston in 1696. [SCS]

SCOTT, ANDREW, born in Paisley, Renfrewshire, died in
Portland, USA, during September 1818. [DPCA]

SCOTT, ARCHIBALD, born 1795, a butcher, landed in Boston
during 1821 from the brig Missionary, Captain Sears.
[USNA/par]

SCOTT, GIDEON, admitted as a member of the Scots Charitable
Society of Boston in 1800. [SCS]; a merchant in Boston,
second son of James Scott a farmer in Shelfhill,

Roxburghshire,1816. [NAS.CS17.1.35/167,636]

SCOTT, HUGH, from Glasgow, admitted as a member of the Scots Charitable Society of Boston in 1731. [SCS]

SCOTT, JAMES, a tailor, admitted as a member of the Scots Charitable Society of Boston in 1703. [SCS]

SCOTT, JAMES, admitted as a member of the Scots Charitable Society of Boston in 1712. [SCS]

SCOTT, JAMES, from Greenock, admitted as a member of the Scots Charitable Society of Boston in 1731. [SCS]

SCOTT, JAMES, from Greenock, admitted as a member of the Scots Charitable Society of Boston in 1748. [SCS]

SCOTT, JAMES, junior, from Glasgow, admitted as a member of the Scots Charitable Society of Boston in 1758. [SCS]

SCOTT, JOHN, a prisoner of war transported to New England on the John and Sarah of London, master John Greene in November 1651. [Suffolk Deeds, 1-56]

SCOTT, JOHN, admitted as a member of the Scots Charitable Society of Boston in 1687. [SCS]

SCOTT, JOHN, from Renfrew, admitted as a member of the Scots Charitable Society of Boston in 1747. [SCS]

SCOT, JOHN, settled in Ryegate, Vermont, on 16 April 1775. [VHS]

SCOTT, ROBERT, a cabinetmaker in Boston around 1866, son of William Scott a slater in Hawick, Roxburghshire. [NAS.SH.1866]

SCOTT, MATHEW, from Glasgow, admitted as a member of the Scots Charitable Society of Boston in 1756. [SCS]

SCOTT, NINIAN, from Greenock on the brigantine Matty, master Thomas Cochrane, on 19 May 1774 bound for New York, arrived 22 July 1774, settled Barnet, Vermont. [HBV]

SCOTT, Captain ROBERT, an officer, arrived in Boston on 22 August 1765 on the Jamieson and Peggy, John Aitken, from Leith. [PAB]

SCOTT, THOMAS, pro September 1663 Salem, Massachusetts

SCOTT, WILLIAM, admitted as a member of the Scots Charitable Society of Boston in 1686. [SCS]

SCOTT, WILLIAM, from Virginia, admitted as a member of the Scots Charitable Society of Boston in 1694. [SCS]

SCOTT, WILLIAM, admitted as a member of the Scots Charitable Society in 1727. [SCS]

SCOTT, WILLIAM, from Glasgow, admitted as a member of the Scots Charitable Society of Boston in 1757. [SCS]

SCOTT, WILLIAM, master of the brig Charlotte of Boston, cnf 27.3.1780 Commissariot of Edinburgh. [NAS.CC8.8.125]

SCROOGIE, GEORGE, admitted as a member of the Scots Charitable Society of Boston in 1689. [SCS]

SEAL, WILLIAM, arrived in Boston on 28 October 1763 aboard the Douglas, master James Montgomerie, from Scotland. [PAB]

SEATON, ANDREW, emigrated via Ireland to New England in 1740, settled in Andover, Massachusetts, and later in Amherst, New Hampshire. [ImmNE#175]

SEATON, GEORGE, admitted as a member of the Scots Charitable Society of Boston in 1731. [SCS]

SEATON, Sir HENRY, arrived in Boston on 22 August 1765 aboard the Jamieson and Peggy, master John Aitken, from Leith. [PAB]

SEATON, JOHN, born in 1724 son of John and Jane Seaton, emigrated via Ireland to New England during 1729, settled in Boxford, Massachusetts, and Washington, New Hampshire, died in 1793. [ImmNE#176]

SEATON, SAMUEL, son of John and Jane Seaton, emigrated to New England during 1729, married Ruth Smith on 2 December 1756, settled in Andover, Mass., and in Amherst, New Hampshire, died in Wenham, Mass., 1796. [ImmNE]

SEIRUIN, GEORGE, 'a youth for education', arrived in Boston from Glasgow on 12 April 1712 aboard the brigantine Success, master Andrew Gibson. [PTA#129]

SELKIRK, ANDREW, a seaman on HMS Drake, son of Jean Selkirk in Barnet, Caledonia County, North America, probate to James Ferguson attorney, January 1822 PCC

SELKIRK, JOHN, son of Robert Selkirk late merchant in Boston, Massachusetts, apprenticed to William Jameson, mason in Edinburgh, for 6 years, on 20 November 1788. [Edinburgh Register of Apprentices]

SELKRIG, ALEXANDER, merchant in Boston, Loyalist, moved to London in 1779. [PRO.AO12.109.278]

SELKRIGG, JAMES, from Shottstown, Lanarkshire, admitted as a member of the Scots Charitable Society of Boston in 1766. [SCS]; merchant in Boston, Loyalist in 1776, settled in Shelburne, Nova Scotia. [PRO.AO12.109.278]

SELKRIG, Mrs, wife of James Selkrig a merchant, with a child, arrived in Boston on 3 June 1766 aboard the George and James, master Robert Montgomery, from Scotland. [PAB]

SELKRIG, ROBERT, a merchant, arrived in Boston on 17 August 1767 aboard the snow Jenny, master Hector Orr, from Glasgow. [PAB]

SEMPLE, HUGH, from Renfrewshire, emigrated to America in April 1774, settled in Ryegate, New Hampshire. [HGP]

SEMPLE, JOHN, from Renfrew, arrived in Boston on 1 June 1768 aboard the snow Jenny, master Hector Orr, from Glasgow, admitted as a member of the Scots Charitable Society of Boston in 1773. [PAB][SCS]

SEMPLE, J., a currier in Ipswich, Massachusetts, husband of Mary Roberton, died there on 5 August 1857. [NAS.SH.13.7.1864]

SEMPLE, ROBERT, merchant in Boston before 1776, returned to Scotland. [PRO.AO13.43.69-89]

SEMPLE, THOMAS, admitted as a member of the Scots Charitable Society of Boston in 1799. [SCS]

SERVICE, GEORGE, merchant in Boston, Loyalist in 1776. [PRO.AO13.83.435]

SERVICE, JOSEPH, arrived in Boston on 19 September 1766 aboard the schooner Blackburn, master Edward Morrison, from Glasgow. [PAB]

SERVICE, ROBERT, from Saltcoats, Ayrshire, admitted as a member of the Scots Charitable Society of Boston in 1765. [SCS]; merchant in Boston, Loyalist in 1776. [PRO.AO13.83.435]

SERVICE, ROBERT, a merchant, arrived in Boston on 2 June 1769 from Glasgow on the Glasgow, Captain John Dunn. [PAB]

SERVICE, SAMUEL, of Sarviss, admitted as a member of the Scots Charitable Society of Boston in 1735. [SCS]

SHAND, DAVID, born on 13 April 1733, son of James Shand in Forgue, Aberdeenshire, admitted as a member of the Scots Charitable Society of Boston in 1766. [SCS]

SHAND, JOHN, son of Alexander Shand a carpenter in Aberdeen, an indentured servant of Robert Cumming a merchant in Boston, Massachusetts, died there in 1738. [APB.3.65]

SHANNON, NATHANIEL admitted as a member of the Scots Charitable Society of Boston in 1691. [SCS]

SHAW, JAMES, admitted as a member of the Scots Charitable Society of Boston in 1713. [SCS]

SHAW, JOHN, from Renfrewshire, emigrated to America in April 1774, settled in Ryegate, Vermont, before 1780. [VHS][HGP]

SHAW, JOHN, born in Greenock during 1811, emigrated to America in 1827, settled in Rockingham, New Hampshire, naturalised there in February 1839. [New Hampshire Nats.]

SHAW, WILLIAM, a clerk, to New England on 22 December 1714. [EMA#54]

SHEARER, THOMAS, admitted as a founder member of the Scots Charitable Society of Boston on 6 January 1657, boxmaster of the Society in July 1667. [SCS]

SHEDDEN, ..., born in 1811, second daughter of Thomas Shedden in Glasgow, and wife of Lieutenant Charles Jackson of the United States Navy, died in Middleton, Connecticut, on 9 July 1833. [SG#3.185/192]

SHERIFF, ANDREW, from Prestonpans, East Lothian, admitted as a member of the Scots Charitable Society of Boston in 1740. [SCS]

SHERIFF, WILLIAM, Commissary at Annapolis, admitted as a member of the Scots Charitable Society of Boston in 1717. [SCS]

SHERLOCK, ROBERT, a merchant, arrived in Boston on 27 June 1763 aboard the snow Jenny, master James Orr, from Scotland. [PAB]

SIM, ALEXANDER, and his family, from Renfrewshire, emigrated to America in April 1774, settled in Ryegate, New Hampshire. [HGP]

SIMSON, ALESTER, a prisoner of war transported to New England on the John and Sarah of London, master John Greene in November 1651. [Suffolk Deeds, 1-56]

SIMPSON, ALEXANDER, admitted as a founder member of the Scots Charitable Society of Boston on 6 January 1657. [SCS]

SIMPSON, ALEXANDER, admitted as a member of the Scots Charitable Society of Boston in 1721. [SCS]

SIMPSON, ANDREW, emigrated to New England during 1720, settled in Deerfield, New Hampshire. [ImmNE#181]

SIMSON, DANIEL, a prisoner of war transported to New England on the John and Sarah of London, master John Greene in November 1651. [Suffolk Deeds, 1-56]

SIMSON, DAVID, a prisoner of war transported to New England on the John and Sarah of London, master John Greene in November 1651. [Suffolk Deeds, 1-56]

SIMPSON, GILBERT, admitted as a member of the Scots Charitable Society of Boston in 1715. [SCS]

SIMPSON, JANE, born in 1843, daughter of William Simpson {1809-1865}, Provost of Whithorn, Wigtownshire, died in Boston on 18 September 1876. [Whithorn g/s]

SIMSON, JOHN, of Moyret, a merchant in Glasgow, then in New London, Connecticut, 1769/1772. [NAS.CS16.1.134/151]

SIMPSON, JOSEPH, a brickmaker, admitted as a member of the Scots Charitable Society of Boston in 1684. [SCS]

SIMPSON, JOSEPH, admitted as a member of the Scots Charitable Society of Boston in 1699. [SCS]

SIMSON, MATHEW, in New London, Connecticut, 1772. [NAS.CS16.1.151]

SIMSON, PATRICK, a prisoner of war transported to New England on the John and Sarah of London, master John Greene in November 1651. [Suffolk Deeds, 1-56]

SIMSON, PATRICK, of Maryland, admitted as a member of the Scots Charitable Society in 1727. [SCS]

SIMPSON, ROBERT, admitted as a member of the Scots Charitable Society of Boston in 1688. [SCS]

SIMPSON, ROBERT, born 1817, son of James Simpson, {1785-1856}, and Helen Williamson, {1780-1869}, died in Boston on 10 June 1841. [Cramond g/s, Midlothian]

SIMPSON, SAMUEL, admitted as a member of the Scots Charitable Society of Boston in 1688. [SCS]

SIMSON, SANDER, a prisoner of war transported to New England on the John and Sarah of London, master John Greene in November 1651. [Suffolk Deeds, 1-56]

SIMPSON, THOMAS, admitted as a member of the Scots Charitable Society of Boston in 1714. [SCS]

SIMPSON, THOMAS, from Bo'ness, West Lothian, emigrated to America by 1718, settled in Deerfield, New Hampshire. [ImmNE#177]

SIMPSON, THOMAS, admitted as a member of the Scots Charitable Society of Boston in 1732. [SCS]

SINCLAIR, ALEXANDER DOULL, born on 15 September 1828 son of Alexander Sinclair and Margaret Doull in Braemore, Berriedale, Caithness, a physician who emigrated to Boston during 1848. [SI#414]

SINCLAIR, HENRY, in Boston by 1737, [Hunter of Hunterstone MSS#54]; admitted as a member of the Scots Charitable Society of Boston in 1738. [SCS]

SINCLAIR, HENRY, son of Magnus Sinclair, of the merchant ship Wentworth, who died in Boston, New England, pro. February 1777 PCC

SINCLAIR, JAMES, in Boston during 1790, son of Donald Sinclair, a merchant, and Isobel Lamont in Inveraray, Argyll. [NAS.SH.1790]

SINCLAIR, JAMES, a blacksmith in Kilmacolm, Renfrewshire, then in Boston, father of a natural son Thomas Laird born 26 November 1850. [Kilmacolm OPR]

SINCLAIR, JAMES, born on 11 July 1827 son of Thomas Sinclair and Margaret Robertson in Penicuik, Midlothian, emigrated to New Haven, Connecticut, around 1855. [SI#409]

SINCLAIR, JOHN, settled in Exeter, New Hampshire, wife Deborah, father of James, John, Mary and Meribah, died 1699, pro 14 September 1700 New Hampshire. [NNQ#6/187]

SINCLAIR, JOHN, from Caithness, admitted as a member of the Scots Charitable Society of Boston in 1739. [SCS]

SINCLAIR, MALCOLM, youngest son of Archibald Sinclair in Balfron, Stirlingshire, died in City Hospital, Boston, on 11 April 1876. [EC#28573]

SINCLAIR, ROBERT, from Greenock, admitted as a member of the Scots Charitable Society of Boston in 1752. [SCS]

SINCLAIR, SOLOMON, a prisoner of war transported to New England on the John and Sarah of London, master John Greene in November 1651. [Suffolk Deeds, 1-56]

SINCLAIR, WILLIAM, admitted as a member of the Scots Charitable Society of Boston in 1728. [SCS]

SKINNER, JOHN, born in 1772, emigrated from Scotland to America in 1801, a shoemaker in Norwalk, Connecticut, in 1812. [1812]

SKINNER, WILLIAM, admitted as a member of the Scots Charitable Society of Boston in 1706. [SCS]

SLATER, GEORGE, a millwright, arrived in Boston on 26 July 1764 aboard the snow Douglas, master Robert Manderston, from Greenock. [PAB]

SLATER, PETER{?}, baptised on 8 April 1722 in Orphir, Orkney, son of Alexander Slater and Janet Groundwater, admitted as a member of the Scots Charitable Society of Boston in 1750. [SCS]

SLATER, SAMUEL, a cotton spinner, died in Rhode Island on 20 April 1835. [DGC:3.6.1835]

SLOANE, ELIZABETH, from Wigtownshire, married William McKenzie from Wigtownshire, in Wakefield, Massachusetts, on 24 December 1872. [EC#27554]

SLOOPER, JAMES, from Alloway, Ayrshire, admitted as a member of the Scots Charitable Society of Boston in 1733. [SCS]

SLOSS, JOHN, from Fairfield, admitted to the Scots Charitable Society of Boston in 1696. [SCS]; probate 2 March 1721 Fairfield, Connecticut

SLOZER, CHARLES, from Edinburgh, admitted as a member of the Scots Charitable Society of Boston in 1762. [SCS]

SMALL, ALEXANDER, in Boston, Suffolk County, Massachusetts, 1809. [NAS.RD4.293.814]; admitted as a member of the Scots Charitable Society of Boston in 1801. [SCS]

SMART, ALEXANDER, admitted as a member of the Scots Charitable Society of Boston in 1690. [SCS]

SMART, CATHERINE, born in 1836, immigrated into Massachusetts aboard the Isabel Stewart, a bark, on 16 July 1849. [LAP]

SMIBERT, JOHN, born in Edinburgh during 1688 son of John Smibert and Alison Bell, admitted as a member of the Scots Charitable Society of Boston in 1729, [SCS], a painter who died in Boston on 2 April 1751. [WA]

SMIBERT, WILLIAM, MD in Boston, admitted as a member of the Scots Charitable Society of Boston in 1765. [SCS]

SMITH, Reverend ANDREW, admitted as a member of the Scots Charitable Society of Boston in 1692. [SCS]

SMITH, ANDREW, from Douglas, Lanarkshire, settled in Ryegate, Vermont, on 6 October 1774, died there later that month. [Whitelaw pp., VHS]

SMITH, CECILIA, youngest daughter of John Smith in Dysart, Fife, wife of James McNair, from Dysart and Dunfermline, then in Bridgeport, Connecticut, died there on 9 January 1893. [FFP]

SMITH, DUNCAN, born in 1741, a farmer from Paisley, Renfrewshire, emigrated from Greenock to Salem on the Glasgow Packet, master Alexander Porterfield, in April 1775. [PRO.T47/12]

SMITH, GEORGE, admitted as a member of the Scots Charitable Society of Boston in 1719. [SCS]

SMITH, HENRY, a prisoner of war transported to New England on the John and Sarah of London, master John Greene in November 1651. [Suffolk Deeds, 1-56]

SMITH, JAMES, a sugar baker, admitted as a member of the Scots Charitable Society of Boston in 1684. [SCS]

SMITH, JAMES, born in Glencairn, Nithsdale, Dumfriesshire, during 1669, married Ann ... [1658-1741], died in Boston on 2 April 1732. [Imm.NE#183]

SMITH, JAMES, admitted as a member of the Scots Charitable Society of Boston in 1709. [SCS]

SMITH, JAMES, from Douglas, Lanarkshire, settled in Ryefield, Vermont, on 8 October 1774. [VHS]

SMITH, JOHN, born in Dunbarton during 1649, a sailor who settled in Boston during 1682, [PRO.HCA.Vol.81, Lopez V.Anthony, 1698]; admitted as a member of the Scots Charitable Society of Boston in 1684. [SCS]

SMITH, JOHN, admitted as a member of the Scots Charitable Society in 1727. [SCS]

SMITH, JOHN, from Birsay, Orkney, admitted as a member of the Scots Charitable Society of Boston in 1755. [SCS]

SMITH, JOHN, from Brechin, Angus, settled in Andover, Massachusetts, by 1878. [NAS.NRAS.2182]

SMITH, PETER, from Brechin, Angus, settled in Andover, Massachusetts, by 1878. [NAS.NRAS.2182]

SMITH, ROBERT, from Glasgow, admitted as a member of the Scots Charitable Society of Boston in 1730. [SCS]

SMITH, ROBERT LESLIE, born during 1863, son of John J. Smith and Isabella Walker, died in Providence, Rhode Island, on 21 February 1895. [St Andrews g/s, Fife]

SMITH, THOMAS, admitted as a member of the Scots Charitable Society of Boston in 1702. [SCS]

SMITH, THOMAS, admitted as a member of the Scots Charitable Society of Boston in 1714. [SCS]

SMITH, WILLIAM, a lockmaker, arrived in Boston on 27 June 1763 aboard the snow Jenny, master James Orr, from Scotland. [PAB]

SMITH, WILLIAM, in Cambridge, Massachusetts, during 1784. [NAS.CS17.1.3/140]

SMITHSON, JOHN, from Barbados, admitted as a member of the Scots Charitable Society of Boston in 1699. [SCS]

SMOLLETT, BENJAMIN, a surgeon, emigrated from Dunbarton to Plymouth, Massachusetts, during 1687, settled in Connecticut. [Anc.H.NE]

SOMERS, CLAUD, born in 1730, from Cambuslang, Lanarkshire, emigrated with his family to America, settled in Barnet, New Hampshire, during 1775. [HGP]

SOMERVILLE, JOHN, from Glasgow, admitted as a member of the Scots Charitable Society of Boston in 1743. [SCS]

SPEED, WILLIAM, admitted as a founder member of the Scots Charitable Society of Boston on 6 January 1657. [SCS]

SPEED, WILLIAM, born 1755, emigrated to New England, died in Boston 21 August 1808. [ImmNE#186][Copps Hill g/s]

SPENCE, PETER, from Orkney, admitted as a member of the Scots Charitable Society of Boston in 1764. [SCS]

SPENCE, ROBERT, admitted as a member of the Scots Charitable Society of Boston in 1805. [SCS]

SPENCE, THOMAS, from Orkney, admitted as a member of the Scots Charitable Society of Boston in 1760. [SCS]

SPENCER, ARCHIBALD, a male midwife from Edinburgh, who settled in Massachusetts in 17... [SA#179]

SPRATT, JOHN, a merchant from Wigtown, Galloway, admitted as a member of the Scots Charitable Society of Boston in 1685. [SCS]

SQUIRE, WILLIAM, a physician who settled in Massachusetts, died in 1731. [SA#180]

STANFORD, PETER, born 1805, died in Connecticut 16 December 1858. [Minigaff g/s, Kirkcudbrightshire]

STARK, ARCHIBALD, born in Glasgow during February 1687, son of James Stark and Katherine Hamilton, educated at Glasgow University, emigrated via Londonderry to New England in 1720, married Elizabeth Nicholas, settled in Londonderry, New Hampshire, and later in Derryfield, New Hampshire, died on 25 June 1758. [Imm.NE#187]

STARK, JESSIE, daughter of James Stark in Newton, Kirkcaldy, wife of John Millar, died in Somerville, Boston, on 10 April 1893. [FFP]

STARKY, ROBERT, admitted to the Scots Charitable Society of Boston in 1696. [SCS]

STARRETT, WILLIAM, born 1700, via Ireland to New England 1735, married Mary Gamble, died Dedham, Maine, 8 March 1769. [ImmNE#187]

STEEDMAN, ROBERT, soldier of Company C, the Maine Infantry Volunteers, died during the US Civil War 1861-1865. [Old Calton, Edinburgh, g/s]

STEEL, ARCHIBALD, from Saltcoats, Ayrshire, admitted as a member of the Scots Charitable Society of Boston in 1748. [SCS]

STEEL, GEORGE, admitted as a member of the Scots Charitable Society in 1723. [SCS]

STEEL, JOHN, in Hull, Nantucket, admitted as a member of the Scots Charitable Society of Boston in 1700. [SCS]

STEEL, ROBERT, from Edinburgh, admitted as a member of the Scots Charitable Society of Boston in 1756. [SCS]

STEEL, Captain THOMAS, admitted as a member of the Scots Charitable Society of Boston in 1686, overseer of the SCS poorbox for south Boston in 1713. [SCS]

STEELE, WILLIAM, emigrated from Greenock aboard the brigantine Matty, master Thomas Cochrane, on 19 May 1774 bound for New York, arrived on 22 July 1774, settled Barnet, Vermont. [HBV]

STEPHENSON, ALLEN, from Glasgow, admitted as a member of the Scots Charitable Society of Boston in 1758. [SCS]

STEPHENSON, JAMES, from Glasgow, admitted as a member of the Scots Charitable Society of Boston in 1733. [SCS]

STERLING, HUGH, born in Glasgow around 1722, settled in New England in 1746. [SG]

STERRETT, JAMES, arrived in Boston on 1 June 1768 aboard the snow Jenny, master Hector Orr, from Glasgow. [PAB]

STETSON, ROBERT, born in 1612, settled in Scituate, Massachusetts, before 1643. [AA#9/97]

STEUART, JAMES, a schoolmaster, member of the Scots Charitable Society of Boston 1684. [SCS]

STEUART, Sir JOHN, of Kettleston, son of George Steuart, surgeon apothecary in Boston, 1752. [NAS.CS16.1.89]

STEVENS, JOHN, from Orkney, admitted as a member of the Scots Charitable Society of Boston in 1750. [SCS]

STEVENSON, ANDREW, admitted as a member of the Scots Charitable Society of Boston in 1713. [SCS]

STEVENSON, GEORGE, admitted as a member of the Scots Charitable Society of Boston in 1799. [SCS]

STEVENSON, JAMES, MD, admitted as a member of the Scots Charitable Society of Boston in 1708. [SCS]

STEVENSON, JOHN, from Neilston, Renfrewshire, admitted as a member of the Scots Charitable Society of Boston in 1762. [SCS]

STEVENSON, ROBERT, a merchant, arrived in Boston on 15 November 1763 aboard the Diligence, master Charles Robison, from Glasgow. [PAB]

STEVENSON, THOMAS, from Renfrewshire, emigrated to New England 1763, settled in Boston, admitted as a member of the Scots Charitable Society of Boston in 1765. [ImmNE#189][SCS]

STEVENSON, WILLIAM, from Glasgow, admitted as a member of the Scots Charitable Society of Boston in 1747. [SCS]

STEWART, ALEXANDER, from Edinburgh, admitted as a member of the Scots Charitable Society of Boston in 1819. [SCS]

STEWART, ARCHIBALD, baptised on 27 September 1738, son of Archibald Stewart in Westray, Orkney, admitted as a member of the Scots Charitable Society of Boston in 1765. [SCS]

STEWART, AUSTIN, a prisoner of war transported to New England on the <u>John and Sarah of London</u>, master John Greene in November 1651. [Suffolk Deeds, 1-56]

STEWART, CHARLES, baptised on 26 May 1725, son of Charles Stewart and Marjory Traill in Kirkwall, Orkney, admitted as a member of the Scots Charitable Society of Boston in 1747. [SCS]

STEWART, CLAUD, from Glasgow, emigrated to America, settled in Barnet, New Hampshire, around 1775. [HGP]

STEWART, DUNCAN, born around 1623, a prisoner of war taken at Dunbar on 3 June 1650, transported to New England as an indentured servant, married Ann Winchurst in 1654, settled in Newbury, Massachusetts, died in Rowley, Essex, Massachusetts, on 30 August 1717. [SG#45.2.50]

STEWART, DUNCAN, Collector of Customs at New London, Connecticut, from 1764, a Loyalist in 1776, in Fort William, Inverness-shire, 1788. [PRO.AO12.104.40][NLS.CH3848]

STEWART, GEORGE, emigrated to New England during 1711, a physician and surgeon in Boston, admitted as a member of the Scots Charitable Society of Boston in 1711, overseer of the SCS poorbox in south Boston in 1713, died after 1730. [SA#180] [ImmNE#189][SCS]

STEWART, GILBERT, admitted as a member of the Scots Charitable Society of Boston in 1687. [SCS]

STEWART, GILBERT, admitted as a member of the Scots Charitable Society of Boston in 1761. [SCS]

STEWART, JAMES, admitted as a member of the Scots Charitable Society of Boston in 1685. [SCS]

STEWART, JAMES, admitted as a member of the Scots Charitable Society of Boston in 1717. [SCS]

STEWART, JAMES, from Edinburgh, admitted as a member of the Scots Charitable Society of Boston in 1740. [SCS]

STEWART, JAMES, admitted as a member of the Scots Charitable Society of Boston in 1830. [SCS]

STEWART, JESSIE, second daughter of David Stewart in Dunfermline, Fife, married Peter Thomson, in Norwood, Norfolk County, Massachusetts, on 17 June 1887. [DJ]

STEWART, JOHN, a prisoner of war captured after the Battle of Dunbar in September 1650, shipped from London on the Unity to Boston on 3 November 1650, an indentured servant at Lynn Ironworks in Massachusetts, purchased by John Pynchon, Springfield, Massachusetts, petitioned Governor Andros on 19 September 1688, died in New England 21 April 1691. [NWI]

STEWART, JOHN, admitted as a member of the Scots Charitable Society of Boston in 1713. [SCS]

STEWART, JOHN, admitted as a member of the Scots Charitable Society of Boston in 1722. [SCS]

STEWART, JOHN, a passenger on the Glasgow Packet, master Alexander Porterfield, bound for Boston, was recruited into the 84 th [Royal Highland Emigrant] Regiment on 23 October 1775. [NAS.GD174/2093]

STEWART, JOHN M. M., a law clerk from Osnaburg Street, Forfar, Angus, then in Quedneet, East Greenwich, Rhode Island, on 10 July 1871. [NAS.RS.Forfar#26/223]

STEWART, MARTHA, wife of John Morton from Dunfermline, Fife, died in Newhaven, Connecticut, on 7 July 1891. [DJ]

STEWART, NEIL, a prisoner of war transported to New England on the John and Sarah of London, master John Greene in November 1651. [Suffolk Deeds, 1-56]

STEWART, PATRICK, admitted as a member of the Scots Charitable Society of Boston in 1694. [SCS]

STEWART, PETER, from Banffshire, admitted as a member of the Scots Charitable Society of Boston in 1759. [SCS]

STEWART, ROBERT, a prisoner of war transported to New England on the <u>John and Sarah of London</u>, master John Greene in November 1651. [Suffolk Deeds, 1-56]

STEWART, ROBERT, admitted as a member of the Scots Charitable Society of Boston in 1694. [SCS]

STEWART, ROBERT, from Glasgow, emigrated via Ireland to New England in 1718, settled in Andover, Massachusetts. [Imm.NE#192]

STEWART, WALTER, settled in Barnet, Vermont, pre 1783. [VHS]

STEWART, WALTER, a druggist and general merchant, West River Street, Rhode Island, 20 August 1877. [NAS.RS.Forfar#33/253]

STEWART, WILLIAM, a prisoner of war transported to New England on the <u>John and Sarah of London</u>, master John Greene in November 1651. [Suffolk Deeds, 1-56]

STEWART, WILLIAM, probate April 1664 Salem, Massachusetts; administration to his widow Sara.

STEWART, WILLIAM, admitted as a member of the Scots Charitable Society of Boston in 1684. [SCS]

STEWART, WILLIAM, admitted as a member of the Scots Charitable Society in 1724. [SCS]

STEWART, WILLIAM MCMORINE, son of William Stewart in Caerlaverock, Dumfries-shire, died in Boston on 25 April 1823. [DGC, 3.6.1823]

STEWART, WILLIAM, admitted as a member of the Scots Charitable Society of Boston in 1828. [SCS]

STEWART, Mrs, widow of John Stewart who was washed overboard during their voyage from Liverpool to New York, was given charity by the Society on 11 February 1756. [SCS]

STIRLING, ALEXANDER, admitted as a member of the Scots Charitable Society of Boston in 1722. [SCS]

STIRLING, DAVID, a prisoner of war transported to New England on the <u>John and Sarah of London</u>, master John Greene in November 1651. [Suffolk Deeds, 1-56]

STIRLING, JAMES, from the Canary Islands, admitted as a member of the Scots Charitable Society in 1716. [SCS]

STIRLING, JOHN, a prisoner of war transported to New England on the <u>John and Sarah of London</u>, master John Greene in November 1651. [Suffolk Deeds, 1-56]

STIRLING, JOHN, admitted as a member of the Scots Charitable Society of Boston in 1698. [SCS]

STIRLING, JOHN, from Glasgow, admitted as a member of the Scots Charitable Society of Boston in 1756. [SCS]

STIRLING, WILLIAM, with his wife and two children, emigrated from Greenock aboard the brigantine <u>Matty</u>, master Thomas Cochrane, on 19 May 1774 bound for New York, arrived there on 22 July 1774, settled Barnet, Vermont. [HBV]

STIRRAT, DAVID, a mariner in Falmouth, Cumberland County, Massachusetts, 6 October 1786, son of David Stirrat, a mason in Gourock, parish of Innerkip, Renfrewshire. [NAS.RS81/12]

STODDART, FREDERICK, born in 1842, son of David Stoddart in Linbridgeford, Middlebie, Dumfries-shire, died in Calais, Maine, on 28 January 1874. [AO]

STRACHAN, GEORGE, born in 1842, son of William Strachan and Lizzie McEwan, died at Valley Falls, Rhode Island, on 17 March 1916. [Brechin Cathedral g/s, Angus]

STRACHAN, JAMES, son of Patrick Strachan, tailor burgess of Aberdeen, and Jean Rait in Aberdeen, a tailor who emigrated to Virginia in 1711, settled in Providence, Rhode Island, died in Jamaica before September 1723. [APB.2.153]

STRACHAN, PETER, born 1812, from Dunfermline, Fife, died in Newport, New Hampshire, on 7 February 1891. [DJ]

STRANG, WILLIAM, from South Ronaldsay, Orkney, admitted as a member of the Scots Charitable Society of Boston in 1739. [SCS]

STUART, GILBERT, born in Perth around 1719, settled in North Kingston, King's County, Rhode Island, before 1751, a snuff grinder, admitted as a member of the Scots Charitable Society of Boston during 1775, with wife Elizabeth Anthony, moved from Newport, Rhode Island, to Nova Scotia in 1775, died in 1793. [NENS#38][SCS][DAB#18/164][SCM#40/5]

STUART, ROBERT, emigrated from Glasgow to New England by 1719, settled in Amherst, New Hampshire. [ImmNE#192]

STUART, JOHN, born in Scotland 1682, emigrated 1718, settled in Windham, New Hampshire, died in 1741. [ImmNE#191]

STURROCK, MARGARET, settled in Frye Village, South Andover, Massachusetts, by 1862. [NAS.RH1/2.698]

SUMMER, JOHN, from Glasgow, admitted as a member of the Scots Charitable Society of Boston in 1731. [SCS]

SUTHERLAND, ALEXANDER, in Nantasket Road, near Boston, 1776.[NAS.GD153.box1]

SUTHERLAND, ANSELL, a prisoner of war transported to New England on the John and Sarah of London, master John Greene in November 1651. [Suffolk Deeds, 1-56]

SUTHERLAND, GEORGE, admitted as a member of the Scots Charitable Society of Boston in 1718. [SCS]

SUTHERLAND, GEORGE, admitted as a member of the Scots Charitable Society of Boston in 1803. [SCS]

SUTHERLAND, JAMES, a plasterer in Boston around 1870, nephew of Margaret Watt in Fochabers, Morayshire. [NAS.SH.1870]

SUTHERLAND, JOSEPH, settled in Horseneck, Connecticut, by 1736. [AA#1/77]

SUTHERLAND, PATRICK, a prisoner of war transported to New England on the John and Sarah of London, master John Greene in November 1651. [Suffolk Deeds, 1-56]

SWAN, JAMES, a merchant in Boston, 1778/1784; admitted as a member of the Scots Charitable Society of Boston in 1798. [SCS] [NAS.CS16.1.174; CS17.1.3/140; CS17.1.17.27; CS17.1.16/195]

SWANSTON, THOMAS, emigrated to America, settled in Barnet, New Hampshire, around 1775. [HGP]

SYM, ANDREW, from Glasgow, admitted as a member of the Scots Charitable Society of Boston in 1741. [SCS]

SYME, JAMES, a merchant in Massachusetts, then in Westminster, 1766. [NAS.CS16.1.125/85]

SYME, JAMES, from Glasgow then in Boston 2 December 1856. [NAS.RS.Forfar#18/146]

TAIT, JAMES, from St Olla, Orkney, seaman on HMS Captain, died in Boston, Massachusetts, pro August 1774 PCC

TANDY, ABEL, emigrated to New England, married Rachel Smith 5 November 1751, settled in Salisbury, New Hampshire, died on 19 May 1797. [ImmNE#193]

TANNHILL, JOHN, a prisoner of war transported to New England on the John and Sarah of London, master John Greene in November 1651. [Suffolk Deeds, 1-56]

TARBET, HUGH, from Glasgow, admitted as a member of the Scots Charitable Society of Boston in 1756, [SCS]; a merchant in Boston, 1769. [NAS.CS16.1.134/294]

TASSIE, WILLIAM, born in 1748, a smith from Glasgow, emigrated from Greenock on the Glasgow Packet, master Alexander Porterfield, to Salem in April 1775. [PRO.T47.12] settled in Groton, Vermont, 1795. [Vermont History#23.96]

TATE, JAMES, admitted as a member of the Scots Charitable Society of Boston in 1731. [SCS]

TATE, JOHN, admitted as a member of the Scots Charitable Society of Boston in 1716. [SCS]

TAYLOR, ABRAHAM, admitted as a member of the Scots Charitable Society in 1724. [SCS]

TAYLOR, ABRAHAM, a shipmaster in Aberdeen, then a ships chandler in Boston 1753. [NAS.CS16.1.92/85]

TAYLOR, ARCHIBALD, and family, settled in Ryegate, Vermont, on 1 February 1775. [VHS]

TAYLOR, ELIZABETH, born during 1738, daughter of Robert Taylor and Jean Innes in Elgin, Morayshire, emigrated to New York in 1772, settled in Stamford, Connecticut. [AA#8/223]

TAYLOR, HUGH, from Orkney, admitted as a member of the Scots Charitable Society of Boston 1757. [SCS]

TAYLOR, JAMES, a prisoner of war captured after the Battle of Dunbar in September 1650, transported from London on 3 November 1650 on the Unity to New England, an indentured servant at the Lynn Ironworks in Massachusetts. [NWI]

TAYLOR, JAMES, from Leith, admitted as a member of the Scots Charitable Society of Boston in 1711. [SCS]

TAYLOR, JOHN, a prisoner of war captured after the Battle of Dunbar in September 1650, transported from London on 3 November 1650 on the Unity to New England, an indentured servant in Kittery, Maine, around 1656. [NWI]; in Berwick, Maine, husband of Martha ..., probate 23 February 1691 Maine Register of Deeds RD5/55. [refers to daughter Katherine Cahan, daughter Mary Taylor, daughter Sarah Taylor, daughter Deliverance Taylor, and Abigail Taylor]

TAYLOR, LAWRENCE, son of James and Margaret Taylor from Markinch, Fife, died in Providence, Rhode Island, on 1 November 1887. [FFP]

TAYLOR, MATTHEW, from Ayrshire, settled in Londonderry, New Hampshire, during 1722. [AA#7/209]

TAYLOR, PETER, baptised 29 December 1728, son of Peter Taylor and Isobel Smith in Stromness, Orkney, admitted as a member of the Scots Charitable Society of Boston 1762. [SCS]

TAYLOR, ROBERT, from Edinburgh, admitted as a member of the Scots Charitable Society of Boston in 1731. [SCS]

TAYLOR, ROBERT, born in Scotland during 1688, settled in Newport, Rhode Island, as a surveyor, died on 26 November 1762. [NHM#2/234]

TAYLOR, WILLIAM, a lad, arrived in Boston on 22 August 1765 aboard the Jamieson and Peggy, master John Aitken, from Leith. [PAB]

TAYLOR, WILLIAM, son of provost Taylor of Kinghorn, Fife, emigrated to America during 1888, settled in Anconia, Connecticut, died 11 December 1889. [FFP, 1.12.1890]

TEAR, ELIZABETH, arrived in Boston on 28 October 1763 aboard the Douglas, master James Montgomerie, from Scotland. [PAB]

TELLER, DAVID, a prisoner of war transported to New England on the John and Sarah of London, master John Greene in November 1651. [Suffolk Deeds, 1-56]

TELLER, WILLIAM, a prisoner of war transported to New England on the John and Sarah of London, master John Greene in November 1651. [Suffolk Deeds, 1-56]

TENLER, DAVID, a prisoner of war transported to New England on the John and Sarah of London, master John Greene in November 1651. [Suffolk Deeds, 1-56]

TENLER, JOHN, a prisoner of war transported to New England on the John and Sarah of London, master John Greene in November 1651. [Suffolk Deeds, 1-56]

TENLER, ROBERT, a prisoner of war transported to New England on the <u>John and Sarah of London</u>, master John Greene in November 1651. [Suffolk Deeds, 1-56]

TERRIS, ANDREW, a prisoner of war transported to New England on the <u>John and Sarah of London</u>, master John Greene in November 1651. [Suffolk Deeds, 1-56]

THOM, JAMES AIMER, graduated MB, CM, from Glasgow University in 1888, later in Olneyville, Providence, Rhode Island. [MAGU#604]

THOMSON, ALEXANDER, a prisoner of war transported to New England on the <u>John and Sarah of London</u>, master John Greene in November 1651. [Suffolk Deeds, 1-56]

THOMPSON, Reverend ALEXANDER, settled in Andover, Massachusetts, and later in Stoningham, Connecticut. [AA#5/104]

THOMSON, ALEXANDER, from Montrose, Angus, admitted as a member of the Scots Charitable Society in 1733. [SCS]

THOMSON, ANDREW, admitted as a member of the Scots Charitable Society of Boston in 1715. [SCS]

THOMSON, ANDREW, admitted as a member of the Scots Charitable Society of Boston in 1722. [SCS]

THOMSON, DANIEL, admitted as a member of the Scots Charitable Society of Boston in 1693. [SCS]

THOMSON, DAVID, born around 1588, married Amias Cole in Plymouth, England, during 1613, settled in Piscataqua, New Hampshire, in 1623, died on Thomson's Island, Boston Harbor, Massachusetts,around 1628. [SG#45.2.75; 46.2.41; 47.4.131]

THOMSON, DAVID, baptised on 16 December 1734, son of David Thomson and Isobel Miller in Stromness, Orkney, admitted as a member of the Scots Charitable Society of Boston in 1763. [SCS]

THOMSON, GEORGE, a prisoner of war captured after the Battle of Dunbar in September 1650, transported from London on 3 November 1650 on the Unity to New England, an indentured servant at the Lynn Ironworks in Massachusetts. [NWI]; admitted as a founder member of the Scots Charitable Society of Boston on 6 January 1657. [SCS]

THOMSON, GEORGE, a soldier at Castle William, deceased by 5 February 1717. [SCS]

THOMSON, HENRY, admitted as a member of the Scots Charitable Society in 1723. [SCS]

THOMSON, JAMES, a prisoner of war captured after the Battle of Dunbar in September 1650, transported from London on 3 November 1650 on the Unity to New England, an indentured servant at the Lynn Ironworks in Massachusetts. [NWI]

THOMPSON, JAMES, born during 1680, an indentured servant, emigrated via Liverpool on the Virginia Merchant, master E. Ball to New England in March 1699. [LRO.HQ325.2FRE]

THOMSON, JAMES, from Orkney, admitted as a member of the Scots Charitable Society of Boston in 1756, a resident of Boston in 1787. [SCS]

THOMPSON, JAMES, a gardener from Hamilton, Lanarkshire, admitted as a member of the Scots Charitable Society of Boston in 1767, a resident of Boston in 1787. [SCS]

THOMSON, JAMES, born during 1733, a coal hewer from Glasgow, emigrated from Greenock on the Glasgow Packet, master Alexander Porterfield, to Salem in April 1775. [PRO.T47/12]

THOMPSON, JOSIAH, admitted as a member of the Scots Charitable Society of Boston in 1798. [SCS]

THOMPSON, Mrs MARGARET, born 1665, widow of William Thompson, emigrated via Londonderry to New England during 1718, settled in Ellington, Connecticut, died on 20 January 1752. [ImmNE]

THOMSON, ROBERT, admitted as a member of the Scots Charitable Society of Boston in 1735. [SCS]

THOMSON, WILLIAM, a prisoner of war captured after the Battle of Dunbar in September 1650, transported from London on 3 November 1650 on the Unity to New England, an indentured servant in Kittery, Maine, around 1656. [NWI]

THOMPSON, WILLIAM, admitted as a member of the Scots Charitable Society of Boston in 1826. [SCS]

THOMPSON, Mrs, and three children, arrived in Boston on 17 August 1767 on the snow Jenny, master Hector Orr, from Glasgow. [PAB]

THORBURN, GRANT, born in Dalkeith, Midlothian, on 18 February 1773, son of James Thorburn a nailmaker, emigrated from Leith to New York on the Providence in 1794, married (1) Rebecca Sickles in 1798, (2) Hannah Whartneby in 1801, and (3) ..... in 1853, a nailmaker, writer and seedsman, admitted as a member of the St Andrews Society of New York during 1824, died in New Haven, Connecticut, on 21 January 1863. [ANY]

THRIPLAND, JOHN, admitted as a member of the Scots Charitable Society of Boston in 1721. [SCS]

TILER, EVAN, a prisoner of war transported to New England on the John and Sarah of London, master John Greene in November 1651. [Suffolk Deeds, 1-56]

TILLOCH, MAGNUS, from Orkney, admitted as a member of the Scots Charitable Society of Boston in 1749, a resident of Boston in 1787. [SCS]

TODD, DAVID, a merchant in Suffield, Hartford County, Connecticut, 1785. [NAS.CS17.1.4/325]

TODD, HENRY, second son of Richard Todd in Balcomie, Fife, died in Boston, Massachusetts, on 25 December 1852. [FH]

TODD, JOHN, admitted to the Scots Charitable Society of Boston in 1726. [SCS]

TOSH, JAMES, from Kirkcaldy, Fife, admitted as a member of the Scots Charitable Society of Boston in 1771. [SCS]

TOSH, JOHN, a prisoner of war captured after the Battle of Dunbar in September 1650, transported from London on 3 November 1650 on the Unity to New England, an indentured servant at the Lynn Ironworks in Massachusetts. [NWI]

TOSH, WILLIAM, a prisoner of war captured after the Battle of Dunbar in September 1650, transported from London on 3 November 1650 on the Unity to New England, an indentured servant who settled on Block Island. [NWI]

TOSH, WILLIAM, New Shoreham, Rhode Island, died in 1685, probate 1685 Rhode Island.

TOUGH, ALISTAIR, a prisoner of war captured after the Battle of Worcester in 1651, transported from Gravesend, Kent, on the John and Sarah of London, master John Greene, to Boston in November 1651, arrived there on 13 May 1652. [NER]

TOWER, PATRICK, a prisoner of war transported to New England on the John and Sarah of London, master John Greene in November 1651. [Suffolk Deeds, 1-56]

TOWER, THOMAS, a prisoner of war captured after the Battle of Dunbar in September 1650, transported from London on 3 November 1650 on the Unity to New England, an indentured servant at the Lynn Ironworks in Massachusetts. [NWI]

TRAILL, GEORGE, from Kirkwall, Orkney, admitted as a member of the Scots Charitable Society of Boston in 1746. [SCS]

TRAILL, HENRY, baptised on 3 September 1720 {?} son of Patrick Traill and Isabel Kaa in Orkney, admitted as a member of the Scots Charitable Society of Boston in 1751. [SCS]

TRAILL, ISABEL, born in Lady parish, Orkney, 2 January 1736, daughter of Reverend Thomas Traill of Hobbister and Sibella Grant, married William Tate in Boston, USA, died on 17 May 1792. [F.7.264]

TRAILL, JOHN, admitted as a member of the Scots Charitable Society of Boston in 1729. [SCS]

TRAILL, JOHN, from Dundee, admitted as a member of the Scots Charitable Society of Boston in 1739. [SCS]

TRAILL, JOHN, from Kirkwall, Orkney, a merchant in Boston, Massachusetts, died before 1750. [Imm.NE#200]

TRAILL, PATRICK, admitted as a member of the Scots Charitable Society of Boston in 1713. [SCS]

TRAILL, PETER, from Kirkwall, Orkney, Lieutenant of the Royal Artillery, admitted as a member of the Scots Charitable Society of Boston in 1762. [SCS]

TRAILL, ROBERT, from Orkney, a merchant in Boston, Massachusetts, before 1756. [Imm.NE#200]; admitted as a member of the Scots Charitable Society in 1731. [SCS]

TRAILL, ROBERT, Customs Controller of Portsmouth, New England, son of William Traill, eldest son of William Traill a merchant in Kirkwall, Orkney, 1772. [NAS.CS16.1.148]; Customs Controller of Piscatuqua, New Hampshire, 1765-, Loyalist, later in London. [PRO.AO13.53.349][NLS.CH3847]

TRAILL, THOMAS, a lad, (to the care of James Traill in Boston) arrived in Boston on 21 October 1763 on board the brigantine Wolf, Captain William Hayes, from Kirkwall, Orkney Islands. [PAB]

TRAN, ALEXANDER, from Glasgow, admitted as a member of the Scots Charitable Society of Boston in 1735. [SCS]

TRAN, ARTHUR, admitted as a member of the Scots Charitable Society of Boston in 1711. [SCS]

TREMBLE, JAMES, from Dunbar, East Lothian, admitted as a member of the Scots Charitable Society of Boston in 1694. [SCS]

TRENT, MONROE, admitted as a member of the Scots Charitable Society in 1724. [SCS]

TRENT, WILLIAM, from Pennsylvania, admitted to the Scots Charitable Society of Boston in 1697. [SCS]

TROTTER, ALEXANDER, admitted as a member of the Scots Charitable Society of Boston in 1716. [SCS]

TRUMBLE, GEORGE, admitted as a founder member of the Scots Charitable Society of Boston on 6 January 1657. [SCS]

TUILL, JOHN, a merchant, arrived in Boston on 3 June 1766 aboard the George and James, Robert Montgomery, from Scotland. [PAB]

TURNBULL, ALEXANDER, in Westbarnmouth, New Hampshire, 1810. [NAS.CS17.1.30/290]

TURNBULL, JANET, born in 1839, daughter of Thomas Turnbull and Isabella Black, wife of John Ballentyne, died in Boston, Massachusetts, on 19 August 1907. [Galashiels g/s]

TURNBULL, JOHN, born on 29 January 1759, settled in Newcastle, Maine.[ImmNE#201]

TURNER, ANDREW, a merchant, arrived in Boston on 15 November 1763 aboard the Diligence, master Charles Robison, from Glasgow. [PAB]; from Greenock, admitted as a member of the Scots Charitable Society of Boston in 1764. [SCS]

TURNER, COLL JOHN, born in Greenock, Renfrewshire, on 3 January 1828, a printer, settled in Edgarstown, Dukes County, Massachussetts, by 1850. [C]

TURNER, ELIZABETH, born in Greenock on 18 April 1804, settled in Edgarstown, Dukes County, Massachusetts, by 1850. [C]

TURNER, ROBERT, from Greenock, admitted as a member of the Scots Charitable Society of Boston in 1733. [SCS]

TYTLER, JAMES, born on 17 December 1745, son of Reverend
George Tytler and Janet Robertson in Fearn, Angus,
educated in Edinburgh University in 1764, a chemist,
balloonist, and editor of the Encyclopedia Britannica in
Scotland, later emigrated to America, died in Salem,
Massachusetts, during 1805. [SA#180][F#5.397]

TYTLER, R., born 1724, Member of HM Council of New England,
died in Boston on 20 May 1771. [SM#33.390]

URE, ANDREW, admitted as a member of the Scots Charitable
Society of Boston in 1827. [SCS]

URE, JAMES, a shoemaker, arrived in Boston on 12 May 1768
aboard the brig Betsy, Captain John Smith, from Greenock.
[PAB]

URQUHART, ANN, born in 1837, immigrated into Massachusetts
aboard the Isabel Stewart, a bark, on 16 July 1849. [LAP]

URQUHART, Reverend JOHN, emigrated to New England in
1774, settled in Warren, Maine. [ImmNE#202]

URQUHART, RODERICK, admitted as a member of the Scots
Charitable Society of Boston in 1720. [SCS]

VANS, HUGH, admitted as a member of the Scots Charitable
Society of Boston in 1722. [SCS]; merchant in Boston
1731,1732, 1734, [NAS.AC7/36/506-512; AC9/1196;
AC7/40/86-115]

VANS, HEW, a merchant in Boston in 1750. [NAS.RD2.168.313]

VANS, JOHN, admitted as a member of the Scots Charitable
Society of Boston in 1742. [SCS]

VAUSS, HUGH, a merchant in Boston, eldest son of John Vauss a
merchant in Ayr, 1731/1743. [NAS.AC7.36.506; AC9.1196;
AC7.40.86; AC9.1297; ACA9.1425][NAS.CS16.1.72]

VEITCH, ANDREW, a tailor, admitted as a member of the Scots
Charitable Society of Boston in 1695. [SCS]

VEITCH, WILLIAM, a laborer, arrived in Boston on 22 August 1765 aboard the Jamieson and Peggy, master John Aitken, from Leith. [PAB]

VELLZON, ANDREW, baptised on 22 December 1725 in Birsay, Orkney, son of William Vellzon, member of the Scots Charitable Society of Boston in 1750. [SCS]

VETCH, SAMUEL, born in Edinburgh on 9 December 1668, son of Reverend William Vetch, admitted as a member of the Scots Charitable Society of Boston in 1700. [SCS]; from Boston to Port Royal, Nova Scotia, appointed Governor there 1710. [NENS#17]

VINIAN, HENRY, from Largs, Ayrshire, admitted as a member of the Scots Charitable Society of Boston in 1766. [SCS]

WADDELL, JAMES, admitted as a member of the Scots Charitable Society of Boston in 1737. [SCS]

WADDEL, JOHN, settled in Ryegate, Vermont, before December 1774. [VHS]

WADDELL, Reverend JOSEPH, born in Shotts, Lanarkshire, 10 April 1771, from New England to Nova Scotia 1797. [NENS#41]

WALKER, ANDREW, admitted as a member of the Scots Charitable Society of Boston in 1702. [SCS]

WALKER, DAVID A., a butcher from Forfar, then in Northburgh, Worcester County, Massachusetts, 22 September 1893. [NAS.RS.Forfar#53/273]

WALKER, JAMES, from Aberdeen, admitted as a member of the Scots Charitable Society of Boston in 1744. [SCS]

WALKER, JOHN, from Glasgow, admitted as a member of the Scots Charitable Society of Boston in 1755. [SCS]

WALKER, JOHN, from Greenock aboard the brigantine Matty, master Thomas Cochrane, on 19 May 1774 bound for New York, arrived 22 July 1774, settled Barnet, Vermont. [HBV]

WALKER, NEIL, born in Leven, Fife, married Barbara Murray there on 13 January 1821, emigrated to USA during 1844, settled in Frye village, Andover, Massachusetts. [PJ, 4.3.1871]

WALKINSHAW, JOHN, admitted as a member of the Scots Charitable Society of Boston in 1685. [SCS]

WALKINGSHAW, WILLIAM, from Glasgow, admitted as a member of the Scots Charitable Society of Boston in 1731. [SCS]

WALLACE, JOHN, from Ayr, admitted as a member of the Scots Charitable Society of Boston in 1700. [SCS]

WALLACE, JOHN, from Glasgow, admitted as a member of the Scots Charitable Society of Boston in 1700. [SCS]

WALLACE, JOHN, from Ayr, admitted as a member of the Scots Charitable Society of Boston in 1728. [SCS]

WALLACE, JOHN, from Saltcoats, Ayrshire, admitted as a member of the Scots Charitable Society in 1771. [SCS]

WALLACE, LACHLAN, from Glasgow, now of Boston, married Annie W. Grant of Boston, in Osgoode, Ontario, on 13 August 1873. [EC#27749]

WALLACE, PETER, born in 1730, emigrated from Glasgow to New England on the Apollo, died in Newbury, Maine, during 1748. [Imm.NE#206]

WALLACE, WILLIAM, formerly of St Croix, West Indies, late of New Haven, America, husband of Catherine, probate March 1831 PCC

WANTWORTH, JOHN, in Portsmouth, New Hampshire, admitted as a burgess and guildsbrother of Edinburgh on 29 August 1764. [EBR]

WARDEN, JAMES, from Greenock, admitted as a member of the Scots Charitable Society of Boston in 1748. [SCS]

WARDEN, JAMES, a merchant in Boston during 1774, son of late James Warden a shipmaster in Greenock, and grandson of deceased Robert Warden. [NAS.RS81/9]

WARDEN, WILLIAM, from Greenock, admitted as a member of the Scots Charitable Society of Boston in 1736. [SCS]

WARDEN, WILLIAM, from Greenock, admitted as a member of the Scots Charitable Society of Boston in 1758. [SCS]

WARDROPE, ELIZABETH HAVEN. In Portsmouth, Rockingham County, New Hampshire, grand-daughter of David Wardrope a merchant in Edinburgh, 1822. [NAS.RD5.227.363]

WARDROPE, JOHN, second son of David Wardrope a merchant in Edinburgh, a merchant who died in Portsmouth, New Hampshire, 30 October 1804. [SM#67.74]

WARREN, JAMES, a prisoner of war captured after the Battle of Dunbar in September 1650, transported from London on 3 November 1650 on the Unity to New England, an indentured servant in Kittery, Maine, around 1656. [NWI]; senior, in Berwick parish, Kittery, York County, New England, probate 24 December 1702 Maine Probate Office 1/85. [ref. to wife Margaret, sons Gilbert and James, daughter Margaret Stagpoal and Grizel, granddaughter Jane Grant, grandson James Stagpoal]

WATERS, ANN, eldest daughter of David Waters in Brems, Caithness, wife of Reverend David Sutherland a Congregationalist minister, died in Bath, New Hampshire, on 3 March 1852. [W#1309]

WATERS, JAMES, born 1840, died in Boston 26 November 1912. [Stronsay g/s, Orkney Islands]

WATERSON, WILLIAM, emigrated from Greenock aboard the brigantine Matty, master Thomas Cochrane, on 19 May 1774 bound for New York, arrived there on 22 July 1774, settled Barnet, Vermont. [HBV]

WATERSTON, ROBERT, a merchant in Boston around 1847, grandson of Robert Cassie a weaver in North Berwick, East Lothian, and Mary Tait. [NAS.SH.1847]

WATSON, DAVID, admitted as a member of the Scots Charitable Society of Boston in 1803. [SCS]

WATSON, JAMES, admitted as a member of the Scots Charitable Society of Boston in 1707. [SCS]

WATSON, JAMES, of New England, master of the Jean and Mary, admitted as a burgess and guildsbrother of Glasgow 13 July 1721. [GBR]

WATSON, JAMES, with his wife and two children, emigrated from Greenock aboard the brigantine Matty, master Thomas Cochrane, on 19 May 1774 bound for New York, arrived there on 22 July 1774, settled Barnet, Vermont. [HBV]

WATSON, JOHN, born in 1755, a cooper from Glasgow, emigrated from Greenock to Salem on the Glasgow Packet, master Alexander Porterfield, in April 1775. [PRO.T47/12]

WATSON, JAMES ANDERSON, born 1882, son of William Watson and Jessie Anderson, died in Boston, Massachusetts, on 31 July 1906. [Cambusnethan g/s, Lanarkshire]

WATSON, JOHN, admitted as a member of the Scots Charitable Society in 1725. [SCS]

WATSON, JOHN, from Mearns, Renfrewshire (?), admitted as a member of the Scots Charitable Society of Boston in 1740. [SCS]

WATSON, JOHN, a surgeon, arrived in Boston on 17 August 1767 aboard the snow Jenny, master Hector Orr, from Glasgow. [PAB]

WATSON, JOHN, born during 1755, a cooper from Glasgow, emigrated from Greenock on the Glasgow Packet master Alexander Porterfield, to Salem in April 1775. [PRO.T47/12]

WATSON, JOSEPH, admitted as an honorary member of the Scots Charitable Society of Boston in 1825. [SCS]

WATSON, WILLIAM, from Glasgow, admitted as a member of the Scots Charitable Society of Boston in 1726. [SCS]

WATSON, WILLIAM, admitted as a member of the Scots Charitable Society of Boston in 1735. [SCS]

WATSON, WILLIAM, in Boston 1771. [NAS.NRAS0888/181]

WATT, ALEXANDER, admitted as a member of the Scots Charitable Society of Boston in 1733. [SCS]

WATT, JOHN, from Aberdeen, admitted as a member of the Scots Charitable Society of Boston in 1753. [SCS]

WATT, ROBERT, admitted as a member of the Scots Charitable Society of Boston in 1720. [SCS]

WATTS, Reverend RICHARD, admitted as a member of the Scots Charitable Society of Boston in 1738. [SCS]; born in 1688, educated at Glasgow University, garrison chaplain in Annapolis Royal, Nova Scotia, from 1727, a minister and a schoolmaster, settled in Bristol, Newport, Rhode Island, in 1738, died there on 15 March 1740. [DCB]

WEATHERSTONE, JAMES, admitted as a member of the Scots Charitable Society of Boston in 1827. [SCS]

WEBB, ..., emigrated to New England, settled in Scituate, Woolwich, Maine, died 1763. [ImmNE]

WEBSTER, JAMES, admitted as a founder member of the Scot Charitable Society of Boston on 6 January 1657. [SCS]

WEBSTER, JAMES, jr., admitted as a member of the Scots Charitable Society of Boston in 1686. [SCS]

WEBSTER, JAMES, admitted as a member of the Scots Charitable Society of Boston in 1699. [SCS]

WEIR, JAMES, from Glasgow, admitted as a member of the Scots Charitable Society of Boston in 1747. [SCS]

WEIR, MARY, born in 1799, immigrated into Massachusetts aboard the bark Isabel Stewart on 16 July 1849. [LAP]

WEIR, NANCY, born in 1823, immigrated into Massachusetts aboard the bark Isabel Stewart on 16 July 1849. [LAP]

WEIR, ROBERT, admitted as a member of the Scots Charitable Society of Boston in 1706. [SCS]

WEIR, WILLIAM, admitted as a member of the Scots Charitable Society of Boston in 1707. [SCS]

WELSH, EDWARD, born in 1850, died in Nantick on 18 October 1872. [Parton g/s, Kirkcudbrightshire]

WELSH, JOHN, admitted as a member of the Scots Charitable Society of Boston in 1731. [SCS]

WELSH, JOHN MILLER, in Andover cnf 1893. [NAS.SC70.1.316]

WEMYSS, JAMES, admitted as a member of the Scots Charitable Society of Boston in 1695. [SCS]

WEMYSS, THOMAS, admitted as a member of the Scots Charitable Society of Boston in 1716. [SCS]

WEST, JAMES, from Aberdeen, admitted as a member of the Scots Charitable Society of Boston in 1765, 1787. [SCS]

WESTLAND, JOHN, born in 1834, a stonecutter from Aberdeen, settled in Quincy, Massachusetts, during 1869, died in Boston 10 July 1872. [AJ#9500]

WESTON, WILLIAM, admitted as a member of the Scots Charitable Society of Boston in 1801. [SCS]

WESTWOOD, CATHERINE, third daughter of Hugh Westwood in Torryburn, Fife, married Robert Thomson, in Portland, Maine, on 10 March 1870. [DP]

WHIPPO, JAMES, from Barnstable, admitted as a member of the Scots Charitable Society of Boston in 1692. [SCS]

WHITE, DANIEL, arrived in Boston on 31 October 1766 aboard the snow Jenny, master Archibald Orr, from Scotland. [PAB]

WHITE, HUGH, a merchant in Glasgow, then in Boston, 1766. [NAS.CS16.1.130/171]

WHITE, JOHN, born in Glasgow during 1672, emigrated via Ireland to New England, died in Lunenburg, Massachusetts, during 1739. [Imm.NE#212]

WHITE, PATRICK, born during 1749, a farmer from Coupar Angus, Perthshire, emigrated from Greenock on the Glasgow Packet, master Alexander Porterfield, to Salem in April 1775. [PRO.T47/12]

WHITE, SAMUEL, from Glasgow, admitted as a member of the Scots Charitable Society of Boston in 1759. [SCS]

WHYTE, HENRY, a merchant and sailor in Boston, 1763. [NAS.CS16.1.117/59]

WHITE, WILLIAM, admitted as a member of the Scots Charitable Society of Boston in 1800. [SCS]

WHITELAW, JAMES, born in 1747, son of William Whitelaw in Whiteinch, a surveyor from Lanarkshire, emigrated from Greenock on 24 March 1773 aboard the Matty, master Thomas Cochrane, landed in Philadelphia on 24 May 1773, agent for the Scots American Company of Farmers, settled Ryegate, Vermont, Surveyor General of Vermont from 1787 to 1804, married (1) Abigail Johnston in 1778, (2) Susannah Rogers in 1790, (3) Mrs Janet Harvey in 1815, he died in Ryegate in 1829. [VHS] [PRO.T47/12][HBV]

WHITING, ANDREW, admitted as a member of the Scots Charitable Society of Boston in 1731. [SCS]

WHITING, JAMES, admitted as a member of the Scots Charitable Society of Boston in 1705. [SCS]

WHITTIER, WILLIAM, born 1710, emigrated to New England 1730, settled in Deerfield, New Hampshire. [ImmNE]

WIGHT, M. J. K., daughter of Robert Wight MD, and wife of Frank Harman in Vermont, died in St John's, Canada East, on 19 April 1877. [EC#29894]

WILDRAGE, Mrs ISABELLA, born in South Ronaldsay, Orkney Islands, during 1740, wife of Captain James Wildrage, died on 23 September 1780, buried in East Cemetery, Portland, Maine. [Imm.NE#212]

WILKIE, ..., to New England in 1753, settled in Warren, Maine. [ImmNE]

WILKINSON, ..., admitted as a member of the Scots Charitable Society of Boston in 1688. [SCS]

WILLIAMSON, DAVID, born in Fife 1764, for 30 years pastor of an Associate Congregation in Whitehaven, New England, died in New York 18 May 1822. [AJ#3839][S.5/237]

WILLIAMSON, PATRICK, purser of the Ludloe Castle, admitted to the Scots Charitable Society of Boston in 1726. [SCS]

WILLIAMSON, PETER, admitted as a member of the Scots Charitable Society of Boston in 1694. [SCS]

WILLIS, JAMES, from Shetland, admitted as a member of the Scots Charitable Society of Boston in 1733. [SCS]

WILSON, ALEXANDER, a brewer, arrived in Boston on 27 June 1763 aboard the snow Jenny, master James Orr, from Scotland. [PAB]

WILSON, ANDREW, a prisoner of war transported to New England on the John and Sarah of London, master John Greene in November 1651. [Suffolk Deeds, 1-56]

WILSON, ANDREW, a mariner, admitted as a member of the Scots Charitable Society of Boston in 1684. [SCS]

WILSON, ARCHIBALD, admitted as a member of the Scots Charitable Society of Boston in 1729. [SCS]

WILSON, ARCHIBALD, a merchant from Inverkip, Renfrewshire, arrived in Boston on 12 May 1768 aboard the brig Betsy, Captain John Smith, [PAB]; admitted as a member of the Scots Charitable Society of Boston in 1769. [SCS]

WILSON, J., from Renfrewshire, emigrated to America in April 1774, settled in Ryegate, Vermont, [HGP]

WILSON, CHRISTOPHER, a prisoner of war transported to New England on the John and Sarah of London, master John Greene in November 1651. [Suffolk Deeds, 1-56]

WILSON, DAVID, a blacksmith in Boston around 1871, son of John Wilson a cabinetmaker in Dundee and Margaret Miller. [NAS.SH.1871]

WILSON, Mrs ELIZABETH, born in Stromness, Orkney, a widow and a pensioner of the Society for 23 years, died on 11 February 1756, probate 14 June 1756. [SCS]

WILSON, JAMES, a merchant, arrived in Boston on 22 January 1766 aboard the snow Peggy, master William Craig. [PAB]

WILSON, JAMES, from Renfrewshire, emigrated to America in April 1774, settled in Ryegate, Vermont, before 1784. [VHS][HGP]

WILSON, JOHN, a prisoner of war transported to New England on the John and Sarah of London, master John Greene in November 1651. [Suffolk Deeds, 1-56]

WILSON, JOHN, born in 1739, a farmer with his son Peter Wilson, born 1761, from Glamis, Angus, emigrated from Greenock to Salem on the Glasgow Packet, master Alexander Porterfield, in April 1775. [PRO.T47/12]

WILSON, JOHN, a tenter in Boston around 1871, son of John Wilson, a cabinetmaker in Dundee, and Margaret Miller. [NAS.SH.1871]

WILSON, MARGARET, born in 1751, from Glasgow, emigrated from Greenock to Salem on the Glasgow Packet, master Alexander Porterfield, in April 1775. [PRO.T47/12]

WILSON, ROBERT, admitted as a member of the Scots Charitable Society of Boston in 1822. [SCS]

WILSON, THOMAS, admitted as a member of the Scots Charitable Society of Boston in 1733. [SCS]

WILSON, WILLIAM, admitted as a member of the Scots Charitable Society of Boston in 1712. [SCS]

WILSON, WILLIAM, admitted as a member of the Scots Charitable Society of Boston in 1715. [SCS]

WILSON, WILLIAM HENRY, from Quebec, admitted as a member of the Scots Charitable Society of Boston in 1826. [SCS]

WILSON, Major ..., from Virginia, admitted as a member of the Scots Charitable Society of Boston in 1693. [SCS]

WILSON, ..., born in 1760, son of John Wilson in Partick, Glasgow, emigrated to Ryegate, Vermont, in 1784. [VHS: Whitelaw pp]

WITHERSPOON, ROBERT, admitted as a member of the Scots Charitable Society of Boston in 1713. [SCS]

WOOD, JAMES, in Newhaven, Connecticut, 1870. [NAS.SH.1870]

WOOD, JOHN, a farmer, with his wife and two children, arrived in Boston on 22 August 1765 aboard the Jamieson and Peggy, master John Aitken, from Leith. [PAB]

WOOD, ROBERT, admitted as a member of the Scots Charitable Society of Boston in 1732. [SCS]

WOODALL, JOHN, a prisoner of war transported to New England on the John and Sarah of London, master John Greene in November 1651. [Suffolk Deeds, 1-56]

WOODRUP, ALEXANDER, from Glasgow, admitted as a member of the Scots Charitable Society of Boston in 1739. [SCS]

WOODROP, HUGH, from London, admitted as a member of the Scots Charitable Society in 1727. [SCS]

WOODROP, JOHN, admitted as a member of the Scots Charitable Society of Boston in 1722. [SCS]

WOODROP, WILLIAM, admitted as a member of the Scots Charitable Society in 1727. [SCS]

WRIGHT, JAMES, admitted as a member of the Scots Charitable Society of Boston in 1713. [SCS]

WRIGHT, JAMES, admitted as a member of the Scots Charitable Society of Boston in 1731. [SCS]

WRIGHT, ROBERT, admitted as a member of the Scots Charitable Society of Boston in 1686. [SCS]

WYATT, ROBERT, admitted as a member of the Scots Charitable Society of Boston in 1802. [SCS]

WYLLIE, ELIZA, daughter of Peter Wyllie, emigrated via Glasgow on the City of Glasgow bound for New York on 18 June 1853 to settle in Boston. [FA, 25.6.1853]

WYLLIE, JANET, youngest daughter of Peter Wyllie in Kinghorn, Fife, widow of David Smith, died in Malden, Boston, during 1901. [FFP, 6.2.1901]

WYLLIE, JOHN, admitted as a member of the Scots Charitable Society of Boston in 1695. [SCS]

WYLLIE, JOHN, a glover in Orleans, Vermont, 15 November 1864. [NAS.RS.Whithorn#4/35, 43]

YOUNG, ALEXANDER, emigrated from Greenock aboard the brigantine Matty, master Thomas Cochrane, on 19 May 1774 bound for New York, arrived there on 22 July 1774, settled Barnet, Vermont. [HBV]

YOUNG, JAMES, in Boston 1726. [Imm.NE#218]

YOUNG, JOHN, from Greenock, admitted as a member of the Scots Charitable Society of Boston in 1748. [SCS]

YOUNG, JOHN, from Old Kirk parish, Greenock, admitted as a member of the Scots Charitable Society of Boston in 1772, a resident of Boston in 1787. [SCS]

YOUNG, MATHEW, from Glasgow, admitted as a member of the Scots Charitable Society of Boston in 1732. [SCS]

YOUNG, THOMAS, arrived in Boston during May 1716 aboard the snow Amity, master Nathaniel Breed from Glasgow. [NWI#1/459]

YOUNG, WILLIAM, admitted as a member of the Scots Charitable Society of Boston in 1722. [SCS]

YOUNG, WILLIAM, admitted as a member of the Scots Charitable Society of Boston in 1729. [SCS]

YOOL, JOHN, a merchant in Paisley, then in Boston 1778. [NAS.CS16.1.174]

YUILL, ALEXANDER, a merchant in Boston, 1781. [NAS.CS16.1.183]

YUIL, ARCHIBALD, from Glasgow, admitted as a member of the Scots Charitable Society of Boston in 1750. [SCS]

YUILE, GEORGE, from Glasgow, admitted as a member of the Scots Charitable Society of Boston in 1746. [SCS]

YUILL, JAMES, from Glasgow, admitted as a member of the Scots Charitable Society of Boston in 1753, [SCS]; a merchant, son of Claud Yuill in Strathaven, Lanarkshire, settled in Boston, Massachusetts, wife Jane Bailey, and son James, later allocated a land grant in Truro, Nova Scotia, 1761, 1763. [NENS#167][NAS.RS42.15.96][NAS.CS16.1.115]

YUILE, JOHN, from Glasgow, admitted as a member of the Scots Charitable Society of Boston in 1759. [SCS]

YUILL, JOHN, in Glasgow then in Boston, son of Alexander Yuill a merchant in Boston, 1781. [NAS.CS16.1.183]

YUILL, ROBERT, admitted as a member of the Scots Charitable Society of Boston in 1711. [SCS]